DIGGING UP JERUSALEM

By the same author

ARCHAEOLOGY IN THE HOLY LAND
DIGGING UP JERICHO

DIGGING UP JERUSALEM

By

KATHLEEN M. KENYON

LONDON & TONBRIDGE
ERNEST BENN LIMITED

FIRST PUBLISHED 1974 BY ERNEST BENN LIMITED
25 NEW STREET SQUARE · FLEET STREET · LONDON · EC4A 3JA
AND SOVEREIGN WAY · TONBRIDGE · KENT

DISTRIBUTED IN CANADA BY
THE GENERAL PUBLISHING COMPANY LIMITED, TORONTO

© KATHLEEN M. KENYON 1974

PRINTED IN GREAT BRITAIN

ISBN 0 510-03315-6

Contents

List of Plates

[All are inserted between pages 128 and 129]

the royal tombs of the period of the Monarchy, but it is difficult to accept this identification

10   The view down the Kedron Valley

11   The outer edge of the Hinnom Valley, where it is curving round to the east to join the Kedron

12   Air view of Jerusalem from the south, taken in the 1960s. The steep slope of the Kedron, flanked on the east by the village of Silwan, is seen on the right, with to the left and in the foreground the line of the Hinnom curving round to join the Kedron

13   View from the east showing the steep west slope of the Kedron Valley. The line of the town wall, first Solomonic then post-Exilic and Byzantine, can be seen on the right at the south-east corner of the temple enclosure, and further south it is followed by the line of houses on the crest of the slope

14   Trench 1 of the 1961–67 excavations down the eastern slope of the eastern ridge. At the top of the trench is the so-called Tower of David, which is in fact Maccabean

15   At Samaria, deep robber trenches of the Hellenistic and Roman periods removed almost all of the foundations of the casemate walls of the period of Omri-Ahab. To the left, the sole remaining stones at the base of the casemate walls are seen. In the centre are the excavations that have traced the trenches that robbed the stones from the Israelite walls

16   The area of the casemate walls at Samaria, showing the only evidence that would have survived if the robber trenches had not been identified

17   The eastern slope of the eastern ridge at Jerusalem, showing the trench laid out in 1961 to trace the defences of early Jerusalem. The houses on the crest follow the line of the walls of the Solomonic extension and of the post-Exilic to 1st century A.D. towns. Beyond the lower end of the 1961 trench is the Spring Gihon, beneath the lower of the two small houses

18   On the right, in the middle distance, is the tower claimed by Professor Macalister to have been built by David; it is in fact Maccabean. In the right foreground is the so-called Jebusite ramp, actually built against the 'Davidic' (really Maccabean) tower. The wall in the centre background is the wall supporting an excavation dump.

19   The face of wall NB, low on the eastern slope, which proved to be the wall of Jebusite Jerusalem, dating from the 18th century B.C. The photograph shows the extreme S.E. angle of the original Trench 1 clearance

20   The original east wall of Jerusalem, wall NB, with the angle as exposed in 1962. On the right is the later wall NA

21   Pottery of the Intermediate Early Bronze-Middle Bronze period from the Mount of Olives

22   The small and carefully rounded shaft of a tomb of the Intermediate Early Bronze-Middle Bronze period on the Mount of Olives

23   The east slope of the eastern ridge of Jerusalem from the north. In the

straight joint. The heavily bossed stones are in Persian style, and presumably date from the post-Exilic period. It is highly probable that the post-Exilic platform was based on that of Solomon

36 Detail of the straight joint between the Herodian masonry on the left and the earlier masonry on the right

37 The casemate in Site H that runs north from the line of the original Jebusite-Davidic north wall, which can be interpreted as Solomonic. Only the walls of heavy stones are original; the patch in the upper right-hand corner is an excavation retaining wall

38 The wall in Site S II on the eastern crest of the eastern ridge, which can be stratigraphically dated to the 8th century B.C., but which is constructed on re-used stones of typically Phoenician type. These stones could well have been derived from a nearby wall of the Solomonic period

39 Ivory carving from Samaria of a miniature size suitable for use on furniture, but illustrative of the half-human, half-animal figures used in contemporary adornment

40 An ivory plaque from Samaria, of which the Egyptian style illustrates the cosmopolitan art to be found in the area of the Israelite kingdom

41 An ivory plaque from Nimrud, to be compared with Pl. 39, as illustrating the current art of western Asia

42 An ivory plaque from Nimrud that (though their scale here is miniscule) can be taken as illustrating the mystical figures that, in the Holy of Holies of the Temple, guarded the Ark of the Covenant

43 In the left foreground is the original wall NB of the Jebusite-Davidic period, with an angular return to the west. The original wall is seen disappearing beneath the later wall, NA, 8th–7th century in date. The wall in the upper left-hand corner is an excavation revetment wall

44 The sloping tips, becoming more and more stony, overlying the buildings in Square A XXIV

45 The first building, circular in plan, to be reached in Square A XXIV

46 Rectangular building on bedrock in Square A XXIV

47 Ashlar steps in Square A XXIV

48 Bronze bucket *in situ* in a cupboard in a wall of the house shown on Pl. 46

49 The bucket shown on Pl. 48, with two other vessels inside it

50 The smaller bucket inside that shown on Pl. 49

51 The bronze jug that was the innermost component of the nest of vessels shown *in situ* on Pl. 48

52 In the background is the shallow cave in the rock scarp, surrounded by massive walls. Within the enclosure so formed was the deposit of pottery seen on Pl. 53

53 Deposit of pottery vessels in the enclosure shown on Pl. 52, probably to be interpreted as a *favissa* associated with the nearby structure interpreted as a sanctuary

54 General view of the extra-mural structure in Squares A XIX–XXI, which is to be interpreted as a cult sanctuary

construction was a staircase leading to a higher terrace, of which nothing is preserved

75   Erosion channels caused by the winter rains on the east slope of the eastern ridge. Some gulleys run the length of the slope. In others, the water has clearly had an underground channel until it burst out at the foot of the slope

76   To the left is the tower, ascribed by Professor Macalister to the Davidic period, but actually Maccabean. (The upper courses are a rebuild by the Department of Antiquities of the Mandate.) In the centre is the so-called Jebusite ramp, a reinforcement of the summit wall that is later than the tower. Above to the right is a small tower which is an early addition to the wall built by Nehemiah

77   To the right is the wall built on top of the scarp shown in Pl. 79, which can be ascribed to the period of Nehemiah. The tower seen in the centre (also seen on the left in Pl. 79), clearly belongs to a reconstruction of this wall

78   The structure called by Professor Macalister 'the Tower of David' shown built over the ruins of the 7th-century houses destroyed by the Babylonians in 587 B.C.

79   In Square A XVIII, opposite P on fig. 28, the steep scarp along the summit ridge had against it a fill of the 6th–5th century period that lapped up against the wall on the crest seen at the top in the centre. This wall can be interpreted as that built by Nehemiah c. 440 B.C. At the top left corner is seen the later tower shown on Pl. 77

80   South-east angle of the Herodian temple platform as it stands up above present-day accumulations. On the left is the elaborate superstructure of a tomb of the Maccabean period, erroneously known today as the tomb of Absalom

81   The north-east corner of the Maccabean tower, erroneously ascribed to the period of David. To the right, the so-called Jebusite ramp is visibly built against this tower

82   The area of the excavations in Site K. The lower house, right of centre, is on the line of the summit scarp. Extending west from this line to approximately the point indicated by the tall cypress, excavations identified terraces that enlarged the area of the town on the eastern ridge during the Maccabean period

83   The portion exposed of the wall bounding the Maccabean terraces on the western side of the eastern ridge, interpreted as the town wall of the period

84   The wall adjacent to the present Citadel, ascribed to the Maccabean period

85   The typical, beautiful, masonry of the Herodian temple platform, seen at the traditional 'Wailing Wall' of the western wall of the temple platform

86   Beneath the present platform of the Haram esh-Sherif in the southeastern area are vaulted chambers known as Solomon's Stables. The

lower courses of the masonry up to above the spring of the vaults, as seen in this view, are certainly Herodian. The interpretation is that when Herod the Great rebuilt the Temple, and extended the area of its court-yards, part of the upper section of the platform was not solid fill but a platform supported on a massive substructure. A comparable example is at Samaria (SS I pp. 123–7)

99   To the right is the eastern pedestrian entrance of a gateway on the
      normal Roman plan, entering Jerusalem from the north. On the left is the
      tower that flanked the entrance. Excavation evidence has shown that the
      gate belongs to the period of Herod Agrippa, A.D. 40–44

100 Street in Herodian style, probably belonging to the period of Herod
      Agrippa, running up the Central Valley. Beyond the street are the
      remains of a staircase leading to a higher terrace

101 South face of wall of very large re-used blocks to the north of the Old
      City, of which the identification is doubtful

102 North face of wall shown on Pl. 101

103 The plan of Jerusalem shown in the Byzantine mosaic floor at Madeba.
      The most interesting points concerning the topography of Jerusalem are
      in the first place the semicircular *place* inside the Damascus Gate, to the
      left, in which stood a column from which the present name of the gate,
      Bab-el-Amud, is derived. Secondly, running south from the *place* are
      two columned streets of which that running straight south still preserves
      fragments of the colonnades. The line of the other, without obvious
      remains of the colonnade, can still be followed to the edge of the Haram
      esh-Sherif

104 Skulls lodged behind collapsed masonry in ruins in Site N that are to be
      dated to the A.D. 70 destruction by Titus

105 Immediately beneath the surface of the terrace in Site K, seen on Pl. 82,
      was the basis of a floor of the 1st century A.D., and an associated drain.
      The building was the latest in the area, as shown by the small amount of
      overlying soil, and in the drain there was evidence of the A.D. 70 destruc-
      tion

106 The Triumphal Arch of the Hadrianic period spanning the street leading
      into the Old City from St Stephen's Gate is partly within the Convent of
      the Sisters of Sion. The northern side entrance and the spring of the
      central arch are seen here; the rest of the central arch spans the present
      street, and is known as the Ecce Homo Arch

107 The Byzantine wall that runs south from the south-east corner of the
      Haram is seen in Square S II. Beneath it is the tunnel by which Warren
      traced it. In the centre is the buttress inserted in 1967 to fill the perilous
      void

108 On the right, the Herodian masonry of the south-east corner of the
      Haram with, on the left, the Byzantine wall built against it

109 Above is rock forming the boundary of a cave in Site D II. Against it is
      built a doorway of the Byzantine period

110 Site M, showing Byzantine walls built on the surface left by quarrying
      which had removed all earlier structures

111 Part of a Byzantine house in Squares S IV–V

112 On the right is the angle of a Byzantine house in Site R. It was cut into a
      dump of rubbish, and the rough wall enclosing it was inserted to prevent
      the dump collapsing

113 The fragmentary remains of the apse of a Byzantine church in Site L

List of Illustrations in Text

xvii

List of Acknowledgements

Plates

The great majority of the photographs were taken by the photographers of the Jerusalem Excavations 1961-67, Miss N. Lord, Miss C. Western, P. Dorrell, and I. Blake.

For the other photographs, permission to publish was kindly given as follows:

Pl. 1 Elia Photographer, Jerusalem.

Pl. 12 E. Schweig, Jerusalem.

Pls. 15, 16, 39, 40 Joint Expedition to Samaria, Palestine Exploration Fund (*Samaria-Sebaste* 1, Pl. XIX. 1, Pl. XIX. 2; *Samaria-Sebaste* 2, Pl. V. 1, Pl. II. 2).

Pls. 41, 42 Sir Max Mallowan (*Nimrud* II, nos. 501, 482).

Pl. 62 Professor N. Avigad (*IEJ* 20, Pl. 29).

Pl. 84 Department of Antiquities of Palestine, *QDAP* XIV, Pl. LIII.

Pl. 85 Miss N. Lord.

Pls. 87, 115 A. Walls.

Pls. 99, 120, 121 Dr J. B. Hennessy (*Levant* II, Pl. XIV, XXII A, XXIV).

Pl. 103 Middle East Archive.

Pl. 106 Middle East Archive.

Pl. 2 is reproduced from W. H. Bartlett, *Walks About the City and Environs of Jerusalem* (publication not dated, but the account is based on a visit in 1847), 2nd edition, opp. p. 89.

Text Figures

Unless otherwise stated, the plans, sections, etc., are reproduced from the field surveys and sections of the Jerusalem Excavations, 1961-67, with the final stages carried out by Brian Johnson. Fair copies have been made by T. A. Holland, Lady Wheeler, and Brian Johnson.

Acknowledgements for the other figures are as follows:

Fig. 1 Frontispiece of *The Survey of Western Palestine, Jerusalem*, C. Warren and E. R. Conder.

3 Warren, *Underground Jerusalem*, p. 140, used as the Frontispiece of the *PEQ*.

4 Ibid., facing p. 69, where it is reproduced from the *Illustrated London News*.

5 *PEFQS* 1873.

6 After *B. and D.*, key map.

7 *B. and D.*, Pl. XIII.

8 After *B. and D.*, Pl. XV.

9 *B. and D.*, Pl. XVIII.

10 Clarendon Press, after *Oxford Bible Atlas*, H. G. May, p. 69.

11 W. F. Petrie, *Tell el Hesy (Lachish)*.

14 Joint Expedition to Samaria, Palestine Exploration Fund, *Samaria-Sebaste* 1, Pl. VII, Section c-d.

16-17 After Vincent, *Jérusalem sous Terre*, Pls. III b, III c.

20 After Warren and Conder, *The Survey of Western Palestine, Jerusalem*, Pl. XXVI.

23, 24 D. Ussiskin, *IEJ* 16, Figs. 4 and 1.

30 *B. and D.*, p. 39.

31 Vincent, *Jérusalem de l'A. T.*, Pl. CII.

32 Warren and Conder, *Survey of Western Palestine, Jerusalem*, Pl. XX.

33 Warren, *Underground Jerusalem*, opposite p. 368. Reproduced from the *Illustrated London News*.

39 *B. and D.*, Pl. V.

40, 41 J. B. Hennessy, *Levant II*, Figs. 1 and 2.

Preface

Digging up Jerusalem records the results of the excavations carried out between 1961 and 1967 and relates them to the results of earlier excavations. The primary sponsor of the 1961–67 excavations was the British School of Archaeology in Jerusalem, with which body on the British side was joined the Palestine Exploration Fund and the British Academy. From 1961 to 1963, the Ecole Biblique et Archéologique de Saint-Etienne shared in the responsibility, as did the Royal Ontario Museum from 1963 to 1967. The principal support to the British side, in addition to that from the sponsoring bodies, came from the Russell Trust, Birmingham City Museum, and the Ashmolean Museum, with welcome contributions from a number of other museums and from universities in the United Kingdom. To this should be added contributions from many overseas museums and universities, amongst which should be especially mentioned the Australian Institute of Archaeology, Melbourne; Trinity College, Dublin; Emory University, Georgia; the Otago Museum, New Zealand; the University Museum, Philadelphia; the University of Sydney; the Southern Baptist Theological Seminary, Louisville, Kentucky; and above all the National Geographic Society of America, which for five years made me a most generous research grant. The contribution of the Ecole Biblique was financed by a grant from the Commission des Fouilles. Support for the Canadian share came from McGill University, Victoria University, University College and St Michael's College, Toronto, Waterloo Lutheran University, Trent University, and Carleton University.

The excavations were directed by myself, in association from 1961 to 1963 with Père Roland de Vaux, O.P., and from 1963 to 1967 with Dr A. D. Tushingham. A very large number of assistants and students took part as site supervisors, specialist surveyors, photographers, in conservation and so on, and in the recording of finds. In addition to the United Kingdom, French, and Canadian nucleus, these assistants came from Jordan, the United States, Australia, Denmark, Japan, Holland, Belgium, Spain, Germany, Argentina, Trinidad, and Saudi Arabia. It was thus in a very real sense an international expedition.

The primary thanks of the Expedition must go to the Department of Antiquities of Jordan and to the municipal authorities of Jerusalem. Throughout the excavations, the old friend of the British School, Dr Awni Dajani, earlier a student at Jericho and my student for his doctorate in London, was Director of Antiquities. His interest in the activities of the British School was constant, and he smoothed all applications for the permissions required for our excavations. He was a very sick man when I went to see him in Amman in July 1967, but he recognized that it was in the interests of science that we should complete our planned programme of excavation after the occupation of Jerusalem by the Israelis in 1967. I must pay a big tribute to my friend and pupil (he continually emphasized this) Awni Dajani.

The municipal authorities of Jerusalem gave us throughout the greatest encouragement and assistance. Successive governors, and especially H.E. Da'ud Abu Ghazezleh, were a great source of strength. The Lord Mayor, Mr Rawhi Khattib, was a close friend and took a great interest in our plans. Of the municipal officers, I must mention especially Mr Yussif Budeiri, the city engineer, to whom we could always turn for advice and assistance.

Our planned excavations for 1967 had to be adjusted to meet the situation created by the June 1967 war. It did in fact prove possible to begin our excavations only a month late. We had to adjust our plan to problems of new one-way streets, new sudden curfews, but, with certain frustrations, we carried out the greater part of our programme. This was only possible because we received the fullest possible support from the Israeli Department of Antiquities and its Director, Dr Biran.

Our excavations were upon the lands of many owners and it was of course only through their goodwill that we were able to work. We are especially grateful for permission to excavate from the Supreme Moslem Council, the Greek Patriarchate, the Armenian Patriarchate, and the Anglican Archbishopric.

The aim of this book is twofold. The main object is to give an account of the results of the excavations in Jerusalem for the interested layman. Secondly, it is an interim report available to professional colleagues until the vast amount of work required for the final report has been completed. This dual aim means that there will be parts that are interesting only to some and parts to others. Professional archaeologists will want to skip the description of methods. The layman may find the detailed discussions of alternative theories tedious. There have been so many controversies about the interpretation of the evidence concerning the plan and history of Jerusalem that the professional must consider the most recent results in relation to them. I can only hope that a reasonable balance has been kept between the needs of different readers.

Both in the chapter concerning our excavation procedure and in this Preface, it has been made clear how very many people had their share in the excavations and whose work was the core of the whole enterprise. To my thanks to them must be added my thanks to those who helped in the production of this book, to Lady McMahon who typed it, to Miss Nancy Lord who prepared the photographs, many of which were her own work in the field, to Lady Wheeler and Tom Holland who did the fair copies of the drawings.

Oxford   K. M. K.
March 1973

Bibliography with Abbreviations

Abel, F. M. *Histoire de la Palestine depuis la conquête d'Alexandre jusqu'à l'invasion Arabe.* Paris, 1952.

Aharoni   Aharoni, Y. *The Land of the Bible.* London and Philadelphia, 1966.

AIHL   *Archaeology in the Holy Land.* See Kenyon.

Amiran, R. and Eitan, A. 'Excavations at the Citadel, Jerusalem.' *IEJ* 20.

Antiquities   See Josephus.

Atlas of the Biblical World. D. Baly and A. D. Tushingham. New York, 1971.

Avigad, N. 'Excavations in the Jewish Quarter of the Old City, Jerusalem 1969/70'; *idem*, 1970. *IEJ* 20.1–2 and 20.3–4.

Benoit, P. 'L'Antonia d'Hérode le Grand et le Forum Oriental d'Aelie Capitolina'. *Harvard Theological Review* 64 (1971).

B. and D.   Bliss, F. G. and Dickie, A. C. *Excavations at Jerusalem 1894–1897.* London, Palestine Exploration Fund, 1898.

Busink, Th. A. *Der Tempel von Jerusalem.* Vol. 1. *Der Tempel Salomos.* Leiden, 1970.

Crowfoot, J. W. and Fitzgerald, G. M. *Excavations in the Tyropoeon Valley 1927.* APEF V. London, 1929.

Crowfoot, J. W., Kenyon, K. M., Sukenik, E. L. *Samaria Sebaste 1. The Buildings at Samaria.* London, Palestine Exploration Fund, 1942.

Crowfoot, J. W., Crowfoot, G. M. *Samaria Sebaste 2. Early Ivories from Samaria.* London, Palestine Exploration Fund, 1938.

Crowfoot, J. W., Crowfoot, G. M., Kenyon, K. M. *Samaria Sebaste 3. The Objects from Samaria.* Palestine Exploration Fund, 1957.

Dunand, M. 'Byblos, Sidon, Jerusalem'. Supplement to *Vetus Testamentum* VII, 1969.

Jerusalem   See Kenyon.

Jérusalem de   See Vincent.
l'A.T.

Josephus, Flavius. *Antiquities of the Jews; The Jewish War or The History of the Destruction of Jerusalem.* In *The Works of Flavius Josephus,* translated by W. Whiston, edited D. S. Margoliouth. London, George Routledge & Sons, 1906.

Kenyon, K. M. *Jerusalem. Excavating 3000 years of History.* London, Thames and Hudson, and New York, McGraw Hill, 1967.

    Royal Cities of the Old Testament, London, Barrie and Jenkins, and New York, Schocken, 1971.

    Digging up Jericho. London, Ernest Benn, and New York, Praeger, 1957.

    Archaeology in the Holy Land. London, Ernest Benn, and New York, Praeger, 3rd edition, 1970.

    'New evidence on Solomon's Temples'. *Mélanges de l'Université Saint-Joseph.* Vol. XLVI. Beirut, 1970.

    'Some Aspects of the Impact of Rome on Palestine'. *Journal of the Royal Asiatic Society,* 1970.

Lachish I   See Torczyner.

Lachish II, III See Tufnell.

Layard, A. H. *Ninevah and Babylon.* London, 1850.

Macalister, R. A. S. *Excavations on the Hill of Ophel, Jerusalem 1923–25.* APEF IV. London, 1926.

McCown, C. C. *Tell en-Nasbeh.* Berkeley and New Haven, 1947.

Mallowan, M. E. L. *Nimrud and its Remains.* Collins, London, 1966.

Marsden, E. W. *Greek and Roman Artillery* I. *Historical Development.* Oxford and New York, 1969.

Mazar The Excavations in the Old City of Jerusalem near the Temple Mount. Preliminary Report of the Second and Third Seasons 1969–1970, B. Mazar. *The Ommayad Structures Near the Temple Mount.* M. Ben-Dov, Jerusalem, 1971.

Moore, E. A. *The Ancient Churches of Old Jerusalem. The Evidence of the Pilgrims.* Beirut, 1961.

Noth Noth. M. *The History of Israel.* English edition London, A. and C. Black, and New York, Harper and Row, 2nd edition, 1960.

Qumran de Vaux, R. *L'Archéologie et les Manuscripts de la Mer Morte.* British Academy Schweich Lectures 1959. London, Oxford University Press, 1961.

Robinson, E. *Biblical Researches in Palestine and the Adjacent Countries.* London, 1867.

Royal Cities See Kenyon.

SS1, 2, 3 See Crowfoot.

Simons Simons, J. *Jerusalem in the Old Testament.* E. J. Brill, Leiden, 1952.

Sukenik, E. L. and Mayer, L. M. *The Third Wall of Jerusalem.* University Press, Jerusalem; London and New York, Oxford University Press, 1930.

Thureau-Dangin, F. *Arslan Tash. Bibliothèque archéologique et historique.* Vol. XVI, 1931.

Torczyner, H., Harding, L., Lewis, A., Starkey, J. L. *Lachish I. The Lachish Letters*. London, 1936.

Tufnell, O., Inge, C. H., Harding, L. *Lachish II. The Fosse Temple*. London, 1940.

Tufnell, O. *Lachish III. The Iron Age*. London, 1953.

de Vaux, R. *The Bible and the Ancient Near East*. Selection from *Bible et l'Orient* (Paris, editions du Cerf, 1967). Translated D. McHugh. London and New York, 1972.

Vincent, L.-H. and Stève, A.-M. *Jérusalem de l'Ancien Testament*. Paris, J. Gabalda et Cie, 1954 and 1956.

V[incent], [L.] H. *Jérusalem sous Terre. Les recentes Fouilles d'Ophel*. London, Horace Cox, 1911.

War   See Josephus.

Warren   Warren, C. *Underground Jerusalem*. London, 1876

*   *   *

APEF   *Annual of the Palestine Exploration Fund*. London.

AV   Authorized Version (Bible).

          Biblical Archaeologist. Published by the American Schools of Oriental Research, Cambridge, Mass.

IEJ   *Israel Exploration Journal*. Quarterly of the Israel Exploration Society, Jerusalem, Israel.

Levant   Journal of the British School of Archaeology in Jerusalem, London.

PEFQS *Palestine Exploration Fund Quarterly Statement*. London.

PEQ   *Palestine Exploration Quarterly*. Published by the
            Palestine Exploration Fund, London.
QDAP   *Quarterly of the Department of Antiquities of
            Palestine*. Oxford University Press, London.
RB   *Revue Biblique*. Published by the Ecole Biblique
            et Archéologique de Saint-Etienne, Jerusalem.
RSV   Revised Standard Version (Bible).

★

CHAPTER ONE

The First Hundred Years

DIGGING UP JERUSALEM began just a hundred years before the recent excavations of the British School of Archaeology and its associates completed the recent campaign in 1967. The Palestine Exploration Fund was founded in 1865. The middle years of the nineteenth century constituted a period in which the great civilizations of western Asia were being revealed by the spade of the archaeologist, and the interest aroused was very great. Archaeologists of many countries were involved, but the contribution of Great Britain was perhaps the greatest. The excavations of Layard at Nimrud (the Calah of Genesis 10:11) and Nineveh uncovered colossal sculptures and reliefs, and, even more important, clay tablets inscribed in cuneiform, which at Nineveh comprised the royal library of Ashur-bani-pal (669–26 B.C.). At Nimrud was found the Black Obelisk of Shalmaneser III (859–24 B.C.) recording his campaigns, and among the kings who offered tribute was 'Jehu, son of Omri' (not in fact his son, but the man who became king of the northern kingdom of Israel by the expulsion of the Omrid dynasty). The Assyrian Galleries of the British Museum are the visible record of Layard's finds.

It was in this climate of excitement at the revelation of remains contemporary with the Biblical record of the history of the kingdoms of Judah and Israel that the Palestine Exploration Fund came into existence. Nowadays, almost every European country has societies to promote the study of archaeology, history, language, and allied subjects in most of the countries of the Mediterranean, western Asia, and farther afield. The Palestine Exploration Fund was the first, in Britain preceding by

1

twenty-one years the foundation of the British School in Athens and by thirty-six years the foundation of the British School at Rome. The study of the Bible had an even greater appeal to the general Victorian public than that of classical antiquity, in spite of the classical basis of education and the interest in classical antiquities stimulated by the eighteenth–nineteenth-century habit of the grand tour. The foundation of societies concerned with excavations in Egypt and the other countries of the Near East had to wait for many years.

The Palestine Exploration Fund was established with great éclat. Queen Victoria became the Patron (as is Queen Elizabeth II). The committee of seventy-eight persons was headed by William Thomson, archbishop of York (his successor is now deputy President; the archbishop of Canterbury, now President, only comes on the scene in 1891), supported by four bishops, four deans, two dukes, five earls, three other peers, and the Speaker of the House of Commons. The archbishop of York presided at the initial meeting. The first list of subscriptions promised amounts to £3,045 11s. 0d., in sums varying, with one exception, from £100 from the queen to 2s. each from Master M. Gurney and Master G. Gurney. The number of those promising subscriptions was 272. The launching of the society was clearly auspicious.

Nevertheless, a warning note was struck at the meeting held in 1866 under the chairmanship of the dean of Westminster. This came from Layard, the excavator of Nimrud and Nineveh himself, then a Member of Parliament, later to be Sir Henry Layard and ambassador in Constantinople. He warned the supporters of the Fund that they could not expect the finds of spectacular sculptures comparable with those from Mesopotamia, on the grounds that the Jewish religion prohibited the representation of the human form and that suitable stone for sculpture did not exist in Palestine. He did not add the fact that the inhabitants of the Jewish states had no artistic skills; when anything elaborate in architecture was required, they brought in foreigners, a subject to which I shall return. Shortage of funds did soon cause anxiety, and this may have been partly due to the lack of spectacular finds that had been expected in the first flush of enthusiasm.

The objects of the Fund were 'the accurate and systematic investigation of the archaeology, the topography, the geology and physical geography, the manners and customs of the Holy Land for Biblical illustration'. Inevitably, however, it was on Jerusalem that most attention was focused. The first representatives of the Fund set out for Jerusalem in December 1865 and arrived there in April 1866. Mention has already been made of an exceptional subscription in the first list of supporters. This was a contribution of £500 from Miss Burdett-Coutts, with the proviso that its use should include the investigation of the best means of providing Jerusalem with water. Since ancient Jerusalem must have had an infinitely better water-supply than existed in nineteenth-century Jerusalem, the investigation of the ancient system and the aqueducts and cisterns that it involved could well help the modern inhabitants. Above all, any such investigation needed an accurate map, compiled to the already well-established standards of the British Ordnance Survey. It was presumably because of this that the work of the Fund in the early years was almost exclusively directed by officers of the Royal Engineers, assisted by a faithful band of non-commissioned officers (fig. 1). The Palestine Exploration Fund publications

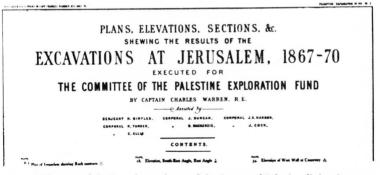

Fig 1   Title page of the Jerusalem volume of the Survey of Palestine, listing Sergeant Birtles and the Corporals who so valiantly assisted Captain Warren in his excavations

do not record the basis on which these soldiers worked for it. Presumably they were seconded on full pay, for the resources of the Fund could not have carried the cost of employing them. Here, unrecorded, is the first British government subvention to Palestinian archaeology, matching that of a frigate to bring back the sculptures of the Nereid and other monuments in 1842–44 and in 1857 of the Mausoleum in Asia Minor. The officers sent to carry out the initial survey were Captain Charles Wilson and Lieutenant Anderson. To them is due the beginning of the accurate mapping of Palestine. In their journey from Beirut to Jerusalem and on to Hebron, they carried out a remarkable survey. In the words of the Statement of Progress prepared by the archbishop of York, the dean of Westminster, and Professor Owen for the meeting of the Fund on 23 July 1866:

> By accurate observations for time and latitude, made at forty-nine separate points between Beyrut and Hebron, and by a line of azimuths carried through the country from Banias to Jerusalem, a series of detailed maps has been formed, on the scale of one mile to an inch (the scale of the English Ordnance Survey) of the whole backbone of the country, from north to south, including the Lake of Genesareth and all the watercourses descending to its western shores.

The Survey of Western Palestine in fact developed into a major activity of the Fund in subsequent years, but at this stage it was just a preliminary to the planning, by Wilson, and the excavation, by Warren, of Jerusalem.

Jerusalem figures prominently in the original list of the objectives of the Fund's researches. The original Prospectus in its list of research starts off

> 1. *Archaeology*—Jerusalem alone would furnish an ample field in this department. What is above ground will be accurately known when the present survey [financed by Miss Burdett-Coutts] is completed, but below the surface hardly anything has yet been discovered.

A list of problems follows (see below, p. 7). The Jerusalem that the founders of the P.E.F. had in mind was relatively well known in England, for in the nineteenth century many travellers had visited Palestine and had recorded their impressions, in the best cases with much accuracy. The best-known artistic records of Jerusalem and of the neighbouring areas are those of David Roberts, whose journeys through Egypt, Sinai, Palestine, and Syria started in 1838. The actual remains he drew with accuracy, but there is always a romantic exaggeration of heights and valleys, and usually a completely invented foreground. W. H. Bartlett, who visited Jerusalem in 1842, was a beautiful artist, whose drawings have a remarkable accuracy, though the needs of the artist again overemphasize declivities. The views of Roberts and Bartlett combine to give a picture of the Jerusalem that the P.E.F. planned to investigate, which is shown in Charles Wilson's plan. This Jerusalem is the present Old City, with its intact medieval walls, a Jerusalem still in 1939 virtually circumscribed by these walls on all sides except the west (Pl. 1). The nineteenth-century views show that there was almost nothing outside these walls. This is still today the Old City of Jerusalem.

Within the walls was the accumulation of millennia. The exception was that the south-east sector was occupied by the great Moslem sanctuary of the Dome of the Rock, certainly covering the site of the Temple of Solomon (see below, p. 110). Though Jerusalem had been under Moslem domination from A.D. 636, with the exception of the relatively brief episode of the Crusades, in a remarkable religious tolerance which characterized Jerusalem until very recent years, the city was divided into separate quarters, a Moslem Quarter on the east, a Jewish Quarter in the west-central area, and in the rest of the western area a Christian Quarter, divided into Armenian, Greek, and Latin sectors. Jerusalem was not a flourishing city at the time of the visits of the travellers of the mid-nineteenth century. All refer to half-ruinous buildings and miserable hovels crowded along insanitary lanes. The most poverty-stricken area was that of the Jews, the most prosperous that of the Armenians, concentrated within the walls that still today constitute a separate enclave. The views published by these travellers suggest that there were waste spaces bordering the walls in many places, and indeed such exist today in the north-east and south-west quarters. But there can be little doubt that the core of the city was closely built up. Bartlett's view of the Pool of Hezekiah (so-called; it has in fact nothing to do with Hezekiah), looking east towards the Dome of the Rock (Pl. 2), has much in common with our view taken from rather further east (Pl. 3). A view looking west along David Street, the main street that runs east from the Jaffa Gate towards the Haram esh-Sherif on which the Dome of the Rock is situated, shows how closely built up the area is. That this is not the result of modern development is shown by the fact that many of the buildings in this core area of Jerusalem are medieval to sixteenth–seventeenth century, with beautifully carved architectural details.

This was the Jerusalem to which the P.E.F. sent its surveyor, Captain Charles Wilson, R.E., and its excavator, Lieutenant Warren, R.E., to investigate 'for Biblical Illustration', for it was the only Jerusalem that the nineteenth century knew. The investigators of Jerusalem had as their textual background in the first place, obviously, the Bible. The Biblical account is singularly lacking in precise details that can enable one to locate topographical features. Secondly, they had the descriptions of Jerusalem given by Flavius Josephus in his *Antiquities of the Jews* and *The Jewish War*. Josephus was a Jew, renegade to Rome in the early stages of the first Revolt of the Jews (A.D. 67–70), who was a first-class historian. His description of Jerusalem in the first century A.D. has the value of contemporary evidence. For earlier periods he provides valuable evidence, which nevertheless has to be assessed in weight against other evidence, for tradition entered more into his record than it would into that of a modern historian. The difficulty of using his contemporary evidence for Jerusalem of the first century A.D. lies in the fact that he refers to landmarks well known in his time, which we cannot today identify.

Captain Wilson's survey of Jerusalem, which produced the plan of Jerusalem to Ordnance Survey standards, began in 1865.

In February 1867, Lieutenant Warren arrived to undertake the excavation of the city, very justly entitled in his publication *Underground Jerusalem*. The problems assigned to Warren's programme in the Statement of Progress of the Fund included researches in the vaults, etc., beneath the Haram (Temple) area, excavations to determine the character of the western wall (of the Haram), to ascertain the

> natural features of the ground between the Ecce Homo Arch and St. Stephen's Gate, and between the Jaffa Gate and the Bab es-Silsileh of the Haram; in the Muristan, or Hospital of St. John, south of the Church of the Holy Sepulchre, for traces of the second wall [that of Josephus; to which we shall return] and in front of the Damascus Gate, where there is an old gateway. In the vaults of the Haram enclosure, the western road of the 'triple passage' might be uncovered, the two ancient doorways in the passage under El Aksa opened, the course of the curious passages, discovered by Mons. de Saulcy, in front of the 'triple gateway' traced out, and several cisterns, which appear to have been constructed for other purposes, examined.

I have quoted the passage at length, as illustrating the problems engaging the attention of the P.E.F. As shown in fig. 2 they are all within the area of the Old City. It was here that Warren's excavations were concentrated. Only one of his discoveries, the Ophel wall, was a leader to a Jerusalem outside the area of the Old City (see below, p. 19).

Jerusalem in the mid-nineteenth century formed part of a not very important province of the Turkish empire, in which a process of decay, culminating only in the twentieth century, was already in progress. The foreigner operating in Jerusalem had to have a *firman* from Constantinople. The P.E.F. began operations with such high prestige from its lists of supporters that the bureaucracy of Constantinople had to take notice. In fact, however, the *firman* was ambiguous in its terms, and obstructive local governors could shelter behind its ambiguity. Warren's excavations in Jerusalem had to deal not only with the

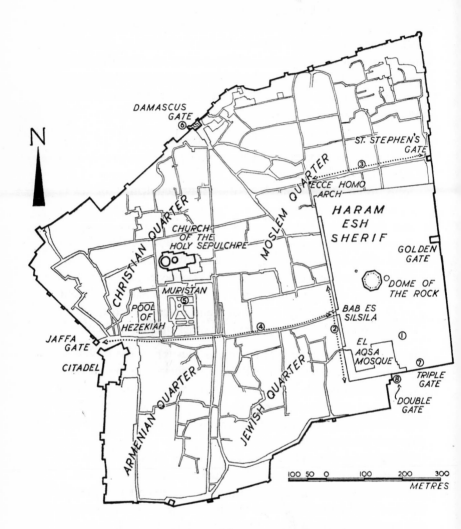

FIG 2   Plan of the Old City, showing sites which the Palestine Excavation Fund suggested should be investigated: (1) Passages and vaults in the neighbourhood of the El Aksa Mosque; (2) western wall of the Haram; (3) area of the Ecce Homo Arch; (4) area between the Jaffa Gate and the Bab-es-Silsileh; (5) area of the Muristan and the Second Wall of Josephus; (6) area in front of the Damascus Gate; (7) the Triple Gate; (8) the Double Gate

excavational difficulties of which no one in London had any conception, but with the devious methods of the Turkish governor and his assistants. With the excavational difficulties, no one in the mid-nineteenth century could have coped better, though by twentieth-century criteria, the results are very limited; but when it came to dealing with troublesome local authorities, Warren was in the top class. No one could possibly have done better.

Warren also had his difficulties with the society that supported him. *Underground Jerusalem* was published in 1876. In it, he refers to the difference between the 'infant society' under whose instructions (and financial support) he operated and the situation in 1876. He says:

> To its early life only I allude, when its swaddling clothes prevented action, when it was feeble and imperfectly organized, directed gratuitously at intervals by one so talented yet so overwhelmed by his professional work, and without a secretary.

He certainly had to deal with an inadequate home organization, in which a number of individuals had very strongly preconceived ideas as to the results he ought to be finding; and it would not be too unfair to describe some of these individuals as cranks. The enthusiasm behind the foundation of the P.E.F. was very genuine, but it took some years for this enthusiasm to be sufficiently organized to raise the required finance. At intervals Warren was paying for expenditure out of his own pocket, at one point in the first year to the extent of nearly £1,000, and a report in *The Times* in 1869 by the eccentric character who adopted the name of 'Rob Roy' referred to the fact that he had had to dismiss one-half of his trained labour force. In the initial stages those organizing the Fund were saying 'give us results, and we will send you money', to which Warren replied 'give me tools, materials, money, food, and I will get you results'. An excavator always has financial worries, but none can have been worse than those of Warren.

As has been said, the interests of the founders of the P.E.F.

were concentrated on the Jerusalem they knew, the Old City. It was natural that the instructions given to Warren placed special emphasis on investigations directed to the problems of the Haram esh-Sherif, for this was generally (and rightly) accepted as being the site of the Biblical Temple. Yet this was the area which the official *firman* appeared specifically to exclude from Warren's activities. In justification of the Turkish, Moslem, attitude, it is fair to quote 'Rob Roy' in *The Times* in April 1869:

> Nor can one wonder that the Turk should refuse a stranger leave to dig quite close to his cherished *Sanctuary*. Even the Dean of Westminster [Arthur Stanley, an enthusiastic supporter of the Fund] would be reluctant to allow a Turkish officer of Engineers to dig by the east buttress of Westminster Abbey.

There were certain ambiguities, due to the complete ignorance of the authorities in Constantinople of the historic sites of Palestine, including confusion between the Haram at Jerusalem and that at Hebron, and on these Warren very cleverly played. He proceeded step by step, establishing precedents and, very literally, burrowed himself in against a wall of opposition that was as recalcitrant as the physical obstacles that he encountered.

One cannot describe his excavations round the temple walls in sequence, for at most stages he had a series of shafts in process of excavation. One can best give an impression of his work and his difficulties by describing his excavations in relation to the different walls of the temple platform. There is a very clear-cut distinction in problems between those of the east and south walls and those of the west and north walls. The former are outside the Old City, the latter within it, and the conditions of excavation completely different.

On the east, Warren established the fact that the lower parts of the platform walls are deeply buried in layers of loose debris, almost all of it accumulated after the construction of the walls. He could not investigate the wall by a trench against its face, for the Pasha, Nasif, held firmly to the prohibition that he was not to excavate in the area of the Haram esh-Sherif. He was therefore obliged to carry out mining operations, with a shaft at a distance from the wall and galleries running up to it. This would be a difficult enough operation in any case. The successful accomplishment of a large number of operations is a miracle made possible only by the skill of Warren and his non-commissioned officers. The account of the excavations aimed at investigating the Golden Gate (Pl. 4), the great Roman-style gate in the east wall of the Haram, can be taken as a classic description of Warren's excavations. Outside the gate is a Moslem cemetery (Pl. 4). The only point at which a shaft could be sunk was 143 feet to the east. At a depth of 81 feet below the ground-level at the base of the gate, a shaft was driven in towards the Haram. Rock was soon struck, and followed upwards. At 68 feet it is recorded that 'the work became very dangerous, the gallery being driven through a mass of loose boulders alternating with layers of shingle, which on being set in motion runs like water'. At 97 feet a massive wall was reached, which defied all attempts at penetration. This wall in fact remains one of the problems that has to be fitted into the history of Jerusalem. One attempt was made by turning back with a gallery to the north, and then running in towards the Haram, but 'the shingle suddenly came in with a rush, quickly filling up six feet of the gallery, and burying some of the tools'. It is not surprising that Warren says

> We also cannot work more than a certain number of days at a time at a difficult place, as the constant danger causes the nerves to become unstrung after a time, and then a few days at safer work is required; only those who have experienced the peculiar effect of the rattling of the debris upon the frames, with the prospect at any moment of the boards being crushed in by a large stone, can appreciate the deterring influence it has upon the workmen. The non-commissioned officers have to keep continually to the front, or the men will not venture up.

It is an incredible story of bravery and determination. In fact, Warren himself says of Sergeant Birtles, his most prized non-commissioned officer,

> Indeed, our work was of such a nature that, I may say, every
> week Sergeant Birtles had to act in such a manner as would, on
> active service, have ensured him the Victoria Cross, or, under
> other circumstances, the Albert Medal; but here it simply
> came into the routine of our work . . .

The incredible difficulties of these operations were considerably
increased by the difficulty and expense of obtaining wood for
the mining frames, not available in Palestine. It was a bitter
moment for Warren when, after some six months of work,
the P.E.F., straitened for money, declared that mining frames
were not necessary. As with so many other decisions of the
supporting organization in England and the opposing local
authorities, Warren met this with sublime disdain.

The shafts and galleries to the east of the Haram showed the
level of the rock upon which the Temple had been founded. The
spectacular point is the south-east angle, where the magnificent
Herodian masonry descends to a depth of 80 feet below the
surface (as usual, revealed only by a shaft and a gallery 20 feet
long running in to the foot of the wall). The discovery of a
builder's mark in Hebrew characters on the stones sunk into
pre-existing levels was hailed as a most exciting find. The illustration of this shaft has achieved fame as the frontispiece of the
PEFQS and its successor the *PEQ*, with its depiction of a lady being
lowered in a chair to visit the base of the wall (fig. 3). It is not
described how gentlemen visitors descended. It may have been
by a rope ladder, but Warren refers to the exertions of hand-
over-hand descending and climbing a rope. I myself found visiting
all our sites in Jerusalem exhausting enough, but life was easy
compared with Warren's day.

The excavations along the east side traced the wall of the
platform to its culmination at the south-east angle, where it
stood out over the valley to a height of 170 feet. From that point,
the rock was traced rising steeply up to the west, up to the place
where today the blocked Double Gate is visible, with rock close
to the present surface. From that point, it slopes steeply down to

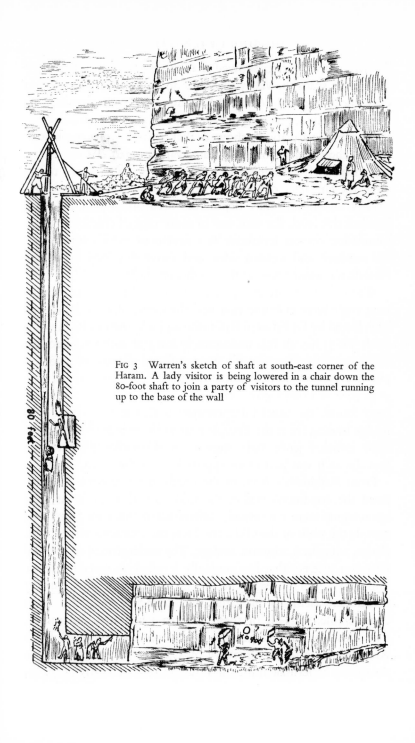

FIG 3 Warren's sketch of shaft at south-east corner of the Haram. A lady visitor is being lowered in a chair down the 80-foot shaft to join a party of visitors to the tunnel running up to the base of the wall

the west, and Warren showed that the present south façade of
the Haram spans the valley that runs down the centre of the Old
City, the Tyropoeon Valley of Josephus. The western wall of the
Haram is built appreciably up the slope of the western ridge.

Warren's excavations showed that towards the south-west
corner, the character of the Haram wall changed. To the east, it
was virtually free-standing to its base. As it sloped down to the
west, the character of the foundations changed. Here there was
already a considerable depth of occupation accumulation.
Beneath this level, the wall was of more rugged character. These
foundation courses terminate at a pavement, which runs round
the southern and western sides, and above this level is the fine
Herodian masonry seen at the south-east angle.

Warren's most interesting and complicated finds at the south-
west angle were in connection with the spring of an arch that had
been found by Dr Edward Robinson and is known as Robinson's
Arch (Pl. 5; fig. 4). It is undoubtedly integral with the Herodian
masonry of the Haram wall. Warren found the base of a corresponding pier, in similar masonry, indicating an arch with a span
at its base of 12·80 metres. Though no more of this structure has
been found, the usual interpretation is that it forms part of a
bridge leading from the Temple near to the western hill. Excavations initiated since 1961 suggest an alternative interpretation
that the arch was part of an approach from the south.

From Robinson's Arch to the north, the excavators encountered the conditions within the Old City that, as far as their
excavations were concerned, differentiated this area from that
outside the walls of the Old City. Here the problems were vaults,
drains, aqueducts, cisterns, sewage. The underground of the Old
City is a warren, that has gradually levelled up several separate
hills into a near plateau. The process has been gradual, but the
constituent elements in vaults and terracing walls are quite
considerable. Into all of these Warren penetrated and mined.
The most complicated are the vaults connected with Wilson's
Arch, named after its discovery by Captain Wilson who began
the survey of Jerusalem for the P.E.F. in 1865. The Arch (fig. 33)

FIG 4   The spring of Robinson's Arch. The arch and the lower courses of the wall of the Haram are of Herodian masonry. Compare Pls. 5 and 87

is an impressive affair, which in 1966 one could still visit, though admittedly the visit was hazardous, involving a rickety ladder balanced on a bed of the friendly sheikh who occupied the adjacent house.[1] Warren's shaft against the Haram wall was still open, and in it one could see Herodian-type masonry disappearing as far as our torches could penetrate. In its final stage, therefore, Wilson's Arch was associated with Herod's rebuilding of the Temple. It is, however, only one element in a most complicated series of vaults and passages that apparently constitute a causeway crossing the central valley on the line of the earliest wall that joined the western ridge to the original city on the eastern ridge. Its line is approximately that of the present David Street, leading down toward the Haram from the Jaffa Gate. Warren penetrated what he describes as a 'secret passage' along the line of this causeway, for a distance of 250 feet. He gives a vivid description of the difficulties, which included the greatest degree of suspicion and opposition by householders, and sheer physical problems. With his usual surveyor's recognition of the importance of ascertaining the exact position of all that he found, he remarks: 'it is exceedingly difficult to level through a succession of vaults underground, with the earth nearly up to the crowns of the arches, and I cannot be certain of these levels to a foot either way'. Nevertheless, he has given us the information of the existence of this causeway based on vaults that crossed the central valley, though he could only guess at the dates of the component parts, and he had inadequate evidence upon which to base his guesses. No one since has added any more certain information.

It was as he progressed to the north and round the north side of the Haram enclosure that the problems he had to deal with sound the most daunting to us today. The area was seamed with water channels and sewers, and often he had to pursue his topographical objective by following the line of a sewer, probably of ancient origin but still functioning. At the north-west corner of the temple area, Herod had established the fortress Antonia

[1] Since that date, conditions have greatly changed as a result of work carried out by the Israeli religious authority that has controlled the area since 1967.

in succession to the Maccabean fortress Baris. It was most desirable to prove its position. From a cistern under the Convent of the Sisters of Sion, which is probably on the site of Antonia, Wilson had observed a rock-cut passage running south towards the Haram enclosure. The passage is 4 feet wide, with smooth sides, 'and the sewage was five to six feet deep, so that if we had fallen in there was no chance of escaping with our lives'. Warren, however, was determined to follow the passage. For the first 12 feet he did this on a number of old planks. He then reached a magnificent passage 30 feet high. Because the danger of planks was, he admits, excessive, he procured three old doors and, with Sergeant Birtles, set out on a leap-frog procedure. 'The sewage was not water, and was not mud; it was just in such a state that a door would not float, but if left for a minute or two would not sink very deep'. In this way they progressed, with great difficulty in raising the hindermost door from the sucking slime, for a distance of 60 feet, where there was a dam retaining the sewage to the north 4 feet higher than to the south.

> Everything had now become so slippery with sewage that we had to exercise the greatest caution in lowering the doors and ourselves down, lest an unlucky false step might cause a header into the murky liquid – a fall which must have been fatal – and what honour would there have been in dying like a rat in a pool of sewage?

From this point they continued for a further 50 feet, after which the sewage became so firm that they could walk on it. At 200 feet from the beginning of the passage, they reached a blocking, so close under the Governor's Building against the north wall at the Haram, that they could hear voices overhead and dared not penetrate further. This particular exploration of Underground Jerusalem produced no information of immediate value. When, eventually, all the subterranean structures of the Old City are fully investigated, it will fall into place. But as a record of exploration, it is magnificent, and for many of us will induce a feeling of claustrophobia. Warren does not bother to describe the return journey which, at the end of this 200 feet, he and Sergeant Birtles had to face.

The mining operations outside the walls of the Haram and the vault-cistern-sewer penetrations within the Old City very literally put this important early area of Jerusalem on the map. The whole circumference of the Haram esh-Sherif, the modern representative of the Biblical Temple, was very thoroughly examined. The relation of its walls to the surface of the rock was established. Some forays were in fact carried out into the interior of the Haram, but such were the difficulties encountered from local opposition and from the inherent complications of the problem, that these do not really add to our knowledge of Jerusalem. Warren's quite invaluable contribution was on the topography of the Old City. I hope that I have described adequately what he did to show how remarkable was his achievement.

Warren's principal efforts were directed to the temple area, for these were his instructions. However, as a true explorer, he followed up a number of other lines. One of these, a remarkable aqueduct running down the Kedron from Bir Eyub, south of the junction of the Kedron and the Hinnom, remains unexplained. He was also responsible for penetration right through the Siloam Tunnel, running from the Spring Gihon in the Kedron Valley to the Siloam Pool in the central valley. Today, it is a simple matter to walk along the tunnel (pp. 154-8 and Pls. 65, 66), but this is due to clearance in 1911. Warren and Birtles had to wallow through on their stomachs, holding candles in their mouths, as well as surveying instruments that enabled them to produce a remarkably accurate plan. Even to walk through today, with water up to mid-thigh, is an impression that remains with one. Again, the intrepidity of these early explorers deserves the fullest recognition.

The Siloam Tunnel is only one, and the latest, of a series of tunnels and shafts connected with the Spring Gihon. The investigations of Père Vincent in connection with the 1911 excavations showed that the earliest was a channel leading to the foot of a shaft that gave access from the higher slope of the hill to the west. This is described below. It was Warren's discovery, and from the point of view of exploration, it was of a difficulty fully equal to the best of Warren's exploits.

Warren's discovery leading on most directly to the rest of the story of Digging up Jerusalem is that he found that running south from the south-east corner of the Haram there was a wall, certainly of town-wall dimensions, following the crest of the ridge above the Kedron Valley. He followed this wall for 700 feet. At least in the area immediately to the south of the Haram, the wall that he was following was Byzantine. As was his usual practice, he followed the wall by tunnelling. In the 1965–67 excavations in Site s II (fig. 22) we found his tunnel, as an alarming void beneath the final Byzantine wall on the edge of the modern road. The photograph (Pl. 107) shows how we had hurriedly to underpin the wall. The wall that Warren followed was Byzantine, but we know now that it was the successor of a much earlier wall. One of Warren's contributions to the full history of Jerusalem was to show that earlier occupation extended to the south of the present Old City.

This leads on to the next stage in Digging up Jerusalem, the expansion of the area to the south of the Old City. From 1896 onwards, the attention of the P.E.F. was increasingly turned to the Survey of Palestine and the exploration of Palestine and the adjacent areas. In the course of this, some further work was done on Jerusalem, and Lieutenant Conder's map, dated 1873, of the contours in the area of the Old City (fig. 5) can be taken as a culmination of the examination of the underlying topography of the Old City. There were many investigations of ancient remains, tombs, aqueducts, vaults, and sewers, especially by Charles Clermont-Ganneau on behalf of the P.E.F. None of these can be ignored by those working on the detailed history of Jerusalem, but, though the detail with which Clermont-Ganneau records all finds and observations is wholly commendable, for the most part they do not add to the overall findings. The records, nevertheless, are fascinating reading. My greatest

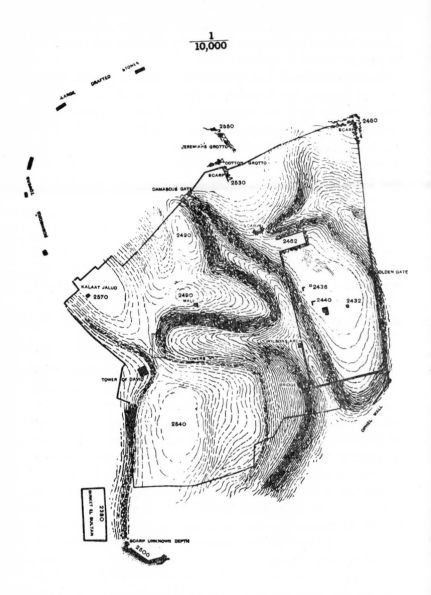

FIG 5 The rock contours beneath the Old City of Jerusalem, as surveyed by Conder

difficulty in perusing the early volumes of the Quarterly Statement of the P.E.F. is not to spend too long on the reports that
are irrelevant to my present study. The perils to health to which
explorers of Palestine at this time were exposed, from which
one of Warren's men had died and several had been seriously ill,
are emphasized by the death in 1874 of one of the leaders of the
Survey, C. F. Tyrwhitt-Drake, at the age of twenty-eight, from
fever contracted during the work.

By 1890, the work of Clermont-Ganneau, Henry Maudslay,
and H. Guthe had shown that remains of ancient structures were
to be found over much of the area south of the Old City, up to
the boundary provided by the valley of the Hinnom, and Warren's
Ophel wall had been traced nearly to the point of junction of the
Hinnom and Kedron. It was to this southern area that the attention of the next main excavations of the P.E.F. was directed.
The direction of the excavations was entrusted to Frederick J.
Bliss, who describes himself on the title-page of the book describing his finds[1] as 'Explorer to the Fund'. He was assisted by an
architect, A. C. Dickie. Bliss was an American who became one of
the assistants of Flinders Petrie. Petrie had recently carried out his
remarkable excavations at Tell el-Hesi, which marked the beginnings of stratigraphical excavation in Palestine. Bliss had worked
with him there and continued the excavation of the site after
Petrie returned to Egypt. Bliss had learnt from Petrie the importance of pottery, but he did not attempt to use Petrie's method of
excavating by layers. He presumably did not consider them suitable for Jerusalem, as indeed such primitive stratigraphical
methods were not.

Bliss in fact followed closely at Jerusalem the methods of
Warren. He dedicates his book thus:

To Major-General Sir Charles Warren, K.C.B.
My dear Sir Charles,
    When as a lad in my father's summer house in Lebanon I used
to listen to the account of the excavations you were conducting

[1] B. and D.

in the Holy City, little did I think that I should have the honour, many years after, of taking up your work. While digging at Jerusalem, Mr Dickie and I had the luck to employ two of your old workmen, and we found that the mighty deeds of 'the Captain' had taken their place in the local folk-lore. We feel great pleasure in dedicating this volume to our predecessor in the work.

Faithfully yours,
F. J. Bliss.

By 1961, no recognizable folklore about 'the Captain' or his successors survived, but traces of their work were to be found everywhere. Mention has already been made of Warren's tunnel beneath the wall along the eastern crest. Bliss defines his aims thus: 'Our chief work was the tracing of the lines taken by the south walls of Jerusalem during various periods . . .'. With quite embarrassing regularity we found a 'B. and D.' tunnel almost everywhere we dug, especially round the lower end of the Tyropoeon Valley. Plate 6 shows our clearance of a gateway found by Bliss at the south-east apex of the defences. The tunnels by which Bliss had traced the walls in either direction are clearly visible. The plan made by Dickie in these cramped circumstances, by the light of lanterns or candles, is so accurate that our surveyor remarked that it was hardly necessary for him to replan it. Moreover, the sheer mechanics of 'driving' (the word always used) the tunnels passes belief. The limits of height and width must have made the removal of enormous blocks of stone incredibly difficult, and the evacuation of the soil and stones back for scores of yards from the tunnel-head is equally incredible. Plate 97 shows the tumble of stones excavated by us in Site N (fig. 36), lying on a Herodian street. Bliss and Dickie had traced this street from the mouth of the Tyropoeon, a distance of 1,400 feet, and Pl. 7 shows their tunnel which had successfully carved its way through the tumble of stones.

Bliss's first project was to trace the wall running south from the south-west angle of the Old City which corresponded to

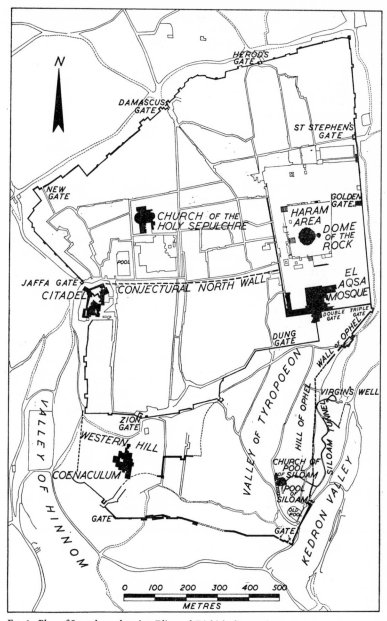

Fig 6 Plan of Jerusalem, showing Bliss and Dickie's discoveries

Warren's Ophel wall running south from the south-east corner of the Haram. Henry Maudslay in 1874 had traced a rock scarp up to 45 feet high running south for 650 feet, then south-east for 350 feet. A long, relatively straight line of scarp like this can be taken as evidence of the line of a wall. It probably served two purposes: to add to the height of the wall and as a quarry for the wall constructed on its top. On occasion, quarrying at the foot of a town wall may belong to a later period, usually suggested by irregularities and the lack of a defined scarp following the line of the wall.

Maudslay's final point suggested a rock-cut ditch turning to the north-east. This was the point at which Bliss took up the search. He traced lines curving round the western ridge, and he also showed that a line, sometimes a scarp only, but sometimes a wall, continued to the south-east. Bliss's method was explicitly that of shaft and tunnel. But the record of his finds is clear. One can always deduce when the buildings and walls that he found were Byzantine, as were many of those in his extensions up the western ridge. Stratigraphical evidence in the modern sense does not exist, but the supreme merit of the records, those of Bliss and his architect Dickie, is the description of architectural and masonry details. One must accept the sequence of walls traced to the east as lacking any stratigraphical evidence for dating, but the detailed description of the masonry makes it quite possible to claim links with other sections of walls for which there is stratigraphical evidence. Modern excavators can learn many lessons from Bliss and Dickie, however much they shudder at their methods.

It takes but a few words to describe the fact of the tracing of the southernmost wall of ancient Jerusalem. The actual process was laborious in the extreme. Shafts and galleries totalling a length of 800 feet were required to cover a distance of 400 feet. The various features encountered leading back into the town – streets, aqueducts, drains – were all followed, almost all by tunnelling. One aqueduct had to be planned by sending a small boy to crawl ahead with the end of the measuring tape and a candle.

In due course the shafts and tunnels carried the excavators

along the line of the Hinnom Valley to its junction with the central valley, the Tyropoeon. There they found a massive wall linking the tips of the two ridges running south from the Old City of Jerusalem. The tracing of the wall was one of the more hazardous parts of the enterprise. We find remarks like: 'Indeed the road caved in outside the terrace at H2, and we were obliged to fill up our tunnel in a hurry'. The difficulties were great, but in spite of them the excavators progressed across the valley. Figure 7 gives an idea of the method and of the enormous labour involved, and the exactitude of the drawings of the masonry shows how it can be interpreted in modern terms. One must emphasize once more the importance of this great step forward in the recording of archaeological structures.

To the north of this wall across the central valley lies the Pool of Siloam, and inevitably Bliss followed clues in that direction. The full problems of the Pool of Siloam are discussed below (pp. 158-9). Following in the steps of Warren, Bliss's basic aim was to establish the physical features of the contours of the valley leading down to the Pool of Siloam. Again in the Warren tradition, he traced these contours by a series of shafts. On a line about 430 feet north of the south end of the present Pool, he sank a series of shafts down the western slope of the valley, and began the ascent of the eastern side. His method is shown on fig. 8. The difficulties encountered are nicely illustrated by the statement:[1] 'The gallery from shaft 7 to the east was driven up the rapidly ascending cliff till the candle ceased to burn'. The Silwani workers of the 1890s were clearly of tougher stuff than our workmen in 1965 who were most unwilling to crawl along a solidly built water channel found 200 yards to the south. In this series of shafts, shaft 8 struck a paved street. Mention has already been made (above, p. 22) of our discovery of the tunnels by which this street was traced. It was followed both north and south of the shaft, and a well-built drain that lay beneath was also traced north from the town wall at the southern end of the hill, where it ran through the gate mentioned above.

[1] B. and D., p. 114.

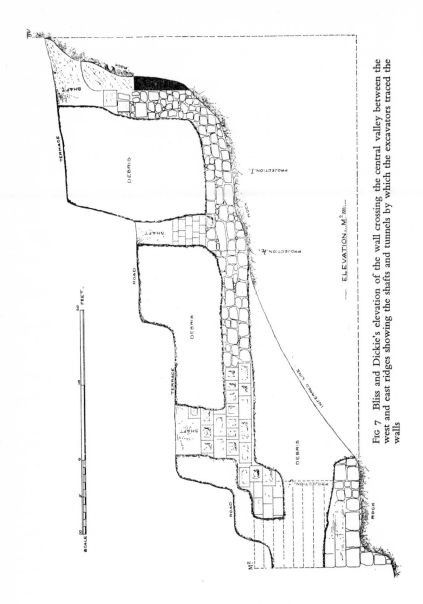

FIG 7 Bliss and Dickie's elevation of the wall crossing the central valley between the west and east ridges showing the shafts and tunnels by which the excavators traced the walls

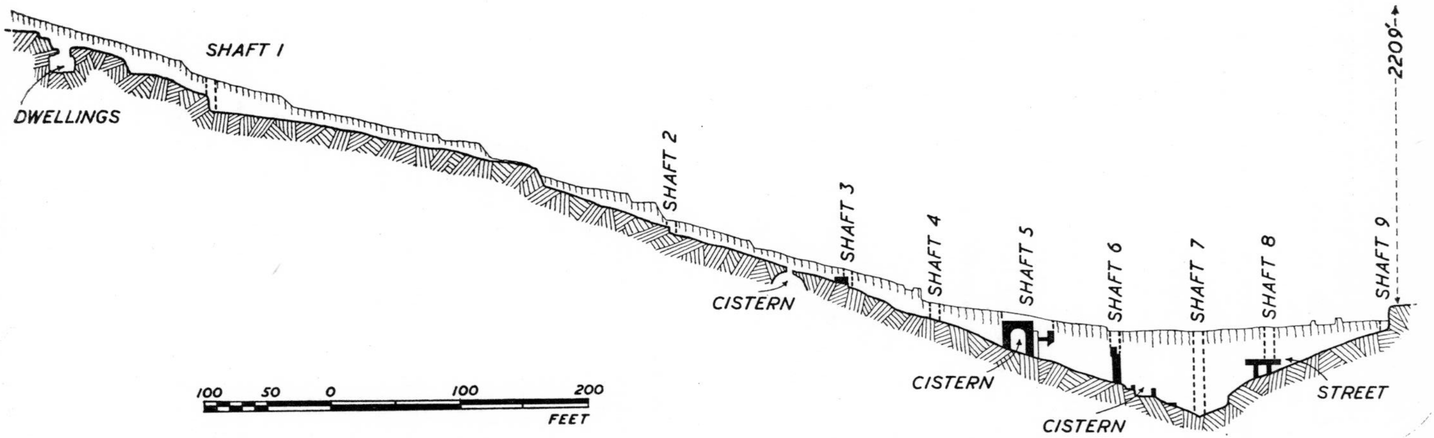

FIG 8 Section across central valley, as established by Bliss and Dickie's shafts

In tracing this road, the excavators struck the structures, probably of the Herodian period, associated with the Pool of Siloam. Equally interesting was their find of a church associated with the Pool. The church is first described by Antoninus Martyr (*c.* A.D. 560–70), and was probably built by Eudoxia, wife of the Emperor Theodosius, during her exile in Jerusalem (A.D. 450–60). I illustrate the plan (fig. 9), for even to Dickie it seemed a great achievement to recover it. The church lay beneath from 12 to 22 feet of debris. On the merely organizational side there were difficulties, for the overlying surface was in three ownerships: 'the west end [of the church] to a certain 'Atallah, most of the rest of the church to one Salim, while a part of the north aisle was held in common by the peasants of Siloam'. The shafts and tunnels in the three areas had to be kept separate, for each owner jealously claimed the stones that emerged from beneath his land. The dimensions of the church were 150 feet by 100 feet, but it needed tunnels more than 500 feet in length to reveal the plan. Bliss says: 'it was not till the excavations were finished that we were aware how completely the remains fitted together to form a coherent plan'. One can well believe it, but it remains a marvel that the surveying was so accurate that a coherent plan could emerge. Even quite adequate photographs were taken, deep in the depths, of the mosaic floor of the church, long before the day of flashlights.

Bliss literally put the southern part of ancient Jerusalem on the map. The wall that he traced across the mouth of the Tyropoeon virtually joined that previously traced down the summit of the eastern ridge. What contemporary technique could not enable him to do was to date the various wall periods and structures that he discovered. He made a very scholarly assessment of the evidence in the light of current knowledge,[1] with full use of all textual material, and often his identifications are very probable. His criteria are, however, those of building techniques, and for the earlier periods he had no comparative material. His dismissal of rock-cut dwellings as primitive, and therefore Jebusite, is

[1] *B. and D.*, pp. 313 ff.

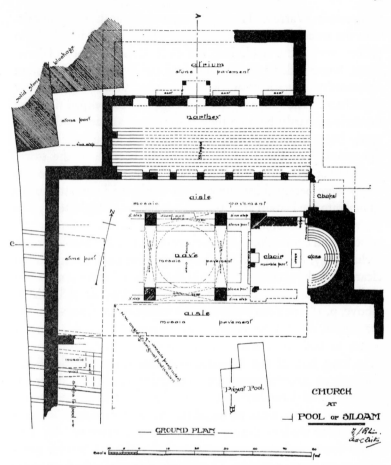

FIG 9   Plan of church above Pool of Siloam

understandable, but in fact our evidence shows that they were
Byzantine. For the periods of the Jewish monarchy, he had no
certain comparisons, and the natural inclination to provide a wide
area for the Jerusalem of the period led him to assign stages in the
wall enclosing the western ridge to the Solomonic and later
monarchical period; this was wrong, but very comprehensible.

In the history of the exploration of Jerusalem, nothing was
on the scale, or of the importance, of the work of Bliss and his

predecessor Warren. The achievements of both were heroic.

In the succeeding years, there were probably few in which no probes were being made into the underground history of Jerusalem. Some added a small element to our knowledge. The next noteworthy investigation, in 1911, was British – the Parker expedition. The objects and findings of the expedition are mysterious, partly because they were never, as such, published; partly because the explorers were rumoured to be searching for the treasures of the Temple; and partly because of the story, probably at least in some degree factual, that, because the organizers were betrayed by one of their workmen in an attempt to tunnel into the Haram area, they had to escape by night to a yacht conveniently moored in a Mediterranean harbour. The whole episode, and excavations, does not redound to the credit of British archaeology. Some good did, however, emerge. The expedition cleared out the accumulated silt in the Siloam Tunnel; instead of wallowing through on one's stomach today, as did Birtles (above, p. 18), one can walk through knee-deep in freely-running water (Pls. 65, 66). Secondly, they allowed Père L.-H. Vincent access to their sites. Père Vincent is one of the most famous in a long line of the Dominican archaeologists of the Ecole Biblique et Archéologique de Saint-Etienne, unrivalled for his knowledge of Jerusalem over many decades. I have the clearest memories of his visits to Samaria, my first participation, as a very junior student during 1931–35, in a Palestinian dig, and of his charm and elegance (he was small and *petit*), but his questions were very searching. Those who disagreed with him came in for a terrific pounding, though always couched in the most polite terms. Anyhow, the organizers of the Parker expedition continued to be referred to as 'les savants messieurs', perhaps because they never published anything with which Père Vincent could disagree. Fortunately, Père Vincent rescued and published quite a lot of evidence. He replanned the Siloam Tunnel and discussed its problems. He replanned the earlier (see below, p. 84) and later accesses to the Spring Gihon and he published some very interesting fourth-millennium tomb groups accidentally discovered. A considerable amount was in fact salvaged from a very unsatisfactory enterprise.

The Parker expedition was exceptional by any standards. The next excavations, in 1913–14, were of a very different standard. They were directed by R. Weill on behalf of Baron Edmond de Rothschild. They represent the first complete clearance of a large area at Jerusalem, at the southern end of the eastern ridge. The site was purchased from its owners, and still lies open, while on the slopes of the valley at its foot a large mound represents the dump of the soil removed, a considerable embarrassment to municipal authorities wishing to widen the road down the valley. Area clearance is potentially an improvement on tunnelling. The excavations revealed a complicated succession of defences along the eastern crest and a maze of cuttings into the rock (Pl. 8). The excavation methods of the time, however, were inadequate to interpret either the successive defences or the maze of rock cuttings. The practice of stratification had not arrived in Palestine. All interpretations were based on the literary evidence of what should be there. A full study of the evidence concerning the defences, based on secure facts from elsewhere, will probably fit these finds into a picture. It is, however, already clear that the interpretation of the rock cuttings can only be guesswork. What one sees today is the result of quarrying at the time that Hadrian built Aelia Capitolina (c. A.D. 135); the evidence for this came from our excavations in an adjoining area. Some of the great cuttings into the rock are pure quarries. Others are earlier cuttings, cisterns and baths of the Hellenistic and Herodian periods, truncated by quarrying. The controversial point is the cuttings that Weill identified as the Royal Tombs of the House of David. The Biblical evidence that David and his heirs were buried *in* Jerusalem[1] has stimulated many searches and fanciful identifications, including that of the so-called Tomb of David shown to

---

[1] e.g., I Kings 2:10: 'Then David slept with his fathers and was buried in the city of David'; I Kings 11:43: 'And Solomon slept with his fathers and was buried in the city of David his father'; similarly for Abijam, I Kings 15:8 and Joash, II Kings 12:21.

tourists today. The particular cuttings revealed by Weill were
certainly unusual, consisting of two rock-cut tunnels side by side
(Pl. 9). They are not like any observed cisterns, though the
plaster that covers the rock shows that they were at some stage
used as cisterns. They are also not like any known tombs of the
period. My own view is that there is absolutely no evidence that
they were the much-searched-for Royal Tombs, and that they
were probably cisterns. I would even go so far as saying that I
doubt that *in* Jerusalem means within the walls of the city, for
burial within the walls of the town was completely contrary to
semitic practice. I would expect the Royal Tombs to have been
on the opposite slopes of the surrounding valleys, probably that
of the Kedron, where magnificent tombs of a later period have
been found. But this is theory only. It is as unsupported by
evidence as was Weill's identification of the tunnels as the Royal
Tombs.

After the 1914–18 War, Britain was quick to renew her interest
in Palestinian archaeology. A Department of Antiquities was
established, and the British School of Archaeology in Jerusalem
was the first successor of the old-established Schools in Athens
and Rome for the training of students and for research in
countries overseas. The links between the new British School of
Archaeology in Jerusalem and the Palestine Exploration Fund
were close. The Fund's interests tended to be concentrated on
Jerusalem, and it initiated the next excavations carried out there
during 1923–25. They were directed by Professor R. A. S.
Macalister. Macalister, a highly respected Irish archaeologist,
entered the Palestine field in 1903, when he began his excavations
at Gezer. His reports of his excavations there are a model of
thoroughness; they lack the stratigraphical method which did
not exist at that date in Palestine. His methods in Jerusalem,
twenty years later, were similar, and here there was the great
problem of a site with stone-built walls, liable to recurrent stone-
robbing, and an underlying rock surface inviting quarrying in
periods of radical movements in the position of the town. The
main area of Macalister's excavations on the summit of the

eastern ridge can be interpreted, in the light of our excavations in adjacent areas, as one in which the quarrying referred to in connection with Weill's excavations further south had removed all evidence before the Roman period. Macalister's attempts to interpret very unconvincing fragments of walls as belonging to the Jebusite-Solomonic periods have no foundation at all. Macalister also exposed a substantial portion of the wall running along the eastern crest, the continuation of Warren's Ophel wall. He interpreted what he exposed as a tower built by David and repaired by Solomon, added onto pre-existing Jebusite defences. As will be seen (below, p. 77), he was hundreds of years out. His method of trenching along the foot of the wall destroys all stratigraphical evidence; it is a major sin in modern eyes, but one must remember that his methods were by then some twenty years old. The reinterpretation of his finds is discussed below (pp. 191-3).

The interest of the Palestine Exploration Fund in Jerusalem was permanent. When J. W. Crowfoot was appointed as Director of the British School of Archaeology in Jerusalem in 1927, the P.E.F. invited him to continue Macalister's excavations on the eastern ridge. Crowfoot's choice of a site was a revolutionary one: the western side of the eastern ridge. His method was also revolutionary. In contrast to the shaft-and-tunnel and area clearance of his predecessors, he cut a trench down into the central valley. John Crowfoot was the first director with whom I worked in Palestine, and I have a great admiration for him. I have a vivid recollection of his description of how, in the disastrous Palestine earthquake of 1927, he was down this trench on Ophel. The earth heaved, but only a few stones fell into the trench. We had many trenches comparable with those of Crowfoot, and all of us can well appreciate what a miracle it was; fortunately during our excavations there were no earthquakes. Crowfoot was the first to discover a line of fortifications on the western side of the eastern ridge, where he was fortunate enough to hit on the position of an imposing gateway. It was built of rough blocks of stone, and on these grounds Crowfoot dated it to the Bronze Age, and considered it to be Jebusite; dating by exact stratification had not yet arrived in Palestine. In fact, the hoard of Maccabean coins, dating to the reign of Alexander Jannaeus (103–76 B.C.), that he found in the gateway provided the true dating.

When in 1919 Britain was made the mandatory power in Palestine, a Department of Antiquities was set up. In the 1930s and 1940, the officers of the department, notably R. W. Hamilton and C. N. Johns, were active in investigating the problems of Jerusalem. Both were trained in classical archaeology, and for the first time the evidence of stratification was used, in conjunction with that of masonry styles, to elucidate the chronology of the structures revealed. Hamilton's main work[1] was against the north wall of the present Old City, where he identified a gate built by Hadrian about A.D. 135, belonging to the Roman city of Aelia Capitolina, beneath the present Damascus Gate, and also provided evidence of the various building periods of the north wall. Johns's work[2] was in the area of the present Citadel, beside the Jaffa Gate on the western ridge. The Herodian origin of the main existing tower is very obvious from the masonry of the lower courses. Johns showed that the Herodian stage was preceded by Hellenistic, or Maccabean, stages. His finds have been supplemented by those of Mrs Amiran in 1968–69.[3] The evidence from the areas excavated by Hamilton and Johns is discussed below (pp. 202–3, 238).

The excavations by the officials of the Department of Antiquities can be seen as the close of an epoch, in more than one sense. In the situation that resulted from the events of 1948, the British officials left. Jerusalem became a frontier town of Jordan, with the boundary between Jordan and Israel running round the north wall from the Damascus Gate and along the length of the west wall; the Jaffa Gate was walled up. Stretching south from the south-west corner of the Old City was an area of

[1] QDAP, X.
[2] QDAP, XIV.
[3] IEJ, 20.

no man's land, extending down to the Hinnom Valley.

It was in this situation that the renewed British excavations were begun, under the aegis of the British School of Archaeology, with many supporters who are detailed in the Preface, and in association with the old inquirer into the history of Jerusalem, the Palestine Exploration Fund. The British School had recently brought to a conclusion its excavations at Jericho. The outstanding finds there had been in the prehistoric period. Jericho had been a site of the greatest importance in the earliest Neolithic. It is a fair guess that no other site in Palestine of this period could compare with it. Certainly many sites of interest must exist, and should be investigated, but to go to them from Jericho would have an element of bathos. As a main dig for the British School, it seemed best to look for something in a different area. The challenge of the problems of Jerusalem provided an immediate answer. Only the excavations of the officials of the Department of Antiquities of the Mandate had approached the problem of dating structural remains by stratigraphy. The problems are described in the ensuing chapter. The basis of the succeeding account is the evidence provided by the excavations of the British School of Archaeology in Jerusalem between 1961 and 1967.

★

CHAPTER TWO

The Topography and History of Jerusalem and its Problems

IN THE FIRST CHAPTER, some reference has been made to the topographical features of Jerusalem. From this point on, we are referring only to ancient Jerusalem, and ignoring the modern spreads to the west and north. The present Old City of Jerusalem has from the air (Pl. 12) a superficial appearance of a plateau. In fact, a walk from the Jaffa Gate along David Street towards the Haram esh-Sherif (fig. 2) shows how steeply one goes down and then climbs sharply up to the platform dominated by the Dome of the Rock in the Haram esh-Sherif, the site of Solomon's Temple. The declivity, which takes its origin in the region of the Damascus Gate, develops rapidly into a deep valley. Sections across it are indicated in the surveys of Warren (fig. 20) and Bliss (fig. 8). The valley was called by Josephus the Tyropoeon, usually translated, unsatisfactorily, as that of the Cheese-makers. The effect of this central valley was to divide the ancient site of Jerusalem into two.

The delimitation of Jerusalem to the east is still starkly apparent. The Kedron Valley has a fairly gentle beginning to the north-east of the Old City. But as it curves round to the south it deepens rapidly. Pls. 10, 13 show its modern contours as it deepens past the north-east corner of the Old City. The delimitation to the west starts visibly only south of the Jaffa Gate. From that point, though there is some masking modern buildings and fill, the Hinnom Valley develops almost equally starkly. Its course is shown on the air view (Pl. 12), which shows that it turns to the east to run into the Kedron (Pl.11).

It was this area bounded by the Kedron on the east and the Hinnom on the west, curving round to run into the Kedron, that was the centre of the expansion of research from the Old City. Warren's Ophel wall, Bliss and Dickie's west and south wall, encompassed it. Warren and Bliss identified the central valley, the Tyropoeon. Research since this time has emphasized the importance of separating the history of the eastern ridge, between the Kedron and the Tyropoeon, and that of the western ridge, between the Tyropoeon and the Hinnom. The Tyropoeon has its origin in the neighbourhood of the Damascus Gate. The upper part of its course is today followed by the main street running south from the Damascus Gate, the Tariq el-Wad, which slopes down as does the valley, but, as Warren's shafts and tunnels showed, there are many feet of debris below the street, and indeed beneath the Roman street, the line of which the modern street follows.

Both the eastern and western ridges on which ancient Jerusalem was built were thus well defended by steep valleys. Only to the north is there no actual boundary. Here, the ridges merge into the central backbone of Palestine, the watershed between streams running into the Mediterranean and those running into the Jordan Valley. The main line of this backbone is north and south, but at this point it bends to the west, and the Jerusalem ridges run off from it to the south.

Of the two ridges, the western is superficially the more attractive, for it is higher and wider than the eastern ridge, which is in the area south of the Old City and has a summit only about a hundred yards across. The western ridge was for long considered to be the site of the original Jerusalem, and on it is situated the traditional Tomb of David, though there is no evidence at all for this attribution. The view that the first Jerusalem was on the western ridge dates back to the time of Josephus, writing in the first century A.D., who calls it Mount Zion, and thus must have considered it to be David's town. Archaeological evidence is quite clear that this is wrong, and that the Jerusalem of the time of David lay on the eastern ridge. Josephus was a careful historian, and it remains an unexplained mystery why he was confused in this important matter.

As will be seen, the archaeological evidence is clear that the first Jerusalem was on the eastern ridge. The reason is a perfectly simple one. Only a settlement on the eastern ridge had access to a perennial water-supply. Rainfall in Palestine is completely seasonal. From about April to November there is virtually none. In the winter months it can, in the hills, be abundant, but to conserve the water over the succeeding months needed cisterns. In the old days, as late as the time of the Mandate, no one was allowed to build a house without a cistern to take the rainwater draining off the roof. The number of rock-cut cisterns of the Hellenistic, Roman, and Byzantine periods found in excavations suggest that there were similar regulations then. But cisterns are only efficient if they have an impervious lining. Mud mortar has the disadvantage that the mud in due course dissolves. Lime mortar as a lining for cisterns appears, on archaeological evidence, only to have been invented about 1000 B.C. In the preceding millennia, every permanent settlement had to be within reach of a perennial water-supply.

The only perennial sources in the vicinity of Jerusalem lay in the Kedron Valley. The Kedron itself, the Hinnom, and in the old days the Tyropoeon, before it was choked with debris, ran with water, but only during winter torrents. Feeding the Kedron Valley were, and are, two springs, the Spring Gihon (referred to in I Kings 1 : 33 and II Chronicles 32 : 30) and Bir Eyub. The latter lies south of the defensible position of Jerusalem, so Gihon is the only spring that converted the physically attractive possibilities of the site into one inviting permanent settlement. Access to Gihon was the reason for the first Jerusalem. Gihon still runs today, its waters for the most part channelled through the Siloam Tunnel. We used them during our excavations, with a donkey carrying four 4-gallon tins climbing up the path to our excavations above, but the water was not very popular with our workmen. This is not perhaps very surprising, as seepage from the whole present occupation on the eastern ridge must contaminate it. It nevertheless remains a fact that the Spring Gihon is the basic factor in the existence of the earliest Jerusalem.

The wider geographical point to be considered is why Jerusalem achieved such importance. It was not ancient as settlements in Palestine go. It made no contributions to the beginnings of settlement, as did Jericho. It was of no importance in the Early Bronze Age compared with the important towns of Megiddo, Beth-shan, and Lachish, though there was some occupation of the period on the site. Its importance comes with the first attempt to establish a unified control over Palestine as a whole. Palestine in the Early Bronze Age, the Middle Bronze Age, and the Late Bronze Age was, as far as archaeological and historical evidence goes, a country of city states, under some distant and intermittent control from Egypt, but not unified and the states probably often at war among themselves; the emphasis on town defences certainly suggests this.

Anyone attempting to create an integrated whole out of these loose units had to face the facts of the country's geography. Upon the older city-state system of the second millennium B.C. had been superimposed the effect of the arrival of the infiltrating Israelite tribes. No more than the villages and towns into which they infiltrated were they a unified whole. Under the Judges, groups joined in temporary alliance to deal with enemies. Full co-operation came with the development of the Philistine threat. This was the foundation of the monarchy of David. In this context, he was elected by both the northern and southern tribes.

Geographically, however, his two kingdoms were separate, whatever the origins of the northern and southern tribes, which are outside the scope of the present discussions. The configuration of Palestine constricts routes of communication within very narrow limits. The watershed between valleys conveying water to the Mediterranean and those running east to the Jordan Valley and the Dead Sea runs the length of the country, and is often very narrow. The nature of the terrain is such that

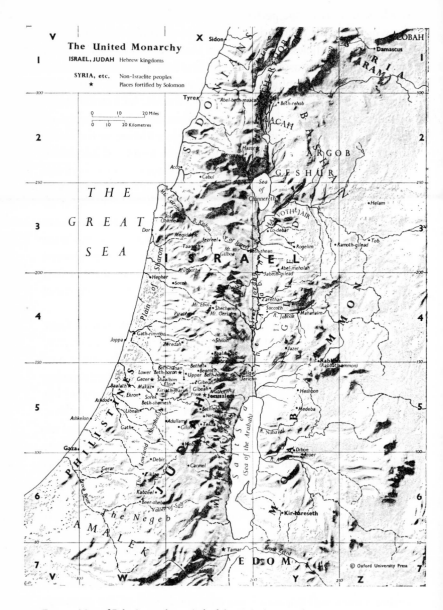

FIG 10   Map of Palestine at the period of the United Monarchy

from the watershed the valleys on either side deepen very rapidly. The summit of the watershed is a backbone which supports the structure of the country. Along it is the main north-south route.

In 1948, the frontier between Jordan and Israel cut the backbone route between Jerusalem and Bethlehem, along which one could drive in fifteen minutes. The alternative route had to climb (in a terrifying manner) up and down the valleys running east from the watershed and took a full hour-and-a-quarter. At the time when the Israelite tribes were approaching unity in the eleventh century B.C., the central route along the backbone was the one point of importance. To the west, in the Mediterranean plain, the Philistines were in control. To the east, the Jordan Valley provided no alternative, for cliffs bounded the Dead Sea on either side. East of the Jordan, alien and enemy powers were in control. The backbone route was essential for uniting David's two kingdoms and, in between the two, Jerusalem controlled the route.

Jerusalem appears first in the penumbra of history in the Amarna Letters (c. 1370 B.C.), in which its ruler, Abd Khiba, protests his loyalty to Egypt. Its importance as a Late Bronze Age town, in the second half of the second millennium B.C., is recorded in the Book of Joshua: 'As for the Jebusites the inhabitants of Jerusalem, the children of Judah could not drive them out: but the Jebusites dwell with the children of Judah at Jerusalem unto this day'.[1] The Jebusites are mentioned a number of times in the Bible, but their only recorded town was Jerusalem. They probably belonged to the Amorite tribes which occupied the hill country, with the Canaanites in occupation of the plains. It is an illustration of the piecemeal infiltration of the Israelites that the Jebusites were still in occupation of Jerusalem at the end of the eleventh century B.C.

During the period in which the Israelite tribal groups remained independent, only joining together in regional confederations to combat enemy threats, the existence among them of enclaves and fortified towns of the earlier inhabitants created no great problems.

[1] Joshua 15:63.

The growing threat from the Philistines, who had occupied the coastal plain soon after 1200 B.C., and who had ambitions to expand over the whole of Palestine, forced the Israelite tribes to combine much more wholeheartedly. Saul, towards the end of the eleventh century B.C., was the first national leader. His resistance to the Philistines ended in defeat and in the death of Saul. In his place, David became the leader of the Israelite tribes. At the stage when David emerges as a renowned warrior, the Israelite tribal groups had coalesced into a northern and a southern group. It is probable that this reflects their route of entry into Palestine, from the southern deserts, with perhaps forays into Egypt, and from the north-east and east. As has already been said, the process was gradual and on a relatively small scale. Archaeologically, there is no point at which one can say that the Israelites had arrived. They infiltrated and adopted much of the existing Canaanite-Amorite material culture.

By the end of the eleventh century B.C., a northern and a southern combination of tribes had emerged. The distinction between them was basically that of their origins. It was emphasized by the fact that the only convenient main road between them along the sharply defined backbone of the hill country was controlled by Jerusalem, still in the hands of the predecessors of the Israelites.

David's reputation as a warrior was such that he was separately elected by both the northern and the southern tribes. Both groups clearly recognized that a unified control was necessary to deal with the military might of the Philistines. David's first capital was at Hebron, in the area of the southern tribes. But it was apparent to him that he must unite his two kingdoms and get rid of the tiresome blockage created by the Jebusite relic of pre-Israelite occupation at Jerusalem.

David's capture of Jerusalem is to be dated *c.* 1005 B.C. Exact dates cannot, in fact, be applied in Palestine until about fifty years later. The Jebusites, who had survived some two hundred years of infiltrating Israelites, met the threat of his attack defiantly.

David's capture of Jerusalem not only enabled him to join together his two kingdoms, but provided him with an ideal site for his capital. It was very literally David's own city, belonging neither to the northern nor to the southern tribes. He was free to do what he liked with it. His aim was to make it both his administrative centre and also the centre for the worship of Yahweh, which was the unifying force in the federation of the Israelite tribes. He made plans to build a temple to house the Ark of the Covenant, but left the execution to his son Solomon on the grounds that Yahweh had declared that as he was a man of war and had shed blood, he should not build the temple.[1] A more prosaic explanation is perhaps that David was so engaged on the expansion of his kingdom, which ultimately reached from Damascus to the Gulf of Aqaba, that he had no time to carry out plans for Jerusalem.

Solomon, therefore, added the Temple to Jerusalem, and palaces for himself and his wives, and one must infer also accommodation for the administration of his kingdom that he set up. The successors of Solomon were of reduced status, for soon after his death in 926–25 B.C., the United Monarchy fell apart into the kingdoms of Judah and Israel. It would seem obvious that the earlier separate origins of the southern and northern tribes, accentuated by the block imposed by Jebusite Jerusalem, broke free from the unity imposed by David and Solomon. For the relatively short remaining period in which the Israelites stayed independent, it was as two separate kingdoms, usually at war with each other.

Jerusalem remained as the capital of the southern kingdom of Judah. Much evidence is given to us in Biblical sources on the activities of successive kings concerning public buildings and especially the walls of the city. The difficulty is that in almost no case (in fact I think that I should say in no case) do the topographical details given enable one to identify the locality of particular constructions. The archaeologist who locates a

[1] I Chronicles 28:3.

structure has therefore a fairly free hand in linking it with the textual evidence.

Jerusalem of the period of the united and divided monarchies was brutally sacked by the Babylonians in their final destruction in 587 B.C. Its destruction is archaeologically recorded. For some sixty years it lay in ruins, inhabited only by 'the poorest of the land';[1] the leaders and the craftsmen who survived the slaughter were carried away into exile in Babylon.[2]

The Persian conquerors of Babylon began to allow the exiles to return c. 538 B.C., and the rebuilding of Jerusalem began. First the Temple was rebuilt by Zerubbabel between 538 and 516 B.C. It was not until nearly a century later that Jerusalem became a walled city again. Nehemiah was allowed to rebuild the walls c. 440 B.C., and his all-out concentration on this is vividly recorded in the Book of Nehemiah.[3] Post-Exilic Jerusalem and Judah remained a vassal of the great powers. When Persia had succumbed to Alexander the Great, Jerusalem came under the control of the kingdoms set up by Alexander's generals, and since it was a frontier area between the Ptolemies of Egypt and the Seleucids of Syria, it both suffered from their struggles and was able to play the influence of one against the other.

The culmination of this stage was the emergence of the Maccabees as national leaders in the first half of the second century B.C. They were so successful in this game of international diplomacy that, by the end of the second century and the beginning of the first century B.C., they succeeded in establishing a virtually independent kingdom. The contributions of the Maccabees to the plan and structures of Jerusalem add a further element to the problems that archaeologists must face.

The culmination of the Maccabean period was the reign of Herod the Great (40–4 B.C.). His claim as a successor to the Maccabean rulers was dubious, and he was half-Idumean (or Edomite), but with the support of Rome under Augustus he

---

[1] II Kings 25:12.
[2] Jeremiah 24:1.
[3] Nehemiah 3.

established his suzerainty over a much-enlarged kingdom. He was a great admirer of Rome and of Augustus, and his rebuildings of the principal edifices of many towns in Palestine, and indeed his creation of new Roman-style towns, provide evidence of his taste. But in his capital at Jerusalem he had to bow to the control of the extremely xenophobic religious leaders. His rebuilding of the Temple was magnificent, but it had to be in the old style. He was responsible for many other buildings in Jerusalem, and for some of them archaeology provides evidence.

The next period for which archaeology provides evidence is that of Herod Agrippa, grandson of Herod the Great, whom the Romans allowed to rule as king in Jerusalem (A.D. 40–44). There is clear archaeological evidence of his ambitious expansion of Jerusalem to the north, and a strong probability of expansion to the south. This period is one of considerable archaeological problems.

Herodian Jerusalem comes to an even more disastrous end at the hands of the Romans than did monarchic Jerusalem at the hands of the Babylonians. The Jews had for years been restive subjects of the Roman Empire. The first Revolt of the Jews broke out in A.D. 66 and terminated in the sack of Jerusalem by Titus in A.D. 70. Like Nebuchadnezzar, Titus left the city in complete ruins, and for this destruction as for that nearly six hundred years earlier, archaeology provides vivid evidence.

The subsequent history of Jerusalem is, however, unlike that following the earlier destruction. The 'poorest of the land' may have remained there after A.D. 70, but they provided a focus of disaffection, even with the presence of the *Legio X Fretensis* on the site of Herod's Palace on the western ridge, disaffection that became so tiresome that after the second Revolt of the Jews *c.* A.D. 130, Hadrian directed that this centre of trouble had to be obliterated. In every sense this was what he did, in the building of Aelia Capitolina on top of Jerusalem. The name of Jerusalem was, for the time being, abolished. Its boundaries were completely changed, and within the area of the new city valleys were filled and, probably, higher areas levelled. The new *enceinte* was laid out on a Roman plan, which survives in part today.

The new city of Aelia Capitolina virtually coincides, as will be seen, with the present Old City. It was the influence of the conversion of the Emperor Constantine to Christianity in A.D. 312 that gave back to the city its old name and gave it a new stimulus to development. Historical evidence and, as will be seen, archaeological evidence, showed that the occupied area spread south beyond the bounds of the Roman city as far as the line of the Hinnom Valley, which curves round from the south-west corner of the Old City to join the Kedron.

This Byzantine expansion was the final phase of the rule of the West over Jerusalem, apart from the brief interval of the Crusades. In A.D. 636 the city fell to the Arabs. There is a certain amount of literary evidence concerning the subsequent lines of the city walls and the fate of the buildings within them. The north wall remained that of the Roman Aelia, but there is uncertainty about the position of the south wall, particularly on the western ridge. The same is true of the century of rule by the Crusaders, from A.D. 1099 to A.D. 1187. It is only in the sixteenth century A.D. that we reach certainty, when Suleiman the Magnificent built the walls of the Old City; his work is virtually intact.

Jerusalem as a city has thus lasted from the time of the Jebusite city, certainly in the second millennium B.C. and probably in the third, until the present day. In this long history, its limits have varied considerably, and it is on the limits of the cities of the successive periods and what evidence has survived of the buildings the limits enclosed, that the rest of this account will be concentrated. The brief historical description just given suggests that broadly we have to establish the evidence concerning (i) the Jebusite city; (ii) the Solomonic city; (iii) the city of the monarchy of Judah; (iv) the post-Exilic city; (v) the Herodian city; (vi) the city of Herod Agrippa; (vii) the Roman city of Aelia Capitolina; (viii) the Byzantine city; and (ix) the Moslem city. Here are problems enough for the archaeologist.

In Chapter 1, the progress of our predecessors in interpreting the history of the site has been described. What was there left for us to do, and why did it seem necessary to mount another expedition, on a very much larger scale than anything attempted by our predecessors, and costing in the aggregate some £70,000?

The basic reason is that the techniques in their day did not enable them to date the structures they found. With tremendous perseverance and often incredible physical courage, they showed us the Jerusalem that lay underground. Warren provided evidence of the magnificent subterranean structure of the temple platform and of the complexities of the Jerusalem that lay beneath the Old City. Bliss and his predecessors traced the walls running south from the Old City and showed the area that was once enclosed by the walls of Jerusalem. Bliss and his successors speculated on the date of the various building stages. Macalister in 1923–25 plumped firmly for a Jebusite-Davidic-Solomonic date for the wall along the crest of the eastern ridge, the line shown in Pl. 14 with Macalister's Davidic Tower at the upper end of our trench down the slope, and the rest of the line followed closely by the houses on the crest. Weill in 1913–14 identified with considerable confidence some of the rock-cuttings he found as the Royal Tombs of the House of David. All this was speculation, not wild speculation, but the considered opinion of scholars using the only evidence available to them – that is to say literary and historical evidence and the fact that they and others had revealed structural remains that had to be interpreted.

When in 1960 one came to consider the evidence concerning Jerusalem, there were a number of problems that struck one as important. Père Vincent, the authority *par excellence* on the history of Jerusalem, where he lived and watched every archaeological investigation for 69 years, and who published a monumental book on the subject,[1] reached the conclusion that earliest Jerusalem was on the eastern ridge, since only a town on that site would have access to a perennial water-supply (see above, p. 38). Père Vincent also suggested that the route of access to

[1] *Jérusalem de l'A.T.*

the Spring Gihon was the shaft and tunnel originally found by
Warren, and that this was the route by which Joab achieved
access into Jebusite Jerusalem and enabled David to capture it.
Père Vincent's arguments were most convincing. But they did
not fit with Professor Macalister's identification of the structure
that he revealed on the crest of the hill, on the line of Warren's
Ophel wall and the line traced on down to the southern tip of the
eastern ridge. Macalister identified this tower as a Davidic
addition to the original Jebusite wall along the crest. Vincent's
interpretation of the shaft and tunnel and Macalister's dating of
the wall on the crest cannot be reconciled, for the staircase at the
head of the passage leading to the shaft comes to the surface some
27 metres outside the line of the supposed contemporary wall.
If anything in ancient town-planning is certain, an elaborate
rock-cut route to a water-supply would provide access from
within the walls of the contemporary town. The episode of
David's capture of the town by Joab's penetration through the
'gutter' or 'water-channel' is not so completely certain owing
to textual uncertainties, but is very probably to be associated
with the same rock-cut access. Equally, a tunnel coming to the
surface outside the walls would not have enabled David to
penetrate the defences that the Jebusites believed to be impregnable. Here, therefore, was a most obvious problem that required
our attention. This was the reason for our Trench 1 in Site A,
which is shown in Pl. 14.

Given that the earliest town was on the eastern ridge, and here
again at the start of the excavations, one was still basing one's
conclusions on probabilities only, one had the fact provided by
the earliest excavators that at some stage a wall had been constructed following a curve of the Hinnom Valley from the south-
west corner of the Old City south and then east to join the
western ridge to the eastern. What was the date of this wall?
Our trenches in Sites F and B (fig. 11) were aimed at dating the
encircling wall, and our trenches in Sites D and E were aimed at
establishing the periods of occupation on the western ridge. Our
choice of sites was considerably restricted by political conditions,

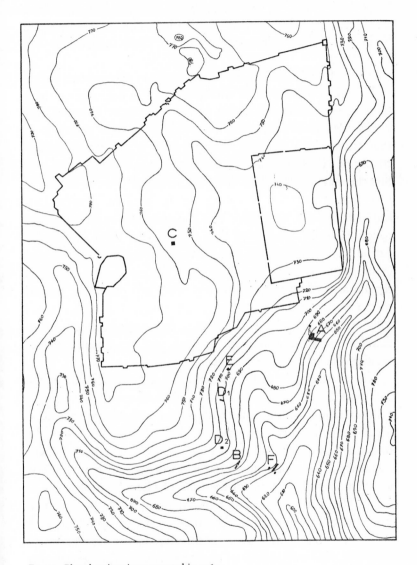

Fig 11   Plan showing sites excavated in 1961

6—DUJ * *

for the summit of the western ridge was, between 1948 and 1967, in no man's land. In Site B, the areas available for excavation were restricted by ancient cemeteries. The conclusions are limited by these circumstances, but these conclusions are important.

Given the implication of Bliss's finds on the western ridge, and his view that the walls enclosing this area belonged to some stage in the Jewish monarchy, at any time from Solomon onwards, Crowfoot's discovery of a gateway on the west side of the eastern ridge (fig. 29) clearly creates a problem. The discovery of a hoard of coins of about 100 B.C. in the gateway shows that the defences to which the gate belonged were in use up to that date. Crowfoot, accepting the finds of his predecessors, found it difficult to believe that the gateway, with its rather rough masonry, was later than the Bronze Age, or Jebusite period, but even if it had to be accepted that the gate remained in use without change of level for a thousand years, it would remain a problem why, if the city walls had joined the eastern to the western ridge some 340 metres south of the gate, it was still necessary to maintain the Bronze Age walls in repair. Here, therefore, was our reason for investigating the defences on the western side of the eastern ridge.

The inconsistency of the evidence for the claimed date of the wall on the eastern crest and the problem of access to the spring concentrated a considerable part of our activities in this area. Mention has already been made of the fact that for none of the stages in Jerusalem's history is there a natural physical northern boundary. This applies down to the north walls of the Old City, in origin, as will be seen, of the time of Herod Agrippa, and in use in Hadrianic and Moslem times; they had to be separated from the higher ground to the north by quarrying and a ditch on a very considerable scale. Macalister, in his excavations of 1923–25, was well aware of the problem, and suggested that some of the wall fragments and rock-cuttings belonged to the Jebusite and Davidic northern defences. The account of the finds did not carry conviction, and the problem of the north wall of earliest Jerusalem was one that demanded attention.

The problems concerning post-Exilic and Maccabean Jerusalem did not, in a preliminary survey, emerge as requiring attention. Until the limits of the Davidic-monarchic Jerusalem were established, there was no reason to suppose that the limits of post-Exilic Jerusalem differed. The tracing of these was, as it were, a follow-up operation. Johns's excavations at the Citadel provided sound evidence for the walls of the Maccabean period in that area. It was hoped that excavations in Site L, in the area belonging to the Armenian Patriarchate in the south-west corner of the Old City, would throw light on the continuation of these walls.

The buildings of the Herodian period are of a magnificence probably exceeding even those of Solomon. An elaborate description of them is given by Josephus.[1] Of the temple building itself, nothing survives. But the masonry of the retaining walls of the platform upon which it stood, enlarging that upon which the Temple of Solomon stood, is a testimony that still survives of the standard of craftsmanship employed (Pl. 85). Warren's excavations gave us the basic information about the platform and on the arches of the viaduct that linked it with the western hill[2]. Here was situated Herod's palace, a new building in addition to the Maccabean palace lower on the same ridge, and one of the towers associated with his palace is visible as the lower courses of one of the towers of the present Citadel (Pl. 90). One of the reasons for our excavations in Site L in the Armenian quarter was the hope that we should find part of Herod's palace, but this was not fulfilled.

The major problem that faced us concerning Herod's Jerusalem was the position of its north wall. The Jerusalem of Herod the Great was the Jerusalem of the time of the Gospels. The Crucifixion took place outside the north wall, and the site of the

---

[1] *War*, V.v. 1–6.

[2] This viaduct has been questioned in the most recent excavations. See below, p. 217.

Holy Sepulchre was nearby. Both sites are claimed to lie beneath the present Church of the Holy Sepulchre. The position of the Church, right in the heart of the present Old City of Jerusalem, is a source of bewilderment to visitors. Josephus gives us some information as to a succession of north walls existing at the time of the Roman attack in A.D. 70. His description is discussed below in Chapter 13, but the basic fact is that gaps in our knowledge of the topography of the city of that time leave us with vital ambiguities. The existence of a waste area south of the Church of the Holy Sepulchre belonging to the Order of St John of Jerusalem was most tempting as the only possible place for excavation in the vicinity of the Church. The willingness of the Order to allow us to excavate there was eagerly accepted, and the resultant Site C (fig. 11) was remarkably productive of evidence.

The problems of the period of Herod Agrippa (A.D. 40–44) were mainly those of his walls. Josephus tells us[1] that he built, though perhaps did not finish, a new north wall. The evidence of Hamilton's excavations pointed to its coincidence with the line of the present north wall of the Old City, but more evidence was needed. There is no literary evidence of any contemporary extension to the south, but our excavations on the western ridge, and especially in Sites F and B, have produced grounds for belief that the expansion to the south at this period was considerable.

Herod Agrippa's Jerusalem had a brief life of less than thirty years. In A.D. 70, came the climax of the Roman defeat of the first Revolt of the Jews, and Jerusalem was captured and sacked after a siege of six months. Plenty of archaeological evidence of this was found, especially in Sites N and K (fig. 36). To control the ruined city, the headquarters of *Legio X Fretensis* was established on the western ridge, in the neighbourhood of Herod's palace, and retaining in use some of its defences.[2] The investigation of this legionary headquarters was one of the objectives of

[1] *War*, V.iv.2 (147–54).
[2] *War*, VII.i (1–2).

the excavation of Site L, but as in every other objective the site was recalcitrant, for the reasons described below (p. 255). A great many of the bricks and tiles stamped L X FRE or its variations were found, but no structures that could be identified as belonging to such a military headquarters.

The uneasy period of the surveillance of the Xth Legion over the ruins inhabited by rebellious Jews came to an end with the second Revolt of the Jews c. A.D. 130, concerning which we have only slight literary evidence. Hadrian clearly decided that Jerusalem was the heart of the rebellion that spread into other Mediterranean lands, and his answer was to abolish Jerusalem by the construction over its ruins of a Roman city. The incidental evidence of this bulldozing operation which our excavations have revealed will be described in due course. The line of the north wall of Hadrian's Aelia Capitolina was indicated by Hamilton in 1937–38 to be on the line of the present north wall of the Old City;[1] the work of Hennessy here is described below in Chapter 13. There is no extraneous evidence for the line of the south wall of Aelia. One of the objectives of our excavations in Site s, south of the Haram, was to investigate this problem.

The evidence concerning the next two centuries of Roman occupation did not suggest any problems to be tackled, nor did our excavations throw any incidental light upon them. The Byzantine period in Jerusalem is in fact much more important than the Roman, for Jerusalem then became a centre of religion for the then civilized world. Our predecessors found many Byzantine remains. We also found them, especially in Sites M and s. Probably the most important were in Site J, to the east of the Damascus Gate within the salient of the walls of the Old City running south from the Haram. One must confess, however, that we were not seeking to deal with problems concerning the Byzantine period. The evidence that we recovered was incidental, but in fact important.

The same must be admitted for the early Moslem and Crusader

[1] *QDAP*, X.

periods. We have a contribution to offer, but the problems of these periods were not our main objectives.

I hope that in preceding pages I have shown that, in 1961, there were many problems worthy of attention if an accurate history of the site of Jerusalem was to be achieved. Certainly, no one excavation could produce all the answers, but our sights have been indicated. Many of the ambiguities that existed when we began our excavations were due to the fact that the greater part of the previous excavations in Jerusalem had taken place at a time when modern archaeological methods were not in practice in Palestine. In the next chapter, the basis of modern methods is described, as well as how we set to work on the excavation of Jerusalem in 1961.

★

CHAPTER THREE

Excavation Methods and the Dig in Jerusalem

THE EXCAVATIONS OF THE 1930S, just described, were concerned with comparatively late stages in the history of Jerusalem, and were in the area of the present Old City or its immediate vicinity. They were carried out by excavators trained in the archaeological techniques that had been developed in England and elsewhere in Europe in the period between the two World Wars. The excavations carried out between 1867 and 1927, which had provided information concerning the area to the south of the Old City, were by older methods. There was certainly development and improvement. Weill, Macalister, and Crowfoot no longer explored by shafts and tunnels. Macalister, in his excavations at Gezer between 1903 and 1909, was fully aware of the importance of pottery for dating archaeological periods, and had endeavoured to produce a pottery sequence from his finds. Crowfoot also was fully aware of this, and endeavoured to interpret the structures he uncovered in terms of building sequence and associated pottery. Nevertheless, excavation by exact stratigraphical methods had not reached Palestine at this time. In contemporary excavations in England it was well established, but it must be emphasized that even in England great improvements have subsequently been made, and the excavators of the 1960s can often regard the work of their predecessors in the 1920s and 1930s as rather primitive; and above all it must be recognized that conditions in a site like Jerusalem were infinitely more complicated than in England, at sites, for instance, like Verulamium and

Housesteads on the Roman Wall. It remains, however, that the interpretations made by the excavators of Jerusalem down to 1930 were not founded on the only ground that is valid for archaeological evidence derived from excavation, which is an observed and exact stratigraphy.

To explain why it was felt necessary to plan a further series of excavations at Jerusalem in 1961, I must here explain what is meant by stratigraphy, and what excavations based on stratigraphical observation can do. Even modern buildings have deposits associated with them. Not even a prefabricated building is set straight onto the existing surface, for if it were, it could blow away in a gale. Walls have to be secured by being set into foundation trenches, usually wider than the wall, but sometimes only just wide enough to accommodate the foundations. When the walls have been built, the interior surface has to be levelled over to take the floor, and similarly the external surface is levelled over. These deposits, the fill of the foundation trenches, and the levelling-over or 'make-up' of the surfaces were put in position when the building was erected. Stray objects may be incorporated in these deposits, for instance coins, fragments of china, pottery or other vessels, objects such as buttons, keys, boot-studs, broken pipe-bowls, and mislaid tools. Many of these objects may be datable. Modern coins can of course be dated by the mint-year that they carry; medieval and ancient coins can also be quite closely dated. Good china can be closely dated, and even the sort of china bought at Woolworth's has patterns which vary over the years. A fragment of a plastic vessel, virtually indestructible, can only belong to a time when this material came into use for common domestic containers. A sequence of forms of the bowls of clay pipes has been established, and often they have initials or trade-marks that can be identified in relation to manufacturers recorded in town-lists for London and elsewhere. A Yale key must be later than c. 1882. The find of any objects of this sort in a deposit associated with a building enables one to say, always provided that the excavation is exact (cf. below, pp. 65 ff.), that the building was not constructed before a certain date. The closeness of the dating obviously varies. Modern coins can be dated to an exact year, older ones in broader terms, the range of which tends to increase with antiquity. A clay pipe can be dated by the period of years during which the town-lists suggest that the particular manufacturer was active. There may be significant points concerning Yale keys; I have not investigated this problem, but those concerned with industrial archaeology, a subject of increasing importance and interest, may have to study it.

The essential point about this evidence is that it gives a *terminus post quem*. An accurately identified deposit containing a datable object cannot have been laid down before the earliest possible date of that object.

It must, however, be recognized that it is a *terminus post quem* only. Changes in fashion in china are relatively slow, and from the time a cup was bought to the time its broken fragments were dropped on a building site may cover quite a span of years. The mortality of clay pipes was probably high, but it is not yet possible to pin down the manufacture within a longish period of activity of the maker. Coins can be dated in themselves, but they have a long life, as a glance at one's small change shows; in Britain one still finds an occasional Victorian coin in circulation (or at least did before the introduction of decimalization), so that a range of nearly a hundred years would be possible. The interpretation depends on commonsense. If there is a single coin, Victorian of 1860, the deposit is later than that date. But if in that level there was a plastic vessel, it could be accepted that just by chance a workman of the mid-twentieth century had in his pocket, and lost, one of the oldest coins still in circulation. If, on the other hand, there were forty coins of 1860, and nothing later, one would be reasonably confident that the deposit, and therefore the building with which it was associated, belonged exactly to that date.

My examples for the evidence of stratigraphy have been drawn from modern periods, for here one can use exact dates. I have used them myself in excavation in eighteenth- and

nineteenth-century Southwark, but I have not the slightest hesitation in claiming that the essential elements in the archaeologist's
approach to this interpretation of nineteenth-century A.D.
Southwark and ninth-millennium B.C. Jericho are the same.

The difference between the archaeological evidence from
modern periods and medieval and ancient periods is not a difference in essence, but a great difference in potentialities. Nowadays,
we are much too tidy. We have hard floors, kept clean. We do
not, except in remote country areas, have to dig rubbish pits,
for the dustman collects our debris. Right down to medieval and
early modern times, things were very different. I shall now turn
to the wealth of stratigraphical evidence that a Near Eastern site
provides, and also to its complications.

The concrete or other hard floor of a modern building is
kept reasonably clean. The floor of most of the houses, perhaps
excluding the palaces, in the general area of western Asia, was
basically trampled-down mud. This would contain fragments of
day-to-day casualties in domestic utensils and implements, and
food debris, especially the bones of animals eaten, grains or seeds
of vegetables eaten, shells, fish-bones, pips, and fruit-stones. The
evidence of all of this, with the help of pottery experts, experts in
flint or metal tools, natural scientists interested in the remains of
early animals and plants, can add up to a picture of the equipment,
resources, and environment of the inhabitants of a site.

The validity of all this evidence stands only if it is certain that
the finds can without doubt be associated with the building to
which they are assigned. There are a series of events associated
with every structure, though evidence of only some of these may
survive – its foundation and construction, its occupation, possibly
in successive recognizable phases, and its destruction. The final
destruction may be rapid, and the ruins may contain objects
belonging only to the final occupation period. Alternatively,
decay may have been slow; a ruined house or hut may have
remained sufficiently intact to be used by squatters for decades
or even hundreds of years; and the objects dropped by these

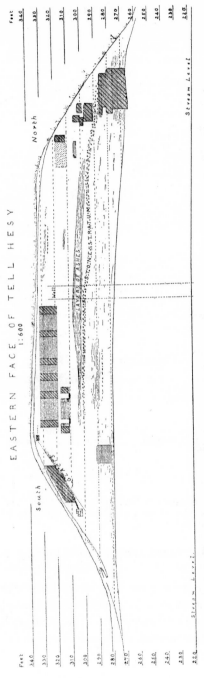

FIG 12 Petrie's section of the east face of Tell el-Hesi, the earliest stratigraphical excavation in Palestine, but illustrating an elementary stage with finds recorded in horizontal levels

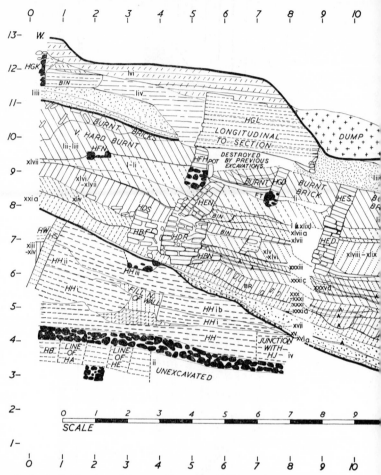

FIG 13 Section at Jericho through houses of the Early, Middle, and Late Bronze Ages, showing how occupation levels are terraced and sloped, creating marked differences in absolute height of contemporary levels

squatters may be mixed with those belonging to the original inhabitants.

A single building, a house built in an Eastern desert or in the marshes of Somerset, will in itself have all these phases. In town sites, in Britain, but infinitely more in the East, house succeeds house over a long period, the destruction phase of one house

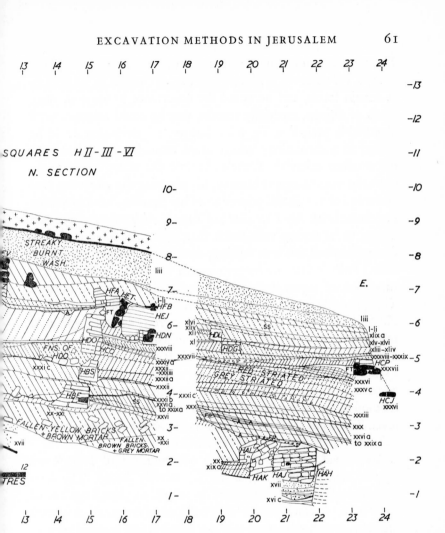

SQUARES H II - III - VI

N. SECTION

merging into the construction phase of its successor, sometimes immediately, sometimes after an interval. The successive house levels built up a mound, known in Arabic-speaking areas as a *tell*, in Turkey as a *hüyük*, in Iran as a *tepe*, all meaning a man-made hill. The layers that made up these *tells* (henceforth I shall treat it as an anglicized loan-word) provide evidence of their history.

This was recognized by Petrie in his excavation of Tell el-Hesi in 1890. He observed in his cuts into the tell changes in the pottery at certain levels, and he noted the occurrence in some of these levels of objects, especially scarabs, that he could associate with identifiable periods in Egyptian history, a history that could be related to a chronology which could ultimately be linked with the modern calendar. Petrie's absolute chronology was many centuries out; Margaret Murray, his admiring disciple (who died at the age of 101 in full possession of her faculties, having written her classic book *My First Hundred Years in Archaeology*), once said 'better to be wrong with Petrie than right with anyone else'. (I do not know if this is in writing, or only my recollection of her *dictat*.) Petrie's dates no longer concern us, but his principle of a succession of layers distinguished by fashions in artefacts does. This principle is shown in fig. 12, his section of Tell el-Hesi. His finds, and those of his disciples, were recorded on the lines of this section. A datum point was established, sometimes arbitrary, sometimes related to sea-level, and finds were recorded relative to this. In 1890 this was a tremendous step forward towards exact recording. Unfortunately, Petrie continued to use the same method in the 1920s. Tell el-Hesi was recorded in feet above sea-level, Tell Ajjul (1930 to 1938) in inches above sea-level, but the difference adds digits but not exactitude.

The broad outlines of Petrie's establishment of periods are sound. The outlines are, however, terribly broad. The least complicated kind of site is one in which the buildings are of mud-brick; thus when a building collapses, there are no structural elements worth salvaging, and the debris is just levelled over in preparation for the next building. But as a site expands, new buildings are constructed at the foot of the previously accumulated mound that are contemporary with others built on earlier ruins. A terraced or stepped occupation is created, sometimes accentuated by the building-up or cutting-back of actual terraces. The complete inapplicability of stratification in ruled horizontal lines with finds recorded in relation to a datum point is illustrated by fig. 13.

The need for a more refined stratification than that of Petrie, and in use by him and his disciples for nearly fifty years, has been discussed only with reference to sites in which the buildings are of mud-brick. The problems of sites at which the buildings are of stone are infinitely more complex. The 1930 inhabitants of the modern village of Sebaste explained to us that if they wanted building stones, it was much easier to dig up a wall of ancient Samaria than to quarry the living rock. For millennia this has been the philosophy of the occupants of areas in which stone is the building material. Sometimes only the portions of ruined walls standing above ground were used; this accounts for the fact that walls standing more than a few feet high are rare. Perhaps more often, and more disastrously for archaeological evidence, the visible base of the wall was followed down below floor-level, and its complete foundations dug out. Examples of this from Samaria are shown in fig. 14 and Pls. 15-16. Plate 15 shows the lines of the trenches left by the removal of the stones; Pl. 16 shows the few stones left *in situ* at the base of the walls. Three points emerge. If the removal trenches, which archaeologists call robber trenches, had not been observed, these walls in which *no* stones remained *in situ* would not have been recorded. Secondly, without the stratigraphical evidence of the level from which the robber trenches descended, the stones in position at the base of deep foundations would have been recorded as belonging to walls at rock-level. Thirdly, the intrusive objects introduced by the stone-robbers, down to the base of their robbing, would have been used as evidence for upper levels. The Samaria walls of which the evidence survives in the foundation courses and in the robber trenches were in fact robbed in two periods, Hellenistic, mid-second century B.C., and Herodian, late first century B.C. An area dug in horizontal spits recorded by height above or below a datum point would therefore have to be given the date of the objects, coins or pottery, thus introduced into levels centuries earlier. Dr Reisner, the excavator of Samaria between 1908 and 1910, a distinguished Egyptologist used to the mud-brick domestic structures of Egypt, in fact declared that

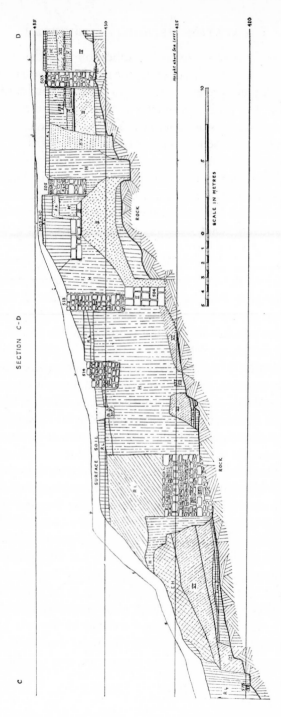

Fig 14   Section at Samaria, showing the deep cuts both of foundation trenches and of robber trenches into earlier deposits

stratigraphical evidence for the site did not survive; the techniques of the day in the Near East were quite inadequate to make
sense of its enormous complexity.

We must here return to the point made above (p. 56), that an
observed and exact stratigraphy is the only way that valid
archaeological evidence can be derived from excavation. The
essential point is that each layer in the soil must be observed, and
finds from it given a separate level number in the excavator's
notebook. The relation of any surface to a wall must be noted:
that it runs up to a wall or is cut by it. If cut by it, this means that
the wall has come down from a higher level, and the finds in
the cut belong to the foundation trench, and must be kept separate. If when a surface is cleaned there is a break in it, this must be
investigated; it may mean that here there was a robber trench of a
wall from which stones have been removed below the contemporary surface, or it may prove to be a pit, for rubbish or perhaps
a burial; again the finds must be kept separate.

All this means that there must be very close supervision of
the whole process of excavations. In the old days, the supervisory
staff usually consisted of the director and an architect who made
the plans, with a *reis* or foreman, often an Egyptian very skilled
in the manual dexterity of uncovering objects and in keeping
the gangs at work, but with no comprehension of stratigraphy.
The modern revolution is that each excavation area, all relatively
small, is supervised by an experienced archaeologist or a student
learning archaeology, who can watch all that is going on and
record it in the site notebook. As an example I can cite our 1961
trench down the eastern slope of the eastern ridge. It was laid
out in squares of 5 metres, two squares wide, seven squares in
extent (Pl. 14), incidentally a very difficult task since the slope
was such that a 5-metre tape could not be held horizontally, even
by the tallest member of the party. One site supervisor was in
charge of each pair of squares side by side. The reason why
Square A xv marked the limit of the trench (with the fortunate
result to which I shall return) was that at this point I had used up
all my site supervisors. The interrelation of sites to be excavated

and site supervisors was close. We could only excavate those sites for which one could provide archaeological control. The other side of the picture was financial. Each year one had to calculate how many sites one could afford to dig, and one could only accept a proportion of enthusiastic applicants, in relation to the number of sites one could afford to dig.

The set-up in Jerusalem was therefore that each site had a site supervisor. He or she recorded the observed levels in his or her notebook. Perhaps I have not so far done justice to a very important element – our Jericho workmen. When we started at Jericho, our workmen were, of course, all untrained. Many worked with us all seven seasons. A few became very highly skilled, able to identify and follow surfaces with great accuracy, able to dig trenches with beautifully vertical sides, and to clean things up for photography. A very few even reached the stage of being able to identify stratification. Their reputation spread, and they became professionals, going from excavation to excavation and provided with a livelihood, if not continuous at least recurrent, which most of the inhabitants of Jericho lacked. They were invaluable at Jerusalem. There again, our basic labour force was untrained locals, a majority from Silwan, though on the sites within the Old City drawn from the refugees who were living in the ruins of the Jewish Quarter. It is strange that the Jerusalem workmen never acquired any real skill, or even interest, though a certain number were good, steady, reliable workmen, who were employed year after year. The answer probably is that the good, steady workmen were the older men, who could not at that stage acquire new skills. Our best Jerichoans came to us as young men or boys, who were receptive to training. The younger ones at Jerusalem were mostly schoolboys, who felt that their education qualified them for better things than manual labour. The Silwanis did not seem to resent the higher status of the Jerichoans, or their higher rates of pay. The element of embarrassment was that *all* Jerichoans considered that they should have this higher status. Some who applied for employment had only been basket-boys on the

Jericho dig, with no skills other than that of avoiding hard work. One had to be very firm in insisting that they could be employed, but only at the grade of the work they were capable of doing.

One of the skills of the Jerichoans to which I have referred was that of cutting clean, vertical sections, that is to say the face formed by the edge of any excavation, either the main edge of the excavated area, or of any subsidiary cuts. The main edge of the excavated area is especially important, for if it is not vertical, the area excavated steadily contracts as excavation proceeds downwards. In excavation at Jerusalem, there are circumstances in which it is physically impossible to have a vertical face for the whole depth of the excavated area. The reason for this is that so much of the fill consists of stone fallen from destroyed buildings. A stone sticking out into the excavated area often cannot be removed without dislodging those above it. Other stones beneath the projecting one similarly cannot safely be prized out, and so gradually the area excavated contracts. I must therefore confess that I enjoyed excavating Jericho more than Jerusalem for just this physical reason. At Jericho, a site at which most of the buildings were of mud-brick, we could dig a trench 50 feet deep with vertical sides,[1] while at Jerusalem there were everywhere these tiresome obstructions of stones that introduced these irregularities.

This emphasis on the need for vertical sides to the excavated areas and to subsidiary trenches is not based simply on the appearance of the excavation and the need to prevent the excavated area contracting as it was carried down, though both of these aspects are important. The basic reason is that one of the most important records of the excavations is drawn sections of the observed levels – surfaces, tip-lines, pits, and so on. These must be recorded by measured drawings of the faces of the excavated areas and subsidiary trenches, drawings made with relation to a horizontal datum, in which each surface is carefully traced. This is emphatically the job of the archaeologist; in recent years, Palestinian archaeologists have accepted the need

[1] Kathleen M. Kenyon, *Digging up Jericho*, Frontispiece.

for sections, but all too often the drawing of the sections has been handed over to the architect, who admittedly can draw a prettier section. I am the worst draftsman in the world, but I always draw all the main sections myself, in collaboration with the site supervisor, since I know the archaeological questions to ask. The site supervisors draw the subsidiary sections, for this is an important part of their training.

The drawn sections are one essential part of the record, for to them, through the level numbers in the site notebooks, are related the finds of the successive levels. The next essential element is the plans of the structures found. For this, on a big dig like Jerusalem, it was necessary to have two surveyors. Usually they were architects, though most of what we found had little architectural merit. The Bronze Age and Iron Age occupants of Jerusalem had very little architectural skill. The walls were, until the Hellenistic period, of roughly dressed stones, laid in rather uneven courses, usually without mortar. They would not have looked so rough originally, as at least the house walls often showed traces of a facing of mud plaster; but the walls were seldom quite straight and the angles seldom an exact right-angle. All this made the surveyors' task more difficult, and to show the character of the walls they had to draw in the individual stones. The plans that they produced are a great credit to their performance of a task which must often have seemed very uninspiring. It must, moreover, be remembered that these plans are the only record of something which has gone forever, for as one digs down to investigate the lower levels, the walls of the upper strata have to be destroyed.

The third essential form of record is the photographs, and one full-time photographer was employed throughout. The photographer had in fact as hard a time as anyone. The bright summer sun of Jerusalem casts strong shadows which make it impossible to take any detailed photographs when the sun is on the site, a difficulty accentuated by the fact that usually by the time we reached any structures we were at a depth of anything from 10 to 40 feet, and the side of the excavation area threw a shadow over part of the structures. All photographs of detail had to be taken before the sun was high, usually before 6 a.m., or after it was low enough to be off the site, usually about 4 p.m. The photographers therefore had a long day, with the middle part of it spent in developing and printing in a very small and stuffy darkroom. They also had on occasion to climb perilously on top of anything available to obtain the required view. I am often asked whether we make full use of colour photographs. The answer is that for lectures, colour transparencies are invaluable for general views. They make all the difference in the world to the visual impact of the site. They are also invaluable for the glossy type of popular publication which one is often asked to do. But the cost of colour plates is still far too high for them to be used in the serious archaeological publication of a site. Moreover, colour photographs need a strong light, and here the problem of shadow obscuring detail is even greater. I have some colour transparencies taken of areas to which I need to refer in lectures, but usually the black and white slide is much better. Therefore, the basic record must be in black and white, with colour transparencies as an adjunct.

So far, I have referred to the site supervisors, who form the essential nucleus, to the surveyors, and the photographer. These are the people who go out into the field. In the background, there has to be a considerable supporting staff. Each day, the finds of the day come in to the dig headquarters. They come in the form firstly of bags of pottery, selected by me as significant from the total pottery sent in from each site. The routine is that every sherd is placed in a basket to which the site supervisor gives two labels showing the level from which the sherds come. The baskets come to the field headquarters, where the sherds are washed by Suleiman and Musa; I can be thus specific since Suleiman and Musa have washed pottery for us since Jericho 1952. The sherds are then laid out on mats, and I select what I consider to be the significant specimens, mainly rims, bases, handles, and decorated wares. Suleiman and Musa then place them in bags, to go to the registration department; the residue is discarded, to form a growing *monte testaccio*, and it was a great relief when the architects repairing the Church of the Holy Sepulchre found that ground-up ancient sherds gave just the colouring they required for the mortar they needed in their repairs; our *monte testaccio* was thereby much reduced. The bags of selected sherds duly reach the registration department, where each sherd is marked in Indian ink with the level number on the label provided by the site supervisor; this is an essential establishment of identity, allowing for free future handling and a precaution against accidents, but a tedious chore for the registration staff. The bulk of the sherds are then tied up in bags, with one label on the string and one inside the bag, as a safeguard against the string breaking, to await further analysis. This is a long-term, and exceedingly laborious, affair, and (in 1971) most of it has still to be done.

Some pottery, vessels of which the form can be mended or reconstructed, merits more immediate attention. They are passed to the draftsman, drawn, and reduced photographs of the drawings are included in the register of finds to be divided with the Department of Antiquities at the end of each season. What are classified as Small Finds – metal objects, pottery figurines, weights, spindle whorls, and so on – are similarly treated.

In my recollection of the day's work in Jerusalem, sorting pottery is indivisibly linked with the sick parade, since the latter took place alongside the pottery mats. Our main responsibility, of course, was dealing with minor injuries incurred during the day, but all sorts of things like boils and chronic ulcers were presented for attention. The diagnostic and bandaging skills of the first-aider concerned had to be considerable. Their qualifications ranged from those of a Red Cross member, through trained nurses to a consultant neurologist of the Radcliffe Infirmary. It has to be admitted that the one in whom the workmen had most faith was *Sitt* Marshall, Dorothy Marshall, whose training was purely Red Cross.

In the background of the archaeological activity is, of course, the way we lived, which in Jerusalem was in fact relatively luxurious. One had to impress on new members how lucky they were. At Jericho most of the party lived in tents, or in rooms in which the rain might come through the ceiling or the spring might come up through the floor. One can recount stories from colleagues in, for instance, Iraq, when most of the tents of the dig camp might be blown down in dust storms. One would not like a beginner in Near Eastern archaeology to expect to find living conditions such as we had in Jerusalem; there would be shocks coming to him. We lived, in fact, in the building of the British School of Archaeology in Jerusalem, then a delightful building in traditional Arab style, though dating only to the early 1900s. The essential background member of the staff was the dig quartermaster, who ran the house with the aid of the excellent Jordanian staff of the School. On a dig of this size a full-time housekeeper is essential, and Theodora Newbould served us faithfully throughout the dig. We therefore lived in a solid building, of which the thick walls mitigated the heat of Jerusalem in the summer months. Nevertheless, a three-month season in a Jerusalem summer is quite hard going.

Work started at 5 a.m. We were called at 4.15 a.m., and at 4.30 had tea and sandwiches, and then drove down to the various sites in an assortment of vehicles. Many of the party found 5 a.m. to 9 a.m. a long stint to do till breakfast. Breakfast was the substantial meal demanded by the appetites created by the preceding work, and was taken at the site headquarters; the breakfast interval was 9 to 9.45 a.m., and the spare quarter of an hour in which one spread out on the floor of the site head-quarters was a godsend. The second stint was from 9.45 to 1.45. This was definitely a warm period, though Jerusalem, at a height of about 2,500 feet above sea-level, is not ordinarily extremely hot. There are exceptions, when the *khamsin*, the hot east wind from the desert, blows. Our worst experience of a *khamsin* was in our first season, when we started in May, July being the ordinary date. We had been digging for a week, when suddenly the temperature went up from 94° F. in the

shade to 104° F., and the trouble was that at that stage we had
not dug deep enough to have any shade. By midday, site supervisors not used to Near Eastern temperatures were definitely
flagging. Enormous comfort was brought to us by Madeline
Parr, wife of the then Assistant Director of the School, who
suddenly appeared with a vast container of iced lemonade. I
don't think that any of those concerned will forget the blessed
gulps of this liquid. The immediate emergency of the *khamsīn*
was dealt with by arranging that the site supervisors worked a
half-day only, and indoor staff members were drafted down to
the site to relieve them. This was the only real heat emergency
that we had to deal with in our seven seasons, but it established
the very acceptable practice that we (and the workmen) had a
break from 12 to 12.10 p.m., during which Suleiman (or Musa
if Suleiman was not available, but Musa was usually adept at
arranging that Suleiman should do the harder work) brought
round lemonade.

At 1.45, everyone converged on the site headquarters. Pottery
boys brought up the baskets and bags of pottery, to be stacked
under the supervision of Suleiman and Musa. The site supervisors would climb up from their various sites. Our cars would
load up, not only with the staff, but with the bags of pottery
and other finds, sorted and bagged as described above (p. 69),
and we would drive off to the School, to settle down to a
substantial lunch. Thereafter, no one was expected to surface
until tea at 4 o'clock, and to put one's feet up on one's bed was
a relaxation that I shall never forget. After tea, there was work
to be done. A considerable part of the photographer's work
came then, and the supervisor of the site to be photographed
and possibly one or two others had to go also. If I was engaged
in drawing the section of a site, I needed the site supervisor, and
again possibly one or two others, to help. Other members of
the staff helped in the registration or conservation departments.
Basically, therefore, work did not finish until it was dark, about
6.30 p.m., or earlier at the end of the season. Thus everybody
had a hard day's work. After dinner at 7 p.m., usually a pretty

delicious meal, most people were free to explore the night life of Jerusalem, of which the highlights were rather limited.

I have mentioned the workmen rather briefly. First in the hierarchy was the foreman, and we were fortunate for most of the time to have for the survey site Abdul Jewad Abassi, otherwise Abu Mohammed, a Silwani. His job was to keep the register of attendance and to give general oversight to the smooth running of the dig. He was also invaluable in negotiations for renting land for excavations. If I felt the rent demanded was exorbitant, I would sweep out indignantly, and leave it to him to persuade the owner to reduce his terms, which he always did. I have never felt it was right that the foreman should hire or fire, since this lays him open to pressure from the workmen and their relatives; this I kept entirely in my own hands, though of course I listened to Abu Mohammed's advice. The workmen to be engaged were in three main categories: the pickmen who did the actual digging, whether with large pick, small pick, or trowel; the hoemen who filled the baskets with the excavated soil; and the basket-boys who carried the baskets of soil to the dumps. The latter are the real headache. A lazy chain of basket-boys can slow down work in a section beyond belief. One of the skills demanded of a site supervisor, in addition to providing the archaeological evidence, is the ability to keep the basket-boys steadily at work. One of the skills of Abu Mohammed was to see that the number of basket-boys on each site corresponded to the amount of soil coming out. As each area of excavation deepened, the number of basket-boys, usually working as a chain passing baskets from hand to hand had to be increased, and at the top end the height of the dump of excavated soil increased, again adding to the number of basket-boys. By the time the lowest levels were reached, one might have two pickmen and two or four hoemen moving soil and forty to fifty basket-boys transporting the soil to the dump. Incidentally, it may be mentioned that 'baskets' is an inexact term. At Jericho we indeed used woven baskets, baggy

two-handled things, of which the nearest English equivalent is a
fish-basket, but their life is short, and in Jerusalem we used a
container of similar shape, still given the Arabic name of *guffa*,
made from old motor-tyres. Their life in strenuous dig conditions is not unlimited, but for a time they can be repaired, and
here I must mention another member of the party, the Haj,
who for three months on end each season sat putting nails into
rubber *guffas;* his only other function was connected with
latrines, for a reason I never understood.

The first stage of getting down to work at the beginning of
each season is that, having made my preliminary assessment of
the number of each category of workmen required, I take on
this number; at Site L in the Old City, Doug Tushingham of
the Royal Ontario Museum, who was in charge in that area,
did the same thing. Abu Mohammed will have passed round
the information that men will be engaged. The result is a milling
throng, if not a howling mob, of those hoping to be employed
Here one comes to the importance of *shehadis*. At the end of
each season, each man and boy is given a chit. These chits are
drafted by site supervisors, on set standards, and signed by
me or Doug Tushingham. For the best workmen, the site
supervisors are allowed to be lyrical. The next grade is 'A has
worked well for X weeks'. Following that is 'B has worked
well under supervision for X weeks'. Next is 'C has worked
for X weeks'. The nadir is as for C, but with at the foot DNEA.
Being interpreted, this is 'Do not employ again'.

After the first season, therefore, I would face the milling
throng, from whatever vantage point the then site headquarters
provided, and select the applicants. The good men were easy,
since usually I recognized them. The junior hoemen and the
basket-boys were more problematical, and here the *shehadis*
came into operation. I had to consider them carefully, not only
from the point of view of whether this was a good man or
boy, but also whether the *shehadi* belonged to him. When a
small boy produced a *shehadi* saying that he had worked as a
hoeman for three seasons, I naturally rejected it, and tore it into

pieces, to the applicant's great mortification, and no doubt to that of the owner of the *shehadi*.

The other exhausting occasion connected with the workmen was the fortnightly pay-day (Pl. 73). The wages book would have been prepared by whichever member of the staff had this task, for most seasons Theodora Newbould, in conjunction with Abu Mohammed. Paying took place at all the main sites, to avoid wasting too much working time. The perambulatory paying party consisted of myself, Theodora, Abu Mohammed, and Suleiman to carry the table and stools. Each gang was accompanied by the site supervisor. I would call out the name and the amount due. Theodora and the site supervisor counted out the money, while I supervised the signing or the thumb-prints, in the latter case the thumb being firmly pressed down by Suleiman. Complaints, of course, were innumerable. Most were concerned with dissatisfaction with wage gradings; that they were being paid as boys when they were really men. Other complaints were that they had worked more hours than were recorded by Abu Mohammed. The only way to get through the proceedings was to be completely authoritarian. Wages flung back on the table were just swept up, and if the complainant realized he was being silly, he would have to come back the next day. The really tiresome ones were just paid off firmly. There is much to be said for a dictatorship.

★

CHAPTER FOUR

Pre-Israelite Jerusalem

OUR MAIN EXCAVATIONS at Jerusalem started with a trench down the eastern slope of the eastern ridge (Pl. 14), for here one could establish a relation with the Spring Gihon, which is shown above (p. 38) to be vital to the existence of Jerusalem. We had here a clearly defined objective. We had reason to doubt the correctness of the identification of the wall on the crest of the ridge as being that of the periods of the Jebusites and of David, from its situation in relation to the earliest access to the spring (see above, p. 48). Our trench was laid out from the foot of the tower (Pl. 18) claimed by Professor Macalister in his excavations in 1923–25 to be an addition by David to the Jebusite town wall (see above, p. 33). Cutting the trench here had the disadvantage that we knew that the earlier excavations would have disturbed the stratification by trenches below the general level at which clearance had been suspended. To have cut our trench further south, however, would have meant cutting through an important pathway leading from the summit of the ridge to the Silwan Valley and village. The Silwanis are fairly patient in such matters, but this seemed unfair.

Our trench showed that along the face of the tower Macalister had in fact dug a trench. It is a cardinal sin in modern archaeology to dig a trench along the face of a wall, for thereby one cuts through the surfaces related to the wall, either as running up to it, or as having been cut by it. One hears ultra-modern excavators saying that this is all old-hat, and I regret to learn that this tendency is growing amongst Israeli archaeologists, who are doing so very much (I write in 1971) to investigate problems of

Palestinian towns. I remain utterly convinced that without the visual evidence in observed and measured sections of the relation of surfaces to structures one is building one's interpretation on sand, and frightfully shifting sand, responsive to all the convulsions, terrestrial, psychological, and political, to which the Near East has been liable for millennia.

The evidence in our Trench I, therefore, running down the slope from the so-called Tower of David could not be stratigraphically satisfactory or complete. One could theoretically project sloping lines of deposit against the face of the tower, and be pretty certain that the datable objects in this fill were later than the structure, but this was not proof. What was proof was that as we cleared the lower levels, we found that the tower rested on the ruins of earlier buildings. These buildings formed part of a complex surviving to the east of the tower, which we were able to investigate in detail. Without any doubt, they dated to the seventh century B.C., and were most probably destroyed by the Babylonians in the early sixth century B.C. They are described below (pp. 161 ff.). This evidence put any association of David or the Jebusites with this structure completely out of court. All the constructions following the line of the eastern crest of the eastern ridge belong to the post-Exilic-Hellenistic-Maccabean period.

Looking back on Trench I, one can say that it plunged down into the unknown. The previous (Macalister) interpretation was suspect, but had not yet been disproved; this came in the latter part of the first season. I suppose that my conviction that full command of the only available water-supply, the Spring Gihon, must have dictated the position of the town walls of Jerusalem on the eastern side, was the reason that I laid out Trench I for a distance of 48 metres east of the so-called Tower of David. I was clear that one must investigate the slope thoroughly. The original end of Trench I at a horizontal distance of 48 metres (given a slope of approximately 45 degrees, I should have to turn to a mathematician to say what the walking/climbing distance was) from the wall on the crest was quite accidental, as I have explained (above, p. 65). It did, however, touch the western side of a wall that was very much earlier than anything excavated so far, and the evidence was clear that this wall, revealed in a very short section, belongs in origin to the Middle Bronze Age, perhaps as early as 1800 B.C.

Trench 1, therefore, takes us back to c. 1800 B.C. Our excavations suggest that a case can be made out that there was a walled town from this date. Jerusalem enters written history much later, at the time of the fourteenth-century Amarna letters. But archaeology in fact takes us back very much earlier, into the third millennium. Third millennium in archaeological terms is Early Bronze Age. Finds made by Macalister on the crest of Ophel, the eastern ridge, were consigned to the Palestine Exploration Fund, his sponsors, and have now reached the University of London Institute of Archaeology. It is certain that there was an 'Early Bronze Age presence', and that there was some settlement at Jerusalem in the third millennium B.C.

Our 1961–67 excavations have confirmed the 'presence', but they have not defined the extent, except by negative evidence. In the excavation of Trench 1 down the eastern slope in Square A on the plan (fig. 18), there is only one small area that one has to identify as Early Bronze Age. Apart from this, Early Bronze Age finds were confined to caves low on the slope. People of the period, that is to say the greater part of the third millennium B.C., were visiting Jerusalem, living on its outskirts in caves or in mud houses, but the small main settlement was on the summit of the ridge, where, as already explained, destructions in the Herodian-Hadrianic-modern excavation periods have removed all evidence.

The urban civilization of the Early Bronze Age is to be expected at Jerusalem. It was a period of city states in Palestine. The contemporary third-millennium phases in Egypt and Mesopotamia produced kingdoms and successive empires (or hegemonies). Palestine produced nothing on this scale. Archaeological evidence, with some slight support from literary Egyptian and Mesopotamian records, indicates that in Palestine towns of modest importance exercised a modest control over smaller settlements in their neighbourhood. There is in fact no evidence that Jerusalem exercised any particular influence or had any dependent settlements. At this stage of our knowledge, one can say that there was a Jerusalem of the third millennium B.C. and tombs of the end of the fourth millennium show that people were there at that period. One must in fact conclude that on the site of present Jerusalem there was a settlement in the third millennium but one of moderate importance.

It is very easy for an archaeologist to fall into such terms as Pre-Pottery Neolithic, Pottery Neolithic, and so on, down to my present point of the end of the Early Bronze Age, somewhere about 2300 B.C. The third millennium B.C. is a nice, comfortable period for western Asia. We, as archaeologists, accept the well-documented Egyptian evidence, and we seize enthusiastically on all evidence for the absolute dating (i.e., in terms of the regnal years of rulers in Egypt, and we are prepared to float up and down with the datings of the experts in this respect). Such evidence for absolute dating is to be found in the presence of recognizably Egyptian objects in stratigraphical association with native Palestinian objects, which are thereby dated in terms of Egyptian chronology. The other method of linking events on Palestinian sites with events recorded in Egyptian written history does not help as regards the Early Bronze Age, since the Egyptian records are not sufficiently precise.

Even in Egypt there are intervals in which adequate documentation is lacking or scanty. One such gap comes at the end of the period of the Old Kingdom, lasting until the re-establishment of unified control under the XIIth Dynasty, a period of disturbance lasting in Egypt from c. 2185 B.C. to c. 1991 B.C. A major element in this period of disturbance was the incursions of Asiatics. Such incursions almost certainly came through Palestine. At this time, the other third-millennium centre of imperial rule, Mesopotamia, was also suffering from the incursions of uncivilized peoples, in the Sumerian and Akkadian records identified as the Amurru, the Amorites of the Old Testament. Written history thus tells us that western Asia and Egypt were struggling against threats to urban civilization during the last centuries of the third millennium B.C., and that these threats came from the nomads or semi-nomads of the Syrian-Arabian desert, the equivalent of the modern beduin. In Mesopotamia and Egypt there were mighty empires, in northern and coastal Syria strong kingdoms closely linked to the major civilizations of the time. All of these succumbed for a greater or shorter time to the incursions of the non-urban peoples pressing on their boundaries. Urban civilization in Palestine was on a more modest scale than that of its neighbours in northern Syria. It is reasonable to accept that this civilization succumbed more easily, and that there was therefore a longer period of interruption in urban life. This is the period which I call Intermediate Early Bronze-Middle Bronze, abbreviated to E.B.-M.B., though my American colleagues, owing to the accidents of archaeological taxonomy, call it M.B.I.

Our knowledge of Early Bronze Age Jerusalem is too slight to provide evidence of the remarkable break in Early Bronze Age civilization that is seen, for instance, at Jericho,[1] and of which the evidence is seen throughout Palestine in new burial customs and the absence of evidence of town life. In the whole area in Jerusalem that we excavated, there was not the slightest trace of the very characteristic E.B.-M.B. Pottery. Yet one knew that these nomadic invading people had reached the area of Jerusalem, since among the material derived from Warren's excavations (see above, p. 6 ff.) and transferred from the Palestine Exploration Fund to the Institute of Archaeology there was a group of pots marked 'Cave east of Olivet'. None of Warren's publications enabled one to identify the area precisely. The material interested me very much, since the peculiar pottery vessels were the closest that I had seen to the vessels from the E.B.-M.B. Pottery-type tombs at Jericho.[2] The only description

[1] *AIHL*, pp. 135 ff.
[2] *Digging up Jericho*, pp. 197–201.

that I find applicable to these vessels is 'tooth-brush mugs', but as such containers are now old-fashioned, this may be an unacceptable description. I therefore reacted with enthusiasm when in 1965 a police corporal appeared on the site with a bag of pottery. He had been building an extension to his house, and had broken into a rock-cut tomb. The vessels that he produced resembled very closely those from Warren's 'Cave east of Olivet'. The location corresponded well. It lay in a bay of the main west-facing range of the Mount of Olives, where one in fact looked east to the Russian Convent of the Ascension. We therefore immediately mounted a subsidiary excavation, which located eleven tombs of the period (and only of this period) Pls. 21, 22).

The E.B.-M.B. people of Palestine had a tribal organization which is reflected in regional variations, variations which are shown in burial customs, for there is almost no other evidence. At Jerusalem we have evidence of one group, which had some contact with the E.B.-M.B. Pottery-type people at Jericho, but which was more closely related to the people who buried at Khirbet Samieh, 15 miles to the north. 'Who buried' is in fact a most important adjectival phrase. The only evidence that has survived of these destroyers of urban civilization is that of their burial customs.

One is thus justified in taking it that there was a gap between a modest urban Early Bronze Age Jerusalem and an urban Jerusalem of the second millennium B.C., a gap filled by the arrival of tribal nomads, who may have destroyed Early Bronze Age Jerusalem, or at least disrupted the economy upon which it was dependent. These invaders left no trace at all on the site of ancient Jerusalem.

At this point the evidence of Trench 1 low on the eastern slope of Ophel comes into play. The discovery of a wall dating to the eighteenth century B.C. has already been mentioned (above, p. 78). In the first stages of the excavation of Trench 1, we had to deal with tip-lines of soil and stone that in places had built up an accumulation of as much as 5 metres. The stony

FIG 15 Section of the south face of the east end of Jerusalem Trench I. The earliest town wall NB has a foundation trench which contains Middle Bronze Age pottery. It is sealed by levels which must have run to a vanished wall to the east, which are cut into the later wall NA

nature of this fill can be appreciated from the view of the sides of the trench in Pl. 25. This photograph and Pl. 64 show that eventually substantial walls began to appear. With the best will in the world, however, it was difficult to interpret any part of them as town walls. Moreover, the associated pottery was relatively late, eighth–seventh century B.C., too late to be anything to do with David or the Jebusites.

At the very bottom end of the lowest square in the trench we struck a wall which from its very first appearance looked different, even though little more than its west face was within the square (Pl. 19). Moreover, the dating evidence was clear. The wall, of which the field identification label was NB (though it may be renumbered in the final publication), was built at the foot of a rock scarp, cutting into a fill that had sloped over the scarp, with a clear foundation trench (fig. 15). In this foundation trench were sherds that were unmistakably Middle Bronze II and fairly early in it, probably about eighteenth century B.C. The contrast between this pottery and that hitherto found in the upper part of Trench I was very striking.

Plate 19 shows how little of wall NB was exposed in 1961. It was perhaps rash of me to claim at that stage that we had located the east wall of Jebusite and Davidic Jerusalem, but in fact this worked out all right. In 1962 we extended the trench a further 6 metres down the slope (Pl. 20). The wall proved to be 2 metres wide, and to the east of it there were no further buildings. In 1967, we extended the trench to the south, with the usual horrible business of shifting dumps that any such extension is liable to involve. A total length of 12.25 metres of the wall was exposed (Pl. 26). It was impossible to clear further to the south because here was the main path leading from the Silwan Valley to the summit of the ridge.

To the north, the exposed portion of wall NB has a re-entrant angle, and disappears beneath the later wall NA (Pl. 20). As originally exposed, this angle suggested a tower. It seemed a reasonable guess that this might be a gate-tower. It must be expected that there was a gate in the wall, leading to the Spring Gihon. Access in time of war was provided by the shaft described below (p. 84) and illustrated in figs. 16 and 17. This would have been an exceedingly inconvenient route for everyday use, and it is virtually certain that there must have been peacetime access by means of a road leading through a gate in the town wall. It was hoped that the 1967 extension would reveal this gate, but it did not. I remain convinced that the line of the present path must closely approximate to the ancient route from the summit to the spring, and that there must be a gate close at hand. This is a problem to be investigated by the next excavations of the area.

The angle shown in Pl. 26 is not the angle of a gate-tower, for the exposed length of wall to the south is too great for this interpretation. It could be evidence that the wall was built with a succession of offsets and insets, or it could be that it is actually the north-east angle of the Middle Bronze Age and Davidic city.

Before we turn to the other boundaries of early Jerusalem we must consider further the siting of this east wall. Reference has already been made (above, p. 18) to the earliest access route to the Spring Gihon, and the necessary association with this of the earliest fortified Jerusalem (above, p. 48). This route was first discovered by Warren in 1867, and was re-examined and more fully recorded by Père Vincent in connection with the 1911 excavations (see above, p. 30). Figures 16 and 17 are redrawings of the plan and section published by Père Vincent.[1] The excavation of the shaft and tunnels must have posed great problems to those who originally constructed them, and certainly did to the investigators. The latter approached from the bottom end, from the spring where, leading off from the water source, was a rock-cut channel which was stratigraphically earlier than the Siloam Tunnel. Along this Warren and Birtles penetrated, followed thirty-four years later by Père Vincent. The latter was aided by the well-equipped team of the Parker expedition, but Warren and Birtles must have accomplished a remarkable mountaineering feat to ascend the 50 metres-high shaft. From the head of the shaft, an angular passage and then steps, all cut in the rock, with rock-cut roofs, led to a staircase roofed by a stone-built vault, which was so insecure that even such intrepid explorers could penetrate no further. The original engineers apparently started their approach to the spring from above, for at the foot of the vaulted staircase is a shaft which was apparently abortive. They failed to penetrate the exceedingly hard rock stratum of *mezzi jahudeh* that they encountered;

[1] L.-H. Vincent, *Jérusalem sous Terre*, Pls. II and III.

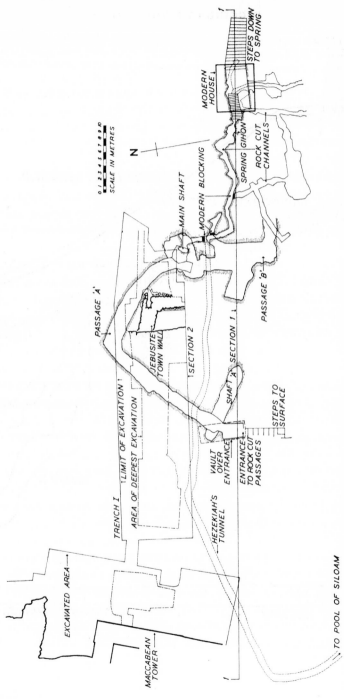

FIG 16 Plan of the earliest access to the Spring Gihon. A channel from the spring runs to a shaft, from the head of which an angular passage leads to steps to the surface, well outside the wall on the crest of the ridge

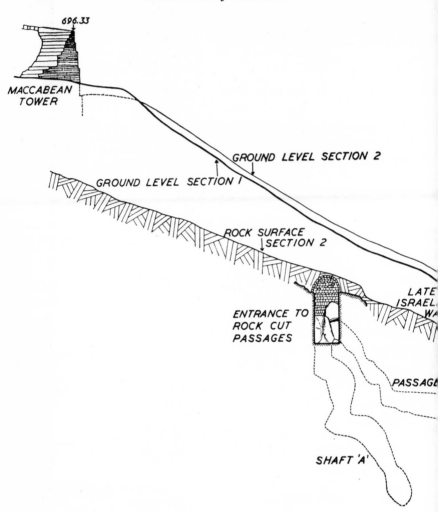

Fig 17 Section of the earliest access to the Spring Gihon. Shaft A was abortive, for hard layers in the rock made it impossible to reach water level. Passage A took its place following an angular line, as the plan in fig. 16 shows, which encountered a fault in the rock that enabled the main shaft to reach the water level

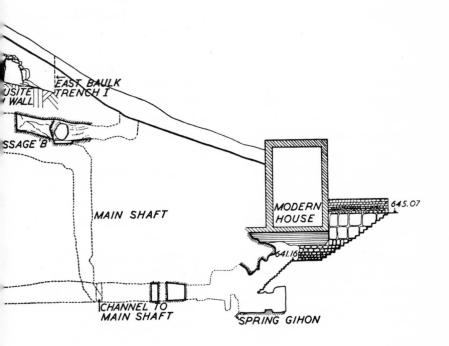

the abortive shaft is seen on the section, fig. 17. The shaft was then abandoned, and the engineers started to descend the slope in a tunnel. After some initial steps, this follows a relatively gentle gradient, first in a north-east direction, with then a sharp elbow back to a south-west direction. It is in fact the underground equivalent to the zigzag track of a path up a steep hill, which must to the engineers have seemed preferable to a more direct staircase, perhaps because of the difficulty of cutting adequate steps in the hard rock. It may have been the intention of the substitute plan, in Père Vincent's view, to accomplish the whole descent in a series of zigzags, but the second arm hit a natural fissure, which enabled a shaft, irregular but workable, to descend to a channel into which water from the spring could flow.

The position of the lower end of this complex was fixed by the situation of the spring. It must have been the choice of the engineers that it was brought to the surface by means of a staircase roofed by a stone-built vault through overlying deposits. We did not attempt to locate this vault, for above its estimated position was an enormous dump of soil from our predecessors' excavations; further excavators with more money to spare might find the clearance of this earliest water-shaft of Jerusalem dramatically worthwhile. Nevertheless, the position of the head of the route to the water was sufficiently clear to make it certain that it came to the surface well outside the wall on the crest of the hill, and it must be accepted as certain that the original engineers would not have chosen to begin their route outside the contemporary walls. The route to the spring just described is not in itself closely dated. Père Vincent dates the sherds from what he describes as the undisturbed silt of the system as 'Canaanite and early Israelite'. Père Vincent was the father of the identification of pottery periods, but in 1911 knowledge of the subject was in its infancy, and recognition of undisturbed silt might have to be looked at critically. One accepts Père Vincent's association of this access route to the water-supply and its dating to the Late Bronze Age-Early Iron Age period, that is to say the Jebusite-Davidic period, because it seems a very likely interpretation, which one need only query if there was strong evidence to the contrary.

I believe, therefore, that the position of the eastern town wall of Jerusalem that we have located is associated with the situation of the Spring Gihon and of the earliest access route to it. If I am right in believing (see above, p. 78) that the Early Bronze Age town (or village) of Jerusalem was confined to the summit of the ridge, the inhabitants may have been insufficiently numerous or skilled to establish a secure access to the spring in face of hostility. From the eighteenth century B.C. onwards, the excavation evidence suggests that control of the spring conditioned the position of the east wall. Placed as it was, well down a steep slope that was markedly uninviting for urban development, it can only be explained by the necessity of protecting the spring. It does not, however, enclose the spring, but only, by a comfortable distance, the access route to the spring that has just been described. This is in fact elementary military sense. If the town wall had been built low enough on the slope to enclose the spring, it would have been so low that it would have been completely commanded by the opposite slope of the Silwan Valley, even by the relatively primitive weapons of archery and slings. This situation is illustrated by Pl. 23. Wall NB is low enough on the slope to protect the tunnel and shaft that provided access to the spring in time of war, sufficiently near to the spring to be able to interfere with an attempt by the enemy to break into the spring from outside, but not so low as to place the wall within range of an enemy on the opposite slope.

The length of wall NB that has been exposed is of course short, and does not provide evidence of the full course of the wall. On the plan (fig. 18), it has been dotted on to the south, to the southern tip of Ophel, as following the same surface contour. It is highly probable that it did follow approximately this line; a salient down the slope merely opposite the spring would have been far too vulnerable to have been good planning. It now seems probable that the line of the continuation to the

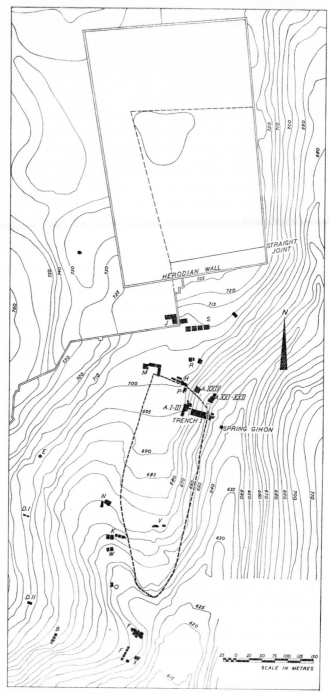

Fig 18   Plan of Jebusite and Davidic Jerusalem

north is given by the angle shown in Pl. 20, shortly beyond which point the wall disappears beneath the much later wall NA. The evidence for this comes from the position of the north wall and from Square A XXIV.

At all periods, the position of the north wall of Jerusalem was arbitrary, in the sense that it was not dictated by physical features. The ascent of the eastern ridge, Ophel, towards the main ridge that forms the backbone of Palestine (see above, p. 37), is gradual, and no feature has been found that would help the defence of the southern part of the ridge, which was vital to the early town because of the water-supply. Successive archaeologists have suggested different positions. We cannot claim to have found the wall, but I think that we have bracketed its position. Our opportunities for examining the surface of the ridge were very much restricted by two circumstances. The area to the west of our clearance at the top of Trench I had been completely stripped in the 1923-25 excavations; reference has already been made to the lack of any sound stratigraphical evidence from these excavations (above, p. 33). To the north of the area so cleared, the gardens of the modern houses are narrow, with frequent dividing terraces. To have organized a wide area of excavation here, transcending boundaries, was beyond my powers of diplomacy and even those of Abu Mohammed. The available area on which we could dig is shown as Site H in the plan (fig. 18). Down the area from west to east ran a path leading to the house of the owners of the plot on the eastern crest. We might have been able to negotiate the question of the path, but along it ran the pipe supplying their water, so the path was inviolate. Most unfortunately, the path skimmed the edge of a complicated succession of very massive walls along the southern boundary of the site. One could disentangle them structurally, but stratigraphical evidence to the north was interrupted by the path, and to the south had been destroyed by the earlier excavations.

Nevertheless, Site H produced conclusive evidence. In the area to the north of the path there were, by great good luck, walls and deposits that had not been disturbed in the Byzantine period, as it appears was the case in most of the 1923–25 area to the south. These deposits showed that the earliest occupation here was about the tenth century B.C.; it could therefore have been Davidic or Solomonic, and our present chronological criteria of pottery could not distinguish between the two.

The crucial point is that the earliest deposits here are in marked contrast with those to the south of this complicated succession of walls. Because of the 1923–25 excavations, we could only examine these in a very limited area, Site P, immediately west of the post-Exilic wall along the eastern crest. The upper layer had been removed in the earlier excavations that traced the line of the wall along the eastern crest. Fortunately, enough remained to show that here there were levels of the Late Bronze Age-Early Iron Age I, absolutely distinct from what was found in the earliest deposits to the north. Some element in the complex of walls along the south side of Site H must have constituted the boundary of the earliest Jerusalem.

The next problem was to trace the line of the wall between Site H and the point where wall NB disappears beneath wall NA. Square A XXIV was excavated with this purpose. It did not find the wall, but the evidence from it was clear that the wall must lie to the south. Like all excavations to the east of the crest of the ridge, the upper level consisted of a featureless fill becoming more and more stony as we progressed downwards, with the first structure reached at a depth of 9·50 metres from the surface. There proved to be only two building levels, both belonging to Iron Age II. They are described in Chapter 7 (below, pp. 131–5). The lowest dates to about the eighth century B.C. (firm dating must await the detailed examination of the pottery); and it was based on bedrock. Here therefore was no trace of any occupation of the time of the Jebusites or David, or indeed of Solomon. The contrast with Squares A I–III only 26 metres to the south where were the massive constructions of the Late Bronze Age, to be described below (p. 95), is complete. We were here certainly outside the earliest Jerusalem, and the

Jebusite-Davidic wall must have followed an oblique course up the slope, as indicated on fig. 18.

Elements have thus been recovered for the basis of a reasonable reconstruction of the plan of the earliest Jerusalem on the east and north sides. The evidence for the western limits depends even more on negative indications. We found, in the first place, very clear evidence that Jerusalem did not spread into the western ridge until a comparatively late date. One of our first objectives was to establish the date of the earliest occupation there. The areas available to us in this region were limited by the zone of no man's land that existed between 1948 and 1967 along the summit of the ridge, and our evidence therefore concerns the lower slopes of the ridge. Our trenches are shown on fig. 11. They all produced unambiguous evidence that there was no occupation before the first century A.D. Early Jerusalem was confined to the eastern ridge. One has therefore to consider a western wall, but not a southern wall, since the east and west sides came to a point where the central valley (the Tyropoeon) entered the Kedron.

Our negative evidence for the line of the western wall is derived from three sites, K, N, and M (see fig. 18), all of them slightly below the present western crest of the eastern ridge. They produced no evidence at all of Bronze Age or Iron Age occupation on the western slopes of the ridge. Site M at its eastern end had possible evidence of a Solomonic extension (below, p. 116), but nothing further west, Site N was confirmatory, though rather low on the slope. Site K was the most conclusive, since it was cut right up to the summit crest. There was some Iron Age pottery in cracks in the rock, but no structures or occupation levels. The main terrace on which Site K was situated was created in the Maccabean period (see below, pp. 193–4).

It therefore seems clear that the western boundary of Jebusite-Israelite-Jerusalem followed the western crest of the eastern ridge. This is the obvious defensive line. The equivalent eastern line had to be abandoned in order to control the water-supply. This seems to me to make sense. My great friend Père de Vaux once remarked that my plans of Jerusalem consisted of a hypothetical line which happened to fit in with a few fixed points. Père de Vaux and I were (and it is very sad to have to write in the past tense) such good friends that I take these remarks as he took mine on his excavations and theories. Nevertheless, I believe that our excavations have produced a plan of earliest Jerusalem that can only be disproved if further excavations produce more factual (by which I mean stratigraphical) evidence. I do not believe that opportunities for such excavations survive, mainly because of ancient quarryings, but also modern building activities. If they do, I wish the excavators luck.

I have defined the limits of Jerusalem of the Middle Bronze Age-Late Bronze Age-Jebusite period as best one can from the archaeological evidence. This early Jerusalem consisted of the summit of the eastern ridge with a sufficient extension down the slope to the east to control access to the Spring Gihon. Evidence of early occupation on the summit area does not exist. This lacuna is mainly because Roman quarrying and Byzantine buildings have destroyed all earlier structures and earlier occupation. For all we know, the original height of the eastern ridge may have been appreciably above that of the surviving rock. There is a secondary element that the stratigraphical technique of the period did not succeed in isolating the few undisturbed deposits. Our evidence from the slope came from Trench I and the wider clearance in Squares A I-III and XXIII at the top, immediately east of the so-called Davidic Tower. Not the whole of the area was excavated to bedrock, owing to the very massive overlying structures. Where bedrock was reached, there were remains of the Middle Bronze Age, presumably contemporary with wall NB. The structural remains were fragmentary, but that was enough to show that the buildings were unimpressive, climbing up the hill following the slope of the rock, which was at an angle of approximately 25 degrees.

This rather modest Jerusalem (on present evidence) of the eighteenth century B.C. was followed by something on a very different scale. Our excavations towards the top of Trench I and in Squares A I–III and XXIII encountered huge stone structures. Some of them belonged to the Iron Age, but the nucleus was certainly Late Bronze Age, which is seen in Pls. 27 and 28. The original nucleus consisted of a fill almost entirely of rubble, built in a series of compartments defined by facings of a single course of stones built on a batter. The fill and the facing courses are seen in Pls. 27 and 28. They lean back to the north against a spine, seen in the background in Pl. 29, to the north of which the batter is in the opposite direction. One must visualize the process as a series of adjoining pyramids built up to produce a platform. The whole structure in Squares A I–III was retained to the east by a north-south wall parallel to the slope. This wall was much more substantial than that which divided the compartments of the fill (Pl. 30), but much too slender to take the thrust of the massive fill; its inadequacy is shown by the bulge and gap in the photograph. It is, however, clear that it had been supported on the downhill side by a lower terrace, of which most of the evidence has been removed by a later terrace of the Iron Age.

This terrace system introduced a revolutionary town-planning element on the area of Jerusalem beneath the crest. In the place of poor-scale buildings following the slope of the rock, a series of terraces were created on which houses of a more civilized type could be built. In the area excavated in which the greatest evidence survived, Squares A I–III, the terraces survived to a height of 4·75 metres above the Middle Bronze Age levels seen at the base of Pl. 28. This terracing expanded the buildings on the crest down towards the Kedron Valley. The date of this revolutionary town-planning operation, presumably to be attributed to the Biblical Jebusites, is certainly Late Bronze Age. A fourteenth–thirteenth-century date is reasonably certain. The sherds providing the dating evidence are terribly fragmentary, and it remains for the final analysis of the pottery to decide whether it is possible to be more precise.

Artificial terraces on such a steep slope run a great risk of collapse. The most striking evidence of this, and also of the long-lasting influence they had in the lay-out of Jerusalem in the area, is the fact that the only buildings upon the upper terrace to survive belonged to the seventh century B.C. These are seen in the background of Pl. 32. There were two stages of Iron Age buildings, but the stone fill seen in the photograph immediately beneath them is entirely Late Bronze Age. All the buildings contemporary with the terraces, and any rebuildings of them down to the seventh century B.C., have completely disappeared in what was probably a whole series of collapses. Within the Late Bronze Age there was certainly the need of a series of repairs. The major collapses were probably to the east, where the thrust of the heavy filling on the steep slope would have a disastrous effect if there was a break in the successive retaining walls; the final breach and bulge of the uppermost retaining wall are shown on Pl. 30. There were also apparently problems to the south of Squares A I–III. Pl. 31 and fig. 15 show the line of collapse and successive repairs within the Late Bronze Age. It is tempting to think that to the south there was an approach to the summit, maintained at a low level after the terraces were built, revetted by a wall which at intervals collapsed. Within the area excavated, however, the whole space was occupied by a gigantic repair belonging to the Iron Age, which is described below (pp. 100–1). The area to the south, with the possibility of uncovering this road up the slope, along which Solomon must have passed after his anointing at the Spring Gihon (I Kings I: 33 ff.), and the head of the early water shaft and tunnel, would be a rewarding one for any future excavator prepared to face the horrors of excavating on this slope, to which in this area is added the overburden of a dump from the 1923–25 excavations. To what extent the terraces continued to the south, with or without the intervention of a sunken approach route, is a matter for conjecture. The probability is that they did, for otherwise something approaching one-half of the superficial area enclosed within the (presumed) line of the walls would have been unsuitable for full urban development because of the steepness of the slope.

As we now know it, Jerusalem of the period preceding its capture by David has a skeleton, but very little flesh. The accumulated evidence suggests that there is little chance of much more information. Our estimation of its early importance is based on literary evidence, especially the inclusion of its ruler, Abd-Khiba, amongst the number of those communicating with Egypt at the time of the Amarna letters in the early fourteenth century B.C. (see above p. 41), and, above all, David's need to capture it to create a united monarchy (see below, p. 98).

★

CHAPTER FIVE

David's Jerusalem

DAVID CAME TO POWER after the death of Saul by election as king first by the southern tribes of Judah about 1005 B.C. and then by the northern tribes of Israel. The reason was his military successes against the Philistines, at whose hands the Israelites had suffered a grievous defeat in the battle of Mount Gilboa, in which Saul, the first man to be acknowledged as king of all the Israelite tribes, and his son Jonathan were killed (I Samuel 1 : 31).

David's capital as leader of the southern tribes was at Hebron. When the northern tribes followed suit seven years later he was in the difficult situation that access between his two kingdoms was controlled by the command of the Jebusite city of Jerusalem over the route along the mountain crest which alone connected the northern and southern parts of Palestine (see above, pp. 39–40). David's capture of Jerusalem is recorded in II Samuel 5 : 6–8.

And the king and his men went to Jerusalem unto the Jebusites, the inhabitants of the land; which spake unto David, saying, Except thou take away the blind and the lame, thou shalt not come in hither: thinking, David cannot come in hither.

Nevertheless David took the strong hold of Zion: the same is the city of David.

And David said on that day, Whosoever getteth up to the gutter, and smiteth the Jebusites, and the lame and the blind, that are hated of David's soul, he shall be chief and captain.

(*AV.* The only significant difference in *RSV* is *water shaft* for *gutter.*)

In the other version in I Chronicles 11 : 4–8, the only additional item is 'And David said, Whosoever smiteth the Jebusites first shall be chief and captain. So Joab the son of Zeruiah went first up, and was chief'.

It can therefore be concluded that the Jebusites considered their defences impregnable against any, still fairly minor, threat from the Israelite tribes. Their defences were penetrated by a water-route, and everything points to this having been the route to the Spring Gihon that has already been described as the earliest access to the essential water-supply of Jerusalem. Joab's feat in climbing the shaft must have been even greater than that of Warren in 1867, for he could have expected an enemy round every corner; he therefore very fully earned his reward of being made 'chief and captain'.

Joab penetrated the defences that we have located on the east side and the lines of which I have suggested elsewhere. The terse Biblical account shows that the penetration took the Jebusites completely by surprise, and the town fell to David.

David's next concern was to secure his position in Jerusalem. This was in fact of very great importance to him. In Hebron to the south or in Shiloh and Shechem to the north, he was dealing with leading towns of confederacies which had selected him as leader but had their own tribal allegiance. Jerusalem was *his* city by right of conquest.

The Biblical reports of David's activities in Jerusalem are brief. In the second book of Samuel they are simply recorded as 'And David built round about from Millo and inwards' (II Samuel 5:9). In the first book of Chronicles it is stated 'And he built the city round about, even from Millo round about: and Joab repaired the rest of the city' (I Chronicles 11:8). He made preparations to provide a home for the Ark of the Covenant in Jerusalem, but in I Chronicles 22:8 and 28:3 it is stated that because he had shed blood Yahweh decreed through his prophets, notably Nathan, that David should not build a permanent home for the Ark. The religious omens, therefore, urged him not to concentrate on the cult centre of Yahweh. It is easy to understand that temporal power and international politics could be a substitute for his interest in the cult centre.

References to David's attention to the defences of Jerusalem are singularly inexplicit. He had captured Jerusalem. He made it his capital. Its defences must have been a matter of major importance to him. Since, as will be seen, the Jebusite wall NB on the east side remained in use until at least the eighth century B.C., and since Solomon's extension to the north was against the Jebusite north wall, it can be taken that he simply repaired the existing walls.

The one part of his work that the record in both II Samuel and I Chronicles emphasizes is his concern with *Millo*. None of the translators of the Bible, down to those of the New English Bible, attempts to interpret the term, but simply transliterates it from the Hebrew, of which the basic meaning is 'filling'. Very many writers on Jerusalem have made suggestions about the building to which the authors of the Biblical accounts are referring. Some have suggested a tower, some the infilling of a ditch, and so on, in different places and for different purposes, and there has been no consensus of opinion. No doubt my suggestion will equally fail to secure unanimous approval.

My candidate is at least certainly a filling that has been found, and equally certainly it was of great importance. This is the terrace structure built by the Jebusites to support the houses on the eastern slope. Its description as a filling needs no comment. Its maintenance was vital to the buildings in this quarter of Jerusalem, and if I am right in suggesting (see above, p. 89) that the inclusion of the eastern slopes within the town continued from the area excavated to the southern tip of the ridge, this 'quarter' may in fact have been almost as large as the level space on the summit of the ridge, as fig. 21 shows. Moreover, the portion of the structure within the area excavated was undoubtedly repaired on a number of occasions within the period of the Israelite monarchy; the Bible records that in addition to the work of David, Solomon (I Kings 9:24; 11:27) and Hezekiah (II Chronicles 32:5) also repaired *Millo*. In the foreground in Pl. 33

is seen a *filling* (I italicize for emphasis) of much larger stones, which is also seen in Pl. 34, where it overlies the earth fill seen in Pl. 31 that repaired the original stone filling; Pl. 31 shows at the base on the right the original stone filling with above it the earth fill, and above again the filling of larger stones. The character of the latter filling is seen even more clearly in Pl. 33, and this emphasizes both the enormous labour of constructing the terrace and the different but almost equally daunting task of excavating it.

The scale held by John Strange, the site supervisor, is 2 metres long, divided into half-metre lengths. This shows the size of the stones involved. The original builders had to convey them from the spot whence they were quarried, probably lower on the slope or on the other side of the Kedron Valley. I have seen donkeys carrying pretty incredible loads, but I doubt whether a donkey could have climbed the slope of the hill carrying such a load. Camels, I suppose, would have been a possibility. Anyhow, the stones did reach the site, and somehow they were manoeuvred into position; here again one doesn't see how, since even elementary mechanical devices such as shere-legs and pulleys would have been very complicated in such a set-up. Sheer manpower may be the answer.

The fact remains that this massive addition to the Jebusite terrace system was created. Our problem was to dissect it. If one had all the space in the world, one could gradually work in from the top, outer edge of the structure and remove the stones in an orderly manner, though even then facing the problem of the weights. In excavation one is confined by the limits of the excavation area. As one goes down, stones engage in the faces of this area and cannot be extricated without endangering the side of the trench or square. An impression of this is given in Pl. 33. Where the site supervisor stands, stones that cannot safely be dislodged start to project from the south wall of the square. In the same photograph one can see how the massive stones of each course project more and more to the east. We did in fact fail to reach bedrock here, having to stop at a level of *c.* 1·40 metres, above that at which, to the north, the less massive structures of the Late Bronze Age terracing enabled us to make a small clearance to bedrock.

It is, in fact, rather difficult to convey to a reader the difficulties an archaeologist trained in the British tradition of excavation based on stratigraphy faces in dealing with problems in which total clearance might reveal grand structures. (I am here thus claiming that these terraces at Jerusalem were grand structures, a grand town-planning conception, though architecturally nothing has survived.) An archaeologist trained in the British tradition cannot throw away the controls of stratigraphy. So I was confined to my squares and trenches, of which the vertical faces gave me the evidence of succession (linked of course to the finds in the recorded levels). One has nevertheless to face the physical and material problems of penetrating through the successive layers.

In the case of the excavation of this addition to the Jebusite terrace system, it was simply a question of removing one stone and levering out the next one. But whatever method the original builders had to place the stone in its original position, we, working from a position some 20–40 feet higher up, had to approach the problem in a completely different way. Our only method was to fragment the stone that the builders had so laboriously hauled into position, so that it could be carried out by the basket-load. Even this fragmenting was not so easy. Wood in Palestine is scarce and of poor quality. Each year we brought out with us hafts for picks and sledgehammers, but the mortality in the latter was enormous when we came to dealing with this massive terrace structure. At this point Abu Mohammed, with his usual excellent local knowledge, suggested that there was someone who would be efficient in this particular respect. I do not remember his name, but he was a tough-looking individual. The toughness of his appearance was irrelevant to his efficiency. Introduced to a difficult stone in the overlapping fill shown in Pl. 33, he would look here and there, and he would sing a little song. (I am emphatic on my evidence of this, but my Arabic is quite inadequate to catch the words of the song.) He then struck the stone a blow at just the right point, and it fell apart into the fragments that we could carry out to the dump. Moreover, I don't think he ever broke a haft. It remains in my mind as an example of complete expertise.

In a stone filling of this sort, there are naturally few finds, and there is also the risk that, as stones are prized out, sherds and small objects may filter through from above. Nevertheless, there was enough evidence that this addition to the terraces was Israelite, and probably tenth century B.C. Whether a more detailed assessment of the sherds will make it possible to assign it to David or Solomon remains to be seen.

Another repair to the early terraces was on the east side, where was the exceedingly massive structure that was the first feature to be revealed as we cut Trench 1 down the slope (Pl. 64). This was, at least as far as its final stages were concerned, appreciably later, and might be the work of Hezekiah, if he is the only later ruler to repair *Millo*. Again, a final assessment of the pottery evidence may provide closer dating.

The Biblical accounts also suggest that David built a palace. In II Samuel 5:11 (*RSV*) it is stated 'And Hiram, king of Tyre sent messengers to David, and cedar trees, also carpenters and masons who built David a house'. The I Chronicles 14:1 account is almost word for word the same. There is no archaeological evidence for this. The probability is that his residence would have been on the summit of the ridge, where, as already described (above, p. 32), all evidence has been destroyed. David must have cleared a space within the Jebusite town, but the size of his residence is unlikely to have been great, for anything grandiose would have taken too much space within the restricted area of the Jebusite-Davidic city. The residence clearly was considered inadequate by Solomon, for he built his own palace. The reference to the masons and carpenters from Phoenicia is interesting evidence of the lack of building techniques among the Israelites, which reappears when Solomon undertook the building of the Temple and his own palaces.

The Jerusalem of David is a key point in the history of Israel. Our excavations have revealed little of it. I am confident that we have delimited it. I believe that the archaeological evidence for anything more does not survive.

The brevity of the Biblical account does not in any case suggest that David devoted much time to Jerusalem. It is probable that the only new structure for which he was responsible was his residence. The I Chronicles 11:8 reference quoted above (p. 99) suggests that he left other work in the city to Joab, and that this consisted only of repairs. This absence of building ambitions in his capital is understandable, since his task was to build a kingdom, and in this he was supremely successful.

The accounts of his conquests are contained in II Samuel 8 and 10 and I Chronicles 18. Both give first place to the fact that he 'smote the Philistines'. In the Chronicles account, he annexed Gath and its district, in the Samuel account he annexed Methegammah (*RSV*). That the Philistines should be his first concern is entirely to be expected, for the tribes elected him as king to save them from the results of the crushing Philistine victory on Mount Gilboa. Strangely enough, he seems never to have attempted to conquer the whole Philistine area and thus extend his kingdom to the coastal plain. There were still independent Philistine states there in the eighth and seventh centuries B.C. The probable explanation is that Egyptian interest in the coastal plain was sufficient to deter an expansionist policy in that direction, even though Egypt was at that time relatively weak. Another element might be that Mediterranean traffic was not then particularly prosperous or lucrative, and that wealth through trade offered greater opportunities through controlling connections between Syria to the north and the Arabian (and even more eastern) trade to the south. Along the fertile strip of table-land between to the west the Jordan Valley and the Arabah and to the east the Arabian desert ran what from time immemorial has been known as the King's Highway. This route provided a connection between the port at the head of the Gulf of Aqaba, and the land route along the Arabian coast, and the rich and civilized states of

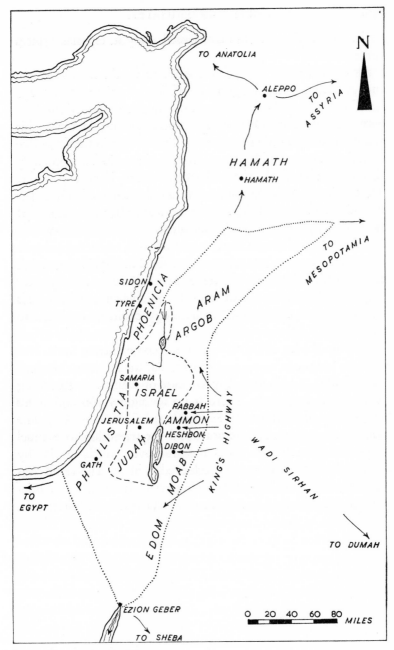

N

TO ANATOLIA

ALEPPO

TO ASSYRIA

HAMATH

•HAMATH

TO MESOPOTAMIA

SIDON

TYRE

PHOENICIA

ARAM

ARGOB

SAMARIA

ISRAEL

RABBAH

JERUSALEM

AMMON

HESHBON

PHILISTIA

JUDAH

DIBON

GATH

MOAB

KING'S HIGHWAY

WADI SIRHAN

TO EGYPT

EDOM

TO DUMAH

EZION GEBER

0   20   40   60   80   MILES

TO SHEBA

FIG 19   Map showing David's conquests

Syria. All the riches of the East passed along it, especially spices and gold.

Along this route were, from south to north, Edom, Moab, and Ammon, petty kingdoms sufficiently strong to 'oppress Israel' in the period of the Judges, before there was any cohesion between the tribes. One would suspect that David turned his attention to these little kingdoms of Transjordan in the first place to deal with any possible menace from that direction, but probably also with a planned scheme to control this important route. The smiting of Moab in both accounts follows that of smiting the Philistines. Edom and Ammon came later, after the records of attacks on Syrian states. It is difficult to believe that this was in fact the course of events, for to capture Moab, and leave a hostile Edom and Ammon while he was involved in a major campaign to the north, does not make sense. The Biblical record does not help us here, and even in the most favourable circumstances it is not a problem upon which archaeology could be expected to throw light.

Third in the list of David's conquests come states in Syria. Not all these states can be precisely identified, for instance Zobah (II Samuel 8:3), which probably lay east of Damascus, stretching towards the Euphrates. There is no ambiguity concerning his subjugation of Damascus (II Samuel 8:4; I Chronicles 18:6). The neighbouring king of Hamath asked for friendship (II Samuel 8:9–10). One can thus assess the area over which David, by military power and prowess, achieved control. The result was certainly a very considerable commercial dividend. For a brief period, Israel became one of the powerful states of western Asia.

★

CHAPTER SIX

Jerusalem at the Time of Solomon

SOLOMON SUCCEEDED his father David *c.* 966 B.C. As far as the Biblical evidence indicates, there were at that stage no disruptive elements that Solomon could not easily deal with; the United Monarchy was a success and was accepted. Solomon's political inheritance was an area vastly exceeding the original area occupied by the Israelite tribes. Inherent in this expansion were commercial riches, and one must accept that these are the basis of Solomon's fame.

Solomon was not a warrior like his father. From all the Biblical records, he was a very civilized person, except that civilization in the oriental world of that time was demonstrated by great luxury. The most dramatic story in the Old Testament of his wisdom and his luxury is that of the visit of the queen of Sheba (I Kings 10:1–13). It is generally (though not universally) accepted that the queen of Sheba ruled an area in south Arabia. She gave to Solomon gifts of gold and spices and precious stones (I Kings 10:10). This tribute from the south was very relevant to Solomon's riches. David had established control over the Trans-jordanian kingdoms through which passed produce from the South and further east (for it is pretty certain that through southern Arabia were transmitted spices and other products from this direction). Therein was the wealth of Solomon's kingdom, which enabled him to undertake grandiose developments in Jerusalem and in other cities which were his especial responsi-bility. Within the period of his reign, the more distant of his father's conquests were lost, notably in Syria, but his rule thrived on the conquests of David. His internal political troubles were not

great. The non-Israelite inhabitants of his kingdom were kept
under firm control, but it is interesting to note that it was admitted
that within Palestine there were still recognizable elements of
'the Amorites, Hittites, Perizzites, Hivites and Jebusites' (I Kings
9:20).

Solomon was clearly an astute diplomatist in the international
field, a field into which David's conquests had enabled Israel to
enter. Probably his most important international success was to
establish diplomatic contacts with Egypt by the age-old method
of dynastic intermarriage. It was no small compliment to Solomon's status that the Egyptian pharoah gave him a daughter in
marriage (I Kings 3:1). One can take one's choice as to why he
regarded her as his principal wife (I Kings 7:8; 9:24; the latter
passage suggests that a palace for Pharoah's daughter took prece-
dence over repairing *Millo*), as between political necessity and the
personal attractions of the lady. Solomon was certainly not a
monogamist; 'he loved many strange women together with the
daughter of Pharoah, women of the Moabites, Ammonites,
Edomites, Zidonians and Hittites' (I Kings 11:1). All these
contacts may have an element of diplomacy in them, and may
be not just evidence of Solomon's promiscuity; but the general
evidence is clear that for diplomatic or personal reasons Pharoah's
daughter was pre-eminent in his harem.

It was not until the fourth year of his reign (I Kings 6:1) that
Solomon began the great building programme at Jerusalem that
was completely to transform a small Late Bronze-Early Iron town
into a city of famed magnificence. In the intervening period he
had to secure his accession against the claims of his elder brother
Adonijah; the details of how he had him murdered and also
those whom he suspected were not loyal to him (I Kings 2) are
unedifying, but very typical of how ancient despots (and indeed
some modern ones) came to power. He had (again there is a
modern ring) to secure recognition from his contemporaries,
and it appears that Egypt's recognition of him as the established
ruler came at an early stage, since it is stated in I Kings 3:1 that
after Solomon had 'made affinity with Pharaoh King of Egypt',

he lodged Pharaoh's daughter in the city of David, that is to say within the limits of the Jebusite-Davidic Jerusalem as defined in the last chapter, until he had finished his new buildings. The recognition of Solomon by his important neighbour Hiram, king of Tyre, ruler in highly civilized Phoenicia, also came early, for Hiram's message of welcome to Solomon clearly preceded the latter's request to Hiram for help in his building projects (I Kings 5:1).

Solomon's building operations at Jerusalem are centred on a House of the Lord to house the Ark of the Covenant. This was a conception that David had failed to achieve. There are obviously many interacting influences in this, including that of David's preoccupations with foreign conquests; the doubts of the still tribal Israelites as to whether Yahweh should have a fixed, monumental, home as opposed to a tent which could be transported as the tribes moved, also played a part. David had, in fact, after it was deduced that Yahweh did not want him to build a permanent home for the Ark in Jerusalem, provided it with a tent (II Chronicles 1:4).

The fact remains that David had hoped to combine his undoubted political control over the northern and southern tribes with the establishment in Jerusalem, his *own* city, of a cult centre housing the focus of the worship of Yahweh, the Ark. In this respect, his reign, so successful in other respects, failed. Solomon, heir to David's conquests and the resultant riches, and helped by the increasing sophistication of the leaders of the Israelite tribes, succeeded. Early in his reign, the concentration of the worship of Yahweh was still in doubt. In II Chronicles 1:3 it is recorded that 'So Solomon, and all the congregation with him, went to the high place that was at Gibeon; for there was the tabernacle of the congregation of God, which Moses the servant of the Lord had made in the wilderness'. One must deduce that there was still divergence of opinion as to the resting-place of the Ark of the Covenant in the tabernacle or tent that had journeyed with the migrating Israelite tribes.

Solomon was, however, very much in accord with his father's

frustrated policy to make Jerusalem the centre of the cult of Yahweh. The rest of II Chronicles I shows his confidence that he had the approval of Yahweh and that his riches were such that he could undertake a grandiose building scheme to provide a house for Yahweh and, as a very clearly linked element, a house for himself and for his principal wife, Pharaoh's daughter. The account of these buildings is given in great detail in I Kings 5–7 and II Chronicles 2–4.

If one had to depend only on the evidence of excavations in Jerusalem, one would have no idea at all of Solomon's building operations. The site of the Temple is not in doubt. Solomon's Temple was ruined by the Babylonians in 587 B.C. About 538 B.C. the first group of the exiles in Babylon were allowed to return. In this interval of less than sixty years, remnants of the inhabitants remained ('none remained, save the poorest sort of the people of the land', II Kings 24:14). The existence of these remnants would have insured a remembrance, even if in the returning group there were not any ancients who themselves remembered the Temple. The first efforts of the returning exiles were concentrated on rebuilding the Temple, which was finished *c.* 515 B.C. From that time onwards until Herod the Great started its rebuilding in the last decades of the first century B.C., there was no gap. The retaining walls of the platform of Herod's Temple are still visible today, now crowned by that supreme example of Moslem architecture, the Dome of the Rock.

Though Herod's temple platform survives, with a level probably close to that of the original one, there is not the slightest trace of his temple building or of its predecessors. Even if it were possible to excavate within the area, which would be a desecration of a site of great sanctity and beauty, it is certain that nothing intelligible would be found. The bare rock is visible beneath the Dome of the Rock, the Akra (the Arabic word for rock) *par excellence*. Any older structures have been swept away in the Roman and Moslem periods that succeeded the final destruction of the Temple by the Romans in A.D. 70.

The platform to which reference has been made is a vital

element in one's conception of the Temple. Solomon built his Temple on the site of the threshing floor of Araunah the Jebusite, where, in David's time, the angel of the Lord halted the plague threatening Jerusalem from the north and south (II Samuel 28:16). Jerusalem was saved at a point outside its walls. The description of the site of Jerusalem has shown that its physical basis was a steep-sided ridge. For a complex on the scale that is indicated by the Biblical account, a platform supported by massive retaining walls is required.

At this point archaeological evidence can make its contribution. There have been many arguments as to whether at the base of the walls of the Herodian temple platform were to be found those of Solomon's platform. The foundations of Herod's walls were revealed in the incredible excavations of Warren (see above, pp. 11 ff.). Such an eminent authority as Père Vincent believed that the lower courses of this great wall were Solomonic. Of this there was no stratigraphical evidence (see above, pp. 55 ff.) and the assumptions based on masonry characteristics are unjustified.

The crucial point is that 32·72 metres north of the south-east corner of the Herodian platform there is a very clear straight joint between the earlier structure to the north and the Herodian addition to the south (Pls. 35, 36). This was revealed by a clearance carried out by the Jordanian Department of Antiquities in 1966. It had in fact been observed by Warren in 1867, but the implications had not been noted. The implications are in fact clear. At the time at which Herod built his platform, he added an extension to the south against an earlier structure. There were certainly a number of vicissitudes in the history of the immediately pre-Herodian Temple, but basically it was the Temple restored by Zerubbabel after the return from the Babylonian exile. It is inconceivable that Zerubbabel, with his very exiguous resources, should have increased the size of the Solomonic platform. It is reasonably certain that he built upon the basis of surviving foundations, and restored the platform as best he could.

This supposition is supported by the structural evidence. The contrast seen in Pls. 35–6 between the Herodian masonry to the south and the much heavier bossed masonry to the north makes it quite clear that two separate building periods are represented. Soon after this structural feature was revealed, it was visited by Maurice Dunand, the doyen of the archaeology of the Phoenician coast. He declared that the older masonry must be dated to the Persian period. He was kind enough to take me to see examples of the masonry he had in mind, at Eshmoun and at Byblos, and I entirely agree with his identification.

Here, therefore, we have at Jerusalem a rebuilding of the temple platform in masonry of the Persian style. What we can see above ground at the moment is not necessarily the work of Zerubbabel, for it looks as if there were several rebuilding periods, but I believe that it represents the restoration, and probably several restorations, of the south-east corner of the platform within the Persian period (sixth, fifth, and early fourth centuries B.C.), and that this is evidence for the south-east corner of the Solomonic platform.

Given that the south-east corner establishes the line of the southern limit of the temple platform, one must then consider the position of the south-west corner. There is no corresponding straight joint in the present west wall. Herodian masonry is visible up to the position of Wilson's Arch, a distance of 180 metres. The most famous section is that which forms the Wailing Wall of the Jews. The presumption is that the original south wall did not extend as far west as does the Herodian one. An alternative would be that on the west side the older wall had been destroyed so low, or was in such a bad condition, that Herod rebuilt it from its foundations. There are two reasons why I prefer the first alternative. The first is based on the relation of the south elevation to the rock contours. Figure 20 shows that the south elevation of Herod's temple platform spans the central valley, with the west wall some 30 metres up the slope of the western ridge. This is improbable for the Solomonic Temple, since we know that the contemporary city was confined to the eastern ridge. The second reason is more complicated, and as

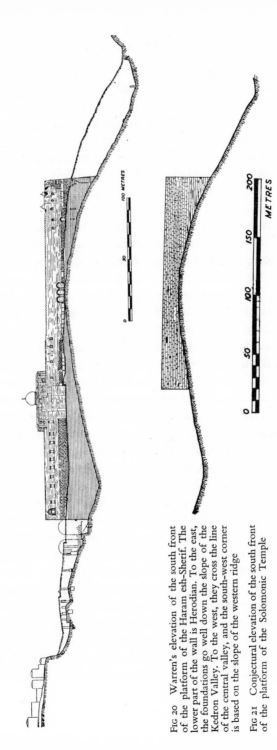

Fig 20 Warren's elevation of the south front of the platform of the Haram esh-Sherif. The lower part of the wall is Herodian. To the east, the foundations go well down the slope of the Kedron Valley. To the west, they cross the line of the central valley, and the south-west corner is based on the slope of the western ridge

Fig 21 Conjectural elevation of the south front of the platform of the Solomonic Temple

will be explained in Chapter 12, I believe that the south-west corner was at the point towards which runs the east wall of the present salient south from the Temple; this salient is much later, probably belonging to the period of Aelia Capitolina, but for the reasons given in Chapter 12, I suggest that it reflects an earlier line. If one projects this line to the point indicated as the south wall of the original platform by the straight joint, one can establish a hypothetical position for the original south-west corner of the platform. The resultant conjectural elevation of the south wall is shown on fig. 21. A plan developed from this south wall (fig. 22) would enable the rock summit, the present Akra, to be enclosed, as surely it must have been, and would allow ample space for the Temple, of which the dimensions were relatively small (see below, pp. 207–8). The plan would also agree with the statement of Josephus (*War*, I. xxi. 1 (401)) that Herod doubled the size of the earlier platform.

The last paragraphs have suggested a hypothetical outline plan for the platform that was the essential setting of Solomon's Temple. The one point that I feel is certain is that the southern wall of the platform was separated by a distance of at least 232 metres from the north wall of David's city, as suggested by the evidence described above (p. 92). It is not entirely obligatory that the city and the new cult centre should be structurally linked. There are, however, a number of reasons for suggesting that they were. The existence of a line of defences along the eastern crest of the eastern ridge has been known since the time of Warren's excavations, which provided the first indication that Jerusalem had at some stage extended to the south of the present Old City (see above, p. 19). This line is pretty closely represented by the houses along the crest seen in Pl. 17. The wall Warren found was Byzantine, but it is now clear that this was the successor of earlier walls.

In the restricted area of Site H (see fig. 22), north of the line of the east-west complex that divides occupation of the Jebusite period from that which is probably tenth century B.C. (see above, p. 92), the earliest wall that we found, based on bedrock, was

of the casemate type, a type in which two parallel walls are linked
by cross walls, thus creating small rooms within the wall complex. Such a method of constructing walls for the Solomonic
period and at least into the ninth century B.C. is attested at
Hazor, Megiddo, Tell Beit Mirsim, and Samaria. The Jerusalem
Site H example (Pl. 37) has interior rooms of smaller size than
elsewhere, but it certainly falls within the same category. The
stratigraphical evidence in Site H was so difficult owing to the
great superimposition of massive walls that the implications of
this casemate wall were not appreciated until the evidence of
Square A XXIV (see pp. 92, 131) made it clear that any extension on the flank of the slope north of the Jebusite-Davidic
north wall (see below pp. 147–8) did not take place until about the
eighth century B.C. Any Solomonic extension must have taken
place only on the crest of the ridge. This is a perfectly reasonable
supposition, since to the north there was no longer the necessity
to control access to the water-supply that demanded the inclusion
within the walls of the difficult terrain of the steep slope. There
the Site H casemate wall seems to fall very satisfactorily into
place.

   Interesting supporting evidence was derived from Site S II
(fig. 22), at a distance of 155 metres north-east of Site H and 105
metres south-west of the present south-east corner of the temple
platform. Here we located Warren's Byzantine wall, with
spectacular evidence of his perilous trench beneath it by which he
followed its line (Pl. 107). Beneath, and several building phases
earlier, was a wall on bedrock, somewhat to the west of the
Byzantine wall, with, projecting east from it (Pl. 38), and running under the Byzantine structure, a wall which probably
belonged to a projecting tower. The date of these earliest walls,
on the basis of the deposits against them, is, on the field estimate of the pottery, eighth century B.C. or earlier. The interesting point is that these walls were constructed of re-used stones
of the character identified as Phoenician at Samaria, with irregu-
larly projecting bosses having unequal margins on one, two,
or three sides. Solomon's use of Phoenician masons is undoubted

(see below, p. 121) and it is a reasonable inference that, close at hand, there was a wall of the time of Solomon, from which the builders of the eighth century B.C. derived their stones. The combined evidence of the various sites therefore indicates that on the east side Solomon joined the town to which he succeeded to the platform of his new Temple by a wall along the eastern crest of the eastern ridge.

The evidence for the west side is slighter. In Site M (see fig. 22), the area crossing the line of the northern boundary which had been suggested by the evidence from Site H, Byzantine quarrying had removed all evidence. Slightly to the north, however, in Square M II there was evidence that a wall of the tenth century B.C. had existed slightly west of the scarp that was probably the original limit of the summit area at this point. This wall did not survive, but against the crest was a deep fill, for which the pottery suggested a tenth-century B.C. date, which was cut by a much later wall. The probability is that this fill had been retained by a wall of the Solomonic period, which very slightly broadened the width of the summit of the ridge in an extension to the north. Beyond that point, any suggestion of the line depends on a hypothesis connected with Herodian quarrying, referred to above (p. 114) and to be discussed below (pp. 221-2).

It will be very obvious that in this effort to define the Solomonic extension to the north there is a very great deal of hypothesis. I am nevertheless confident that the picture is reasonably correct, and that the plan given in fig. 22 in general represents Solomonic Jerusalem. I am still more confident that it will be the greatest good fortune if any more precise evidence is recovered. The reason is quarrying, mainly in the Herodian and Roman periods. The plan on fig. 22 shows the areas on or touching the summit of the ridge, north of the limits of the Davidic city, that we excavated, Sites H, M, R, and S. In all of them except Site H, the evidence from which has already been described, all levels earlier than the first century B.C., and most levels earlier than the Byzantine period, had been completely removed in quarrying for building stone at subsequent periods. We had hoped much

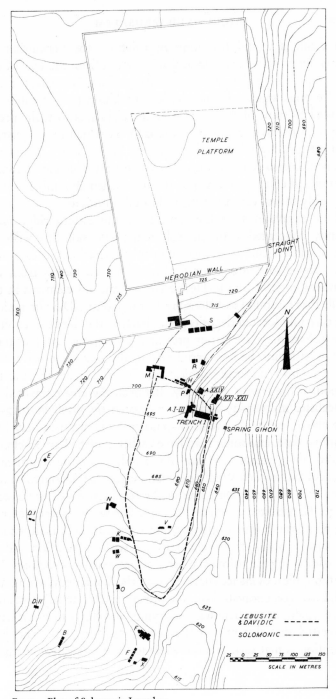

Fig 22 Plan of Solomonic Jerusalem

from Site s 1 (and had long negotiations for permission to
excavate), within the angle projecting south from the wall of the
Haram, forming the present boundary of the Old City; it was
a nice open space with no modern buildings (save a cabin inhabited by some of the more tiresome claimants to their, probably non-existent, rights over the land on which they squatted,
and guarded by what we knew as the 'hoarse dog'). However,
excavation showed that quarrying here started in the Herodian
period and continued down to the time when Byzantine houses,
probably fourth century A.D., were built in this area.

Our excavations on the summit of the eastern ridge were
mainly concerned with the Solomonic extension. Immediately
to the south of Site H, Macalister in 1923–25 carried out extensive
excavations to bedrock for a distance of 110 metres from the
southern edge of Site H. He interpreted various elements in the
walls that he found as belonging to the Jebusite-Davidic period.
He certainly located deposits going back to the third millennium
(see above, p. 78). But our present evidence suggests that most
of the structures he uncovered date to the Byzantine period. At
any rate, no valid stratigraphical evidence can attach them to the
period of the Jewish monarchy. Between the area excavated by
Macalister in 1923–25 and that excavated by Weill in 1912–13
(see above, p. 31–2), twentieth-century buildings (this may be a
minimal date, and some may have earlier ancestry) are so closely
spaced that excavations are impossible. The de Rothschild
finances that backed Weill's excavations secured the purchase of a
large area on the eastern side of the southern tip of the eastern
ridge. The results are seen on Pls. 8–9). The whole aspect shown in
the photograph is that of truncation – truncation of bedrock and
truncation of anything cut into it, with, in addition, deep
quarries going far below the level of pre-existing structures. No
stratigraphical evidence survives from the Weill excavations. We
did, however, excavate from the present surface an adjacent area.
Here, again, at the base was quarrying, and the pottery evidence
suggested that this was in the second century A.D. The presumption is that such areas of early Jerusalem that had not been

destroyed by quarrying at an earlier period were destroyed when the Romans built Aelia Capitolina *c.* A.D. 135, and needed great quantities of building stone.

What our excavations did was to define two elements in Solomon's expansion of Jerusalem, that of the Temple on its massive platform and that of the area linking the platform to the original city *c.* 232 metres to the south.

The Bible records that Solomon built three structures: the House of the Lord (I Kings 6–7); his own house (I Kings 7: 1–12); and the house for his wife, Pharaoh's daughter (I Kings 7:8; 3:1). The description of the Temple is given in great detail, and as has already been said, it is only from the Biblical record that we have any evidence, since no structural evidence survives. What struck the chronicler, however, was much more the interior aspect than that of the exterior. This leaves uncertainties which have allowed of divergent theoretical reconstructions of the building. In this, archaeology has no part to play, except to suggest interpretations from evidence of the world within which Solomon lived, which are especially important as regards the decoration of the interior.

The plan of the Temple was relatively simple, a wide porch leading into a high main hall, flanked, and structurally buttressed, by three tiers of small rooms (I Kings 5:6). Beyond it was the Holy of Holies, separated from the main hall by a screen of chains of gold (I Kings 6:21). There are no details concerning the porch or of the flanking three-tiered rooms which probably served utilitarian purposes, but the interior of the main hall is described in detail.

The main structure was of stone quarry-dressed, and therefore dressed with great precision so that it could be fitted without any mason's work on the site (I Kings 6:7). The interior was completely lined with boards of cedar, though I Kings 6:15 is ambiguous as to whether the floor was of cedar or fir. The cedar facing was elaborately carved; 'And the cedar of the house within was carved with knops [in *RSV*, gourds] and open flowers: all was cedar; there was no stone seen'. (I Kings 6:18). The mere lining of the building with cedar was a great luxury, for the cedar had to be imported from Lebanon (see below, p. 121). But even the cedar lining was not visible, for 'the whole house he overlaid with gold, until he had finished all the house' (I Kings 6:22). In I Kings 6:30 it is even said that he overlaid the floor with gold. One must be forgiven for feeling that this was somewhat ostentatious.

The Holy of Holies, or oracle, in which was housed the Ark of the Covenant (I Kings 6:19), was likewise lined with cedar overlaid with gold. The most striking element in the decoration here, though none but the priests would ever have seen it, was a pair of cherubim carved in olive wood, again overlaid with gold. The cherubim were ten cubits (5 metres) high, with a wing span of ten cubits, with their inner wings meeting and their outer wings touching the walls.

The Biblical account also gives details of the appurtenances of the Temple (I Kings 7:15–51). First come two pillars, Jachin and Boaz of 'molten brass' (RSV, bronze), with capitals of intricate design, and apparently free-standing with no structural purpose; one may perhaps be permitted to think that here there was an incorporation of the *mazzeboth*, the standing stones of the Canaanite religion. Then there was the 'molten sea' ten cubits (5 metres) in diameter, five cubits high, supported by twelve oxen, with many other elaborate details, and the ten portable lavers on bronze stands, and pots, shovels, and basins of 'bright brass' (I Kings 7:40). To all this one adds in the final verses of I Kings 7 candlesticks, flowers, lamps, tongs, bowls, snuffers, basins, spoons, censers, and even the hinges of the doors in gold.

One cannot tell how much of this is the historian's hyperbole. Certainly one cannot expect finds from Jerusalem to produce factual evidence, for the recorded evidence of the sackings of Jerusalem would have removed all such objects of intrinsic worth. Comparable objects from even less thoroughly destroyed cities than Jerusalem do not survive; gold, though essentially indestructible, very rarely escapes the attention of destroyers.

What archaeology can do is to relate the period of Solomon's building activities to that of the contemporary culture of western Asia. The key point is that Solomon asked Hiram, king of Tyre for his help in building a house for Yahweh.

> And behold, I purpose to build an house unto the name of the Lord my God, as the Lord spake unto David my father, saying, Thy son, whom I will set upon thy throne in thy room, he shall build an house unto my name. Now therefore command thou that they hew me cedar trees out of Lebanon; and my servants shall be with thy servants; and unto thee will I give hire for thy servants according to all that thou shalt appoint: for thou knowest that there is not among us any that can skill to hew timber like unto the Sidonians. (I Kings 5:5–6)

This passage is crucial to any attempt to envisage Solomon's creation in Jerusalem. Solomon's subjects had no skills in the niceties of carpentry and Solomon had to turn to Hiram. David had also turned to him both for carpenters and for masons (II Samuel 5:11).

These passages in the Biblical record are the basis of any attempt to visualize the public buildings of Solomon, his Temple and his palaces. The Israelite tribes had no building skills, and in fact archaeological evidence suggests that they never acquired them. A ruler of the status of Solomon, anxious to have a capital that would stand comparison with his contemporaries, had to call in foreign technicians, which he was enabled to do by his riches.

The interpretation of the appearance of the public buildings that Solomon built must come from his relation with Hiram, king of Tyre. Phoenicia in the tenth and subsequent centuries was a place which received cultural impulses from a very large area, from Egypt to the south, with which links had existed from the fourth millennium B.C., to Mesopotamia in the east and Anatolia in the north. Phoenician culture was cosmopolitan and its art eclectic. Such evidence as we have suggests that it was from the artistic culture of Phoenicia that the decoration of Solomon's buildings was derived.

The carvings that decorated the Temple are described in detail. Archaeology can produce nothing quite comparable, which is not surprising since the carvings described are on a grand scale. The finds of ivories from the Samaria excavations were the first to suggest that examples could survive to indicate what the cherubim in the Holy of Holies and elsewhere looked like. The Samaria ivories[1] (Pls. 39, 40) were on a minute scale, the decoration of furniture rather than walls. They did, however, indicate the current style of Phoenician art, for Omri, like Solomon some eighty years earlier, had turned to Phoenicia for his craftsmen and artists. When Samaria was being excavated and published in the 1930s, there was little comparable material, only the finds, not stratigraphically documented, of Layard at Nimrud in 1849, and from Arslan Tash[2] with certainly close links with the Samaria ivories, and very fortunately dated by an inscription to the reign of Benhadad II, a contemporary of Ahab. The evidence was sufficient to link the ivories found at Samaria, associated with the palatial structures of Omri and Ahab (c. 880–850 B.C.), with the wider field of Phoenician-Syrian art. Our knowledge of this art has been enormously increased by the finds from the excavations of Professor Mallowan between 1949 and 1962 at Nimrud.[3] The finds of ivories at Nimrud cover a rather wider chronological range than the periods of the buildings of Solomon at Jerusalem and of Omri and Ahab at Samaria, and also include objects of a different inspiration, from Assyria itself rather than from Phoenicia-Syria. Nevertheless, one is justified in selecting from these finds illustrations of the current art of western Asia that seem to fit well into the Biblical description of decoration of the Temple. I illustrate (Pls. 41, 42) two examples, one of figures related to the cherubim that protected the

[1] J. W. and G. M. Crowfoot, *Samaria-Sebaste 2*.
[2] F. Thureau-Dangin, *Arslan Tash*.
[3] M. E. L. Mallowan, *Nimrud and Its Remains*.

Ark of the Covenant of the Holy of Holies, the figures in the Nimrud ivory being 16 centimetres high, those in the Holy of Holies being 5 metres high.[1]

Solomon's subsidiary interests were his own house and a house for Pharaoh's daughter, very explicitly (see above, p. 119) linked in the same building operation. Here, archaeological evidence can enter the field, first with regard to the plan and appearance of Solomon's palace, and secondly where it was situated.

The Biblical description of Solomon's palace (I Kings 7:1–2) is not very explicit. One element was 'the house of the forest of Lebanon', 50 metres long, 25 metres wide, 15 metres high, with four rows of cedar pillars, and a triple row of windows (I Kings 7:2–5). On the whole, one can deduce that this was probably a separate structure in which some classes of official business took place. The description of his own palace seems to start in I Kings 7:6, with a porch leading into a hall of pillars with, adjacent to it, 'a hall of the throne where he might judge, even the hall of judgment'.[2] These two elements are clearly part of the public building of the palace. From that point one apparently moves to the king's private quarters. 'And his house where he dwelt had another court within the porch [RSV, back of the hall] . . . Solomon made also an house for Pharaoh's daughter . . . like unto this porch [RSV, hall]'.

One can therefore interpret this description as an audience chamber approached through a porch and assembly hall. The audience chamber was intended to be most impressive. The throne was of ivory, overlaid with gold (II Chronicles 9:17). A throne of *solid* ivory is inconceivable from the basic fact that ivory must come from the tusks of elephants, of dimensions inadequate to provide the structure of furniture. Nevertheless, a throne covered by ivory inlay would be a highly expensive

[1] The connections between the decoration of the Temple and the art of western Asia are dealt with in more detail in *Royal Cities*, pp. 47–52.

[2] Translators vary in the use of 'porch' and 'hall', and these quotations are something of an amalgam.

object. To overlay this beautiful and expensive material with gold can again only be classed as ostentatious.

The general plan would, from the Biblical description, remain obscure, if it were not that there is evidence of contemporary palaces. One can call in evidence the fact that Solomon built not only at Jerusalem but at Megiddo, Hazor, and Gezer (I Kings 9:15), using in these towns the same levy (*RSV*, forced labour) as he had used for his constructions in Jerusalem. The interpretation of the finds at Megiddo is not easy, and has long been a subject of controversy. The definition of the structural periods already suggested in the Samaria Report[1] has been very fully confirmed by Professor Yigael Yadin's subsequent investigations.[2] An element that remains certainly Solomonic is Palace 1723, set in a wide courtyard. A very convincing exercise (fig. 23) interprets[3] the building, denuded to its foundations, in terms of contemporary palaces in Syria (fig. 24). In all of these examples,

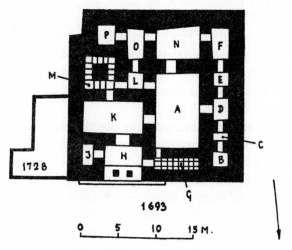

FIG 23   Reconstruction of plan of Building 1723 at Megiddo, suggested to be a Governor's residence on a common Syrian plan

[1] *Samaria-Sebaste 3*, pp. 199–204.
[2] *Biblical Archaeologist* XXIII, 2; *IEJ* 16, p. 278; *IEJ* 17, p. 119.
[3] David Ussiskin, *IEJ* 16.

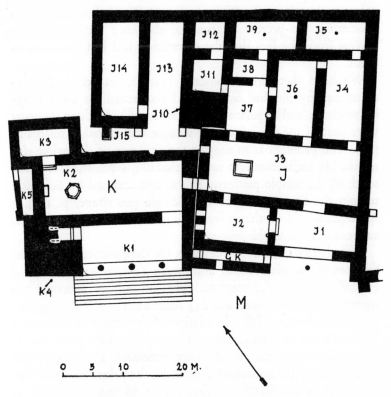

FIG 24   Plan of two palaces at Sendshirli

there is an element of public halls, in which the king meets his
people, and a second element of his private quarters. The subsidiary element of the quarters for his principal wife is suggested
by the Biblical text and the suggestion that two groups were
separately approached is supported hypothetically by structural
elements that could be interpreted as separate staircases. In the
light of this evidence from the countries from which Solomon
drew his inspiration, one can suggest that his palace and that of
his principal wife, Pharaoh's daughter, were on these lines.[1]
The luxury of the appointments of the public portions of the

[1] This problem is discussed in *Royal Cities*, pp. 50 ff.

palace is clear from the Biblical account. The lack of any details concerning the private quarters of the king very reasonably derives from the fact that the chroniclers had had no access to them.

We have therefore Solomon's Temple, set on a platform demanded by physical features and confirmed by archaeological evidence, and his palace and that of his wife. All these elements were part of the same building scheme and probably related in plan. The problem is to suggest the situation of the palace elements. My inclination is to suggest that they lay in the area to the south of the temple platform, in the area enclosed by Solomon to join the Davidic city to the Temple (see above, p. 114), a space presumably hitherto free of buildings. The reason for this suggestion is threefold.

First, there is the problem of space. On the evidence of Josephus, the area of the platform of Solomon's Temple was half that of Herod's Temple; the suggested plan on fig. 31 averages 210 metres from east to west and 245 metres from north to south.[1] The whole feeling of the description of the setting of Solomon's Temple is one of spaciousness. To have fitted in the palace buildings on the platform would have produced a very crowded setting. There are no overall figures for the palace complex, but the house of the forest of Lebanon was 50 metres long by 25 metres wide, and in what is presumed to be the main building, the assembly hall leading to the throne room was 25 metres long and 15 metres wide; beyond lay the dwelling quarters. The area covered must have been very considerable.

The second point is that the 'house of Pharaoh's daughter' seems to be closely associated with Solomon's palace (I Kings 7:9). It is not explicitly stated that the two were structurally connected, but in the suggested comparison with the Megiddo building 1723 and the Syrian examples, it would seem that

[1] The area is thus 61,450 square metres. The dimensions of the present platform which may extend farther to the north than the Herodian courtyard are c. 450 by 300 metres, giving an area of 135,000 square metres. The suggested plan must be approximately right.

quarters for the wife of the king or governor formed part of the same complex. Pharaoh's daughter was a heathen, who could certainly not have lived within the *enceinte* of the Temple. The implication of II Chronicles 8:11 is that she should not 'dwell in the house of David king of Israel', still less in sanctified places 'because the places are holy, whereunto the Ark of the Lord hath come'. Even if one has to find a place for Solomon's palace on the temple platform, that of Pharaoh's daughter was excluded, and my own view is that the palace of Solomon and that of his principal wife were closely, and probably structurally, linked. One could even say that from the point of view of diplomacy (see above, p. 108), it would have been tactless if they were not.

The third consideration is perhaps the most interesting. In Solomon's building operations there emerges the concept of a Royal Quarter. This concept finds its clearest exposition in the lay-out of the new city of Samaria, established by Omri (880 B.C. or 872 B.C., according to alternative chronologies). The whole summit of the hill was occupied by palaces and official buildings, and this same process is seen in Solomon's foundations at Megiddo and Hazor.[1] The archaeological evidence at Hazor and Megiddo suggests that the concept dates from the time of Solomon. At Megiddo, Hazor, and Gezer he had a *tabla rasa*, in each case a site which was virtually unoccupied since the Late Bronze Age, or in the case of Gezer which came to him as the dowry of his wife; here he could do as he wished, and could establish his administrative buildings. There is no suggestion in the Biblical record that he annexed areas within the ancient Jebusite-Davidic city. It is, however, clear that he set up an efficient administration for his kingdom.[2] It seems to me that it is reasonable to suggest that in the newly enclosed area between the north wall of the Davidic town and the platform of Solomon's Temple was a Royal Quarter, in which were to be found the administrative buildings required by the vastly increasing elaboration of Solomon's kingdom, the palace of the king, and perhaps also

[1] This subject is discussed in detail in *Royal Cities*.
[2] I Kings 4:7–19; Y. Aharoni, *The Land of the Bible*, pp. 277 ff.

accommodation for his seven hundred wives and three hundred concubines (I Kings 11:3), though this is a detail upon which I would not insist.

My conclusions are that Solomon constructed on the site designated by David, on the threshing floor of Araunah the Jebusite to the north of the pre-existing town, a temple to provide a sanctuary for the Ark of the Covenant and a home for the worship of Yahweh, a construction that involved the building-up of an imposing platform to provide the required flat area; here we have the Biblical evidence concerning the Temple and the archaeological evidence of the platform (see above, p. 111). In my interpretation, the second element in Solomon's construction was an enclosure of the area on the crest of the ridge to join the pre-existing town to the Temple; the evidence for this is given above (p. 114). In this newly enclosed area, I believe that he established his palace, adjacent to the Temple; the palace of Pharaoh's daughter certainly closely linked with his own palace; the buildings needed to accommodate the bureaucracy required to administer his kingdom; and, perhaps, accommodation for all his other wives and concubines. It seems reasonable to suggest that here we have for Palestine the first stage of a Royal Quarter, in the image of those of contemporary western Asiatic kingdoms, which is echoed in Solomon's own building programmes at Hazor and Megiddo,[1] and achieves full development at Samaria under the monarchy of the Northern Kingdom, some eighty years later.[2] The reason why no material evidence survives has already been made clear (above, p. 118).

[1] *Royal Cities*, pp. 53 ff.
[2] *Royal Cities*, pp. 71 ff.

1 Air view of Jerusalem from south, taken in 1930s. On right, line of Kedron Valley limits ancient Jerusalem. On left, the first part of the Hinnom Valley marks western limits

2 The so-called Pool of Hezekiah, a little east of present Jaffa Gate

3 Skyline, Mount of Olives. Middle distance, Moslem sanctuary of Dome of the Rock, set on platform of the Herodian Temple. Foreground, closely built-up houses of present Old City

4 Golden Gate in east wall of Herodian temple platform. In the foreground is part of the Moslem cemetery which presses closely against walls of Jerusalem on this side

5 On right, eroded stones of great platform that supported Herodian Temple. Bonded into these stones is the spring of Robinson's Arch, that carried an entrance from west. Contrast this 1961 view with photographs shown on Pls. 87, 115 taken after 1967 (pp. 14, 217)

6 Gateway at south-east apex of ancient Jerusalem, first excavated by the Bliss and Dickie excavations 1894–97 and re-excavated in 1961. To left and right the Bliss and Dickie tunnels are visible (p. 22)

7 A street of Herodian period in Site N, with on left the fallen masonry derived from Roman destruction in A.D. 70, and in the centre the Bliss and Dickie tunnel that had traced the street through this tumble of stones (p. 22

8 Area at south end of eastern ridge cleared by Weill excavations in 1912–13. In extreme top left corner, terrace excavated by 1961–67 excavations, which showed that the quarrying was Hadrianic (pp. 263–4)

9 Among the truncated rock-cuttings revealed by the Weill excavations were two long, tunnel-like cuttings. It was suggested that these were the royal tombs of period of Monarchy (pp. 31–2).

10 The view down the Kedron Valley (p. 36)
11 Outer edge of Hinnom Valley, where it is curving round to the east to join the Kedron

12
Air view of
Jerusalem
from south,
taken in the
1960s
(p. 36)

13 View from east showing steep west slope of Kedron Valley (p. 36)
14 Trench 1 of 1961–67 excavations down eastern slope of eastern ridge. At top of trench is the so-called Tower of David, which is in fact Maccabean (pp. 65, 191, 193)

15 Deep robber trenches of Hellenistic and Roman periods at Samaria. To left, sole remaining stones at base of casemate walls. In centre, excavations have traced the trenches that robbed the stones from the Israelite walls (p. 63)

16 Area of the casemate walls at Samaria, showing the only evidence that would have survived if the robber trenches had not been identified (p. 63)

17 Eastern slope of eastern ridge at Jerusalem, showing the trench laid out in 1961 to trace the defences of early Jerusalem (p. 48)

18 On right, middle distance, the tower claimed by Professor Macalister to have been built by David. Right foreground, the so-called Jebusite ramp. Centre background, the wall supporting an excavation dump (pp. 48, 192)

19 Face of wall NB, low on the eastern slope, which proved to be the wall of Jebusite Jerusalem, dating from 18th century B.C. Photograph shows extreme S.E. angle of original Trench 1 clearance (p. 78)

20 Original east wall of Jerusalem, wall NB, with the angle as exposed in 1962. On right, later wall NA (p. 83)

21 Pottery of the Intermediate Early Bronze–Middle Bronze period from Mount of Olives (p. 81)

22 Small and carefully rounded shaft of a tomb of the Intermediate Early Bronze–Middle Bronze period on Mount of Olives (p. 81)

23 East slope of eastern ridge of Jerusalem from north. Middle distance, dumps of the
1961–67 Trench I. The line of defences revealed by this trench is almost in centre of
photograph (p. 89)
24 Original, Jebusite, eastern wall of Jerusalem, NB, from north (p. 83)

25 Centre, the Jebusite–early-Israelite wall NB, with an enormous boulder grooved by a drain. Foreground, late tumble rests direct on levels contemporary with life of wall NB. Above wall NB is wall NA, probably 8th century

26 Original, Jebusite, eastern wall of Jerusalem, NB, from north, with its angle to west disappearing beneath wall NA (p. 83). Walls in background are excavation structures supporting present path up the slope

28 Stone-filled terraces constructed by Jebusites, 13th century B.C. Extreme right, retaining wall, against which a compartmented fill of stones, shown in photograph, served to build up a terrace (p. 95)

27 Compartment walls used in building up the terraces of Jebusite period (p. 95)

29 The build-up of the terraces near crest of eastern slope of Jerusalem (p. 95)

30 Jebusite terraces were supported by retaining walls parallel to slope of hill. This photograph shows how they bulged and collapsed (p. 95)

31 At base, fill and structures of earliest occupation on east slope of eastern ridge. Above, stone fill of Jebusite terraces, c. 13th century B.C., which have collapsed to south on steep slope (p. 96). Resting on them, foundations of Maccabean tower (p. 192)

32 Middle distance, compartmented walls of Jebusite terraces. Above them, where man stands, houses of 8th–7th centuries B.C. (p. 96) Near left foreground, more massive additions to Jebusite terraces, probably to be dated to early Israelite stages

33 The very massive blocks of latest repair of the Jebusite terraces, probably Davidic or Solomonic (pp. 101–3)

34 Earth repair to stone collapse seen in Pl. 31 is cut into and capped by a final repair, probably dating to Davidic or Solomonic period, of very massive stones (pp. 100–3)

35 On left, Herodian masonry of temple platform. Between this and more heavily-bossed stones on right, a straight joint. The heavily bossed stones are in Persian style

36 Detail of the straight joint between the Herodian masonry on left and the earlier masonry on right (pp. 111–12)

37 Casemate wall in Site H that runs north from line of original Jebusite-Davidic north
   wall, which can be interpreted as Solomonic (pp. 114–15)
38 Wall in Site S II on eastern crest of eastern ridge, which can be stratigraphically dated
   to 8th century B.C., but constructed on re-used stones of typically Phoenician type
   (pp. 115–16)

39 Ivory carving from Samaria of a miniature size suitable for use on furniture, but illustrative of half-human, half-animal figures used in contemporary adornment (p. 122)

40 An ivory plaque from Samaria, of which Egyptian style illustrates cosmopolitan art to be found in area of Israelite kingdom (p. 122)

41 An ivory plaque from Nimrud, to be compared with Pl. 39, as illustrating current art of western Asia

42 An ivory plaque from Nimrud that (though their scale here is miniscule) can be taken as illustrating the mystical figures that, in the Holy of Holies of the Temple, guarded the Ark of the Covenant (pp. 122–3)

43 Left foreground, original wall NB of Jebusite-Davidic period, with angular return to west. Original wall is seen disappearing beneath later wall, NA of 8th–7th century (pp. 144–7)

44 The sloping tips, becoming more and more stony, overlying the buildings in Square A xxiv (p. 132)

45 The first building, circular in plan, to be reached in Square A xxiv (p. 132)

46 Rectangular building on bedrock in Square A XXIV (p. 132)

47 Ashlar steps in Square A XXIV (p. 132)

48. Bronze bucket *in situ* in a cupboard in a wall of house shown on Pl. 46 (p. 133)

49 The bucket shown on Pl. 48, with two other vessels inside it (p. 134)

50 The smaller bucket in-
side that shown on
Pl. 49 (p. 134)

51 The bronze jug that
was the innermost
component of nest of
vessels shown *in situ*
on Pl. 48 (p. 134)

52 In background is shallow cave in rock scarp, surrounded by massive walls. Within the enclosure so formed was the deposit of pottery seen on Pl. 53 (pp. 135–6)

53 Deposit of pottery vessels in the enclosure shown on Pl. 52, probably to be interpreted as a *favissa* associated with nearby structure interpreted as a sanctuary (p. 136)

54 General view of the extra-mural structure in Squares A XIX–XXI, which is to be interpreted as a cult sanctuary (p. 137)

55 The *mazzeboth* in the room adjoining the *favissa* on Pls. 52–53 (p. 137)

56 To right, structures east of the rock scarp; the *mazzeboth* are seen in right foreground; their associated floor to left has been removed (pp. 137–8)

57 Area south of cult sanctuary seen on Pls. 52–56. The carefully paved room on left
   centre is unusual. Centre, opening of cave of which contents are seen in Pls. 58–61
   (p. 139)
58 Tumble of pottery within the cave shown on Pl. 57 (p. 140)

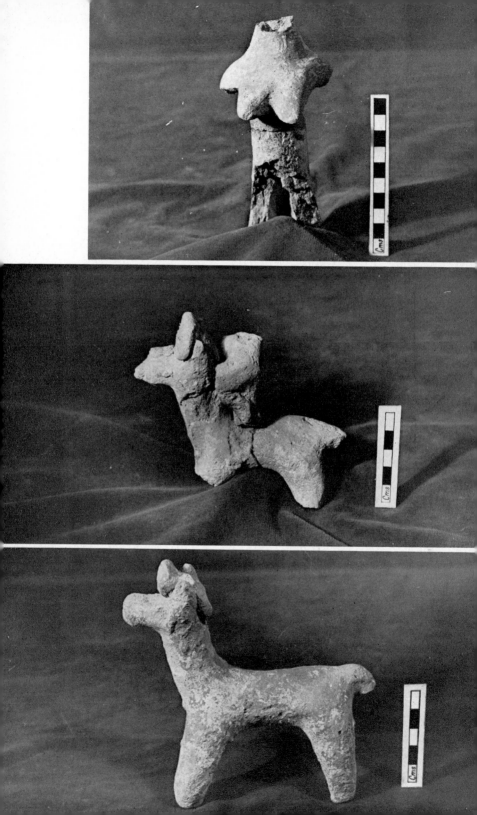

62 Very massive wall, certainly a town wall, excavated in 1969–70, in the area of Jewish
   Quarter on eastern slopes of western ridge (p. 148)

[*Opposite*]
   59 Mother-goddess fertility figurine from the cave (p. 141)
   60 Figurine from the cave of horse with rider, and disk on its forehead (pp. 141–2)
   61 Figurine from the cave of horse with disk on its forehead (pp. 142–3)

13—DUJ * *

63 At lower end of Trench I, the succession of structures showed that the original Jebusite-Davidic wall NB (slightly left of centre) was sealed by a cobbled street (p. 144)

64 The massive substructures on the eastern slope that were in use until the 7th century B.C. to support terraces (p. 161)

65 The Siloam Tunnel near the northern end (p. 154)
66 The Siloam Tunnel in the central area (p. 154)
67 Lower end of Central Valley. Centre, the minaret indicates position of Pool of Siloam. On right, immediately behind tall tree, is scarped end of eastern ridge, scarping which truncated outflow channel from original pool (p. 159)

68 Scarp that truncates southern tip of eastern ridge, cutting away, as seen at its base, the outer side of the outflow channel from Pool of Siloam (p. 159)

69 Original rock-cut channel carrying the overflow from the Pool of Siloam, of which the left-hand, western, wall has been removed by later quarrying (p. 159)

70 Buildings of the 7th century B.C. on crest of eastern slope of eastern ridge (pp. 163–4)

71 Foreground, buildings of 7th century B.C., seen in Pl. 70. To left, collapse of stones that engulfed the buildings in Babylonian destructions of 687 B.C. To right, sloping lines of erosion that completed destruction (p. 170)

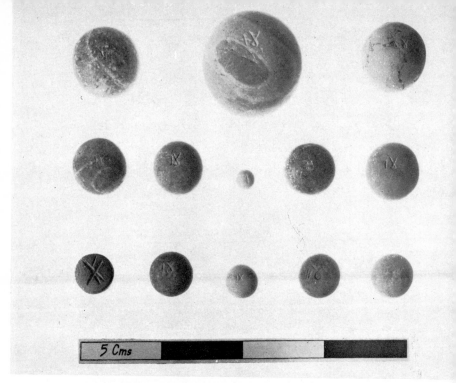

72 Limestone weights inscribed with denominations in shekels and other scales, found in the 7th-century houses shown in Pl. 70 (pp. 162–3)

73 Pay-day, held fortnightly, with the paying party progressing round the various sites with the money bags, pay books, a paraphernalia of table and stools, and supporting staff (p. 175)

74 In the houses of the 7th century B.C., seen on Pl. 70, a secondary construction was a staircase leading to higher terrace, of which nothing is preserved (p. 164)

75 Erosion channels caused by winter rains on east slope of eastern ridge (p. 170)

76 To left, 'Davidic' tower (p. 192). In centre, so-called Jebusite ramp (pp. 192–3). Above
to right, small tower which is an early addition to the wall built by Nehemiah (p. 191)

[*Opposite*]
77 To right, wall built on top of scarp shown in Pl. 79, which can be ascribed to period of
Nehemiah. Tower in centre clearly belongs to a reconstruction of this wall (p. 191)
78 Professor Macalister's 'Tower of David' shown built over the ruins of the 7th-century
houses destroyed by the Babylonians in 587 B.C. (p. 192)

79 In Square A XVIII, opposite P on fig. 29, the steep scarp along summit ridge had
against it a fill of the 6th–5th century period that lapped up against the wall on crest
seen at top in centre (p. 183)

80 South-east angle of Herodian temple platform as it stands up above present-day
accumulations (p. 211). On left, elaborate superstructure of a tomb of Maccabean
period, erroneously known today as tomb of Absalom (p. 226)

81 North-east corner of Maccabean tower, erroneously ascribed to period of David. To right, so-called Jebusite ramp is visibly built against this tower (p. 193)
82 Area of excavations in Site κ (p. 193)

83 Portion exposed of wall bounding Maccabean terraces on western side of eastern ridge, interpreted as town wall of period (p. 193)

84 Wall adjacent to present Citadel, ascribed to Maccabean period (p. 202)

85 The typical, beautiful masonry of Herodian temple platform, seen at the traditional
'Wailing Wall' of western wall of temple platform (p. 211)

86 Beneath the present platform of Haram esh-Sherif in south-eastern area are vaulted
chambers known as Solomon's Stables. Lower courses of masonry up to above the
spring of the vaults, as seen in this view, are certainly Herodian (p. 213)

87 South-west corner of Haram esh-Sherif, of which lower part of masonry belongs to period of Herodian temple platform (p. 215–17)

88 Site s of 1961–67 excavations in angle between platform of Haram esh-Sherif, on right, and salient to south, which may belong to period of Aelia Capitolina, *c.* A.D. 135

89 Site s from west, with on left the salient from south wall of Old City, of which the massive blocks at the base probably belong to period of Aelia Capitolina (p. 263)

90 View of towers of Citadel at Jaffa Gate today. The lower courses of right-hand tower are Herodian. In foreground, buildings of Muristan and dome of medieval church of St Stephen (p. 223)

91 Square s 1 against salient in south wall of Old City. The enormous blocks of lower courses of wall, seen in Pl. 89, rest on bedrock (p. 221)

93 The Church of the Holy Sepulchre (pp. 226–7)

92 General view of Site C, in Muristan, directly south of Church of the
Holy Sepulchre. Excavation site is in centre foreground (p. 227)

94 Detail of the quarry scarp shown on Pl. 91. At the base on the right the quarrying cut through a cistern (p. 221)

95 Foundations of wall, of period of Herod Agrippa (A.D. 40–44), joining western to eastern ridge along line of Hinnom Valley (p. 247)

96 Site C excavated to bedrock, looking west (p. 228)
97 Tumble of stones in Site N, including excellent paving stones on a grand scale, representing the destruction by Titus in A.D. 70 (p. 248)

98 Detail of the 7th-century B.C. quarrying shown at the base of Pl. 96. Above the quarrying was a 7th-century fill (p. 228)

99 To right, eastern pedestrian entrance of a gateway of period of Herod Agrippa on normal Roman plan, entering Jerusalem from north. On left, tower that flanked the entrance (pp. 238–9)

100 Street in Herodian style, probably belonging to the period of Herod Agrippa, running up Central Valley. Beyond street are remains of a staircase leading to a higher terrace (pp. 247–8)

101 South face of back of very large re-used blocks to north of Old City, of which the identification is doubtful (pp. 251 ff.)

102 North face of wall shown on Pl. 101
103 The plan of Jerusalem shown in the Byzantine mosaic floor at Madaba (p. 260)

104 Skulls lodged behind collapsed masonry in ruins in Site N that are to be dated to the A.D. 70 destruction by Titus (p. 254)

105 Immediately beneath surface of terrace in Site K, was the basis of a floor of the 1st century A.D., and an associated drain (pp. 254-5)

106 Triumphal Arch of Hadrianic period (northern side entrance and spring of central
arch seen here); spanning street leading into Old City from St Stephen's Gate is
partly within the Convent of the Sisters of Sion (p. 260)

[*Opposite*]
107 Byzantine wall that runs south from south-east corner of Haram is
seen in Square s II. Beneath, tunnel by which Warren traced it.
Centre, buttress inserted in 1967 to fill the perilous void (p. 270)
108 On right, Herodian masonry of south-east corner of Haram with, on
left, Byzantine wall built against it (p. 270)

109 Above is rock forming the boundary of a cave in Site D II. Against it is built a doorway of the Byzantine period (p. 271)

110 Site M, showing Byzantine walls built on surface left by quarrying which had removed all earlier structures (p. 271)

112 On right, angle of a Byzantine house in Site R. It was cut into a dump of rubbish, and the rough wall enclosing it was inserted to prevent dump collapsing (p. 272)

111 Part of a Byzantine house in Squares s IV-V (p. 271)

114 Fragment of a mosaic from the church in Site L (p. 273)

113 The fragmentary remains of the apse of a Byzantine church in Site L (p. 273)

115 South-west angle of the Haram esh-Sherif, showing excavations begun in 1968. Centre left, spring of Robinson's Arch (pp. 217–18). To south of south wall of the Haram on right, Byzantine wall enclosing structures to south (pp. 276–8)

116 Obverse of a gold coin of the Emperor Heraclius, found in Site H (pp. 74–5)

117 Face, not disturbed by subsequent rebuildings, of retaining wall south of Haram esh-Sherif, seen on Pl. 115, with a column *in situ* belonging to building to south (p. 276)

118 Part of retaining wall south of Haram esh-Sherif, in which earlier stones were re-used, and which probably belongs to Ommayad period (p. 276)

119 Paving of Byzantine street, successor of a Herodian street, along south face of Haram
     esh-Sherif (the Herodian temple platform), cut by wall of Ommayad enclosure to
     south (p. 276)
120 Fallen block of stone in area of church north of present Damascus Gate; the halo is
     evidence of Christian association (p. 279)

121 The Crusader roadway through Damascus Gate, blocked by debris that preceded construction of gate of Suleiman the Magnificent (p. 279)

122 In Site L in south-west corner of Old City, the first buildings to be encountered in the 1961–67 excavations, belonged to a Mamluk building of the 13th century A.D. (p. 280)

★

The Kingdom of Judah and its Capital Jerusalem

THE KINGDOM ruled by David and Solomon was one in which personal prowess and reputation played a large part. David had been selected independently by the southern and northern tribes as their leader to combat the Philistine menace. From this dual election and by means of his creation of a physical unity by his capture of Jerusalem, and his establishment there of his capital, David created the United Monarchy. Solomon inherited a great charisma which he maintained, though many of the outlying conquests of David were lost, through his personality and reputation as a man of culture and learning that spread far beyond the boundaries of his kingdom. No doubt all this was backed up by an efficient administration, for otherwise there would not have been the wealth required to finance all his building projects.

Solomon died in 926–25 B.C. This is the first Palestinian date that can be stated with some certainty, though if Egyptian dates in the first millennium B.C. are adjusted, those in Palestine must follow suit, for there is still no internal Palestinian dating evidence. Solomon was succeeded by his son Rehoboam, and the links that joined the southern and northern tribes were immediately shown to be tenuous. The breakaway of the northern tribes left Jerusalem as the frontier capital of the southern group, of Judah as opposed to Israel.

The result of this division, a division going back to the old tribal routes of entry from the south or north-east, was that Judah and its capital Jerusalem were left with far less fertile and productive areas than those in the realm of the new kingdom of Israel. The new kingdom of Judah was also so enclosed by enemies, Israel to the north, the Transjordanian kingdoms to the east, that it was cut off from contact with the flourishing culture of western Asia. The one asset of Judah was that it possessed Jerusalem.

It is not surprising in these circumstances that the archaeological finds in Jerusalem are not spectacular. Since only evidence concerning the basic foundations of the Solomonic temple platform survives, and nothing of the Temple itself, all evidence concerning the structures of the Temple has inevitably disappeared. On the summit of the eastern ridge, the Herodian and Roman quarrying that destroyed the buildings of the Jebusite, Davidic, and Solomonic periods also obviously destroyed all trace of buildings of the kingdom of Judah.

On the eastern slope of the eastern ridge, in the area excavated between 1961 and 1967, a sufficient amount of structural evidence has been recovered to suggest that further excavations in this area could add something to the structural history of Jerusalem. Would-be excavators must, however, be warned that such excavation involves laborious, and even perilous, penetration through layers of rubble and silt that have accumulated following, as will be seen (below, pp. 170–1), the destruction by the Babylonians of the Jerusalem of the kingdom of Judah. I have had my fill of this; I wish well to future excavators, and I am sure that if they have the necessary perseverance they will add details to the history of Jerusalem during the period of the kingdom of Judah.

The main development on the eastern slope is that at some stage the old wall of the Jebusite period, re-used by David (see above, p. 100), was succeeded by a later one which continued to the north where the old wall veered to the north-west. It is seen in Pl. 43. Structurally, the wall has four or five periods. The archaeological difficulties in dating walls on a slope are that the evidence must come from the deposits to the rear, the deposits into which the foundations were cut, and the deposits that accumulated against them. The problem in Jerusalem is that erosion has sheered off all the superstructure of the walls, leaving only their foundations, and has removed almost all the deposits on the uphill side. It may be that when all the finds of the 1961–67 seasons have been worked over in detail, a more exact chronology can be worked out.

Meanwhile, there are some facts. It does not seem that the original wall or its rebuilds were buried in debris until about the eighth century B.C., for on the rock outside was occupation, including an oven (Pl. 25), which seems to go down to that date.

Belonging to approximately the same date is clear evidence in Square A XXIV of expansion to the north of the original boundaries of the town (see above, p. 92). The first occupation here seems to be eighth century B.C., and one must here admit that the dating criteria, almost entirely pottery, are, in the stage of present archaeological knowledge, vague within a century. It may be that, when I have studied the pottery in detail, I shall be able to relate the stage in the rebuilding of the eastern walls to the extension of the town along the eastern slope that is proved by A XXIV, but I am inclined to doubt that the refinement of pottery chronology has reached that stage.

We can, however, state firmly that about the eighth century B.C. the wall on the eastern slope was rebuilt, on a line that ignored the oblique turn to the north-west of the earlier one. The line of the new wall (Pl. 43) very clearly encloses an area on the eastern slope that extends to the north of that originally within the Jebusite-Davidic town. The area exposed in Square A XXIV (see fig. 22) illustrates this expansion.

The point has already been made (above, p. 92) that Square A XXIV lies only c. 26 metres north of the area excavated at the west end of Trench I, and that the evidence in A XXIV is completely different from that in the Trench I area. We are here outside the limits of the terraces established by the Jebusites and maintained by David and Solomon. The excavational and stratigraphical difference is absolute. In Square A XXIV there is no evidence at all of Late Bronze Age (Jebusite) or Early Iron I

(Davidic or Solomonic) occupation. The area was quite clearly outside the original town.

The excavation of Square A XXIV had the usual problems of the sites on the slopes of the eastern ridge. For some 9.50 metres of deposit there was nothing to be recorded except varying degrees of stony wash (Pl. 44). The first reasonably intact foundations to appear, certainly datable within the seventh century B.C., were part of a circular building (Pl. 45). In its walls were sockets for timbers. Palestinian archaeology has produced nothing very similar. One is tempted to think of granaries in, for instance, Roman Britain, where raised floors preserve grain from damp and vermin. Such an interpretation can be supported if this circular building was a successor in function, though different in plan, to the underlying building.

This building (Pl. 46) consisted of rectangular rooms built on bedrock providing evidence of the earliest occupation in this area. On the present provisional assessment of the pottery evidence it dates to ± 800 B.C. It was a very substantial structure, and in the south-west corner of the square was a flight of steps of fine ashlar masonry (Pl. 47) leading to a higher terrace to the west; the perilous state of the overlying fill made it impossible to explore more than a small portion of these steps. The contents of the rooms suggest that they were storerooms. There was an enormous quantity of sherds of typical storage jars (Pl. 8) of Iron Age II. When the building was destroyed, the rooms must have been stacked with these great jars, and the probability is that they contained grain, though since the building was not burnt, which alone would have enabled evidence of grain to survive, this can only be a hypothesis. Nevertheless, I use this hypothesis to suggest the use of the succeeding circular building.

This first building in Square A XXIV also provided a find that, in the light of the general poverty of finds of outstanding objects in excavating in Jerusalem, can be considered as dramatic. Certainly it seemed so to us on the dig. I was virtually never away from the dig during the working hours of 5 a.m. to 2 p.m. However, in August 1966 I did accept an invitation to lunch with the charming General Odd Bull, head of the United Nations Truce Supervisory Commission, at his headquarters at the Government House of the Mandate period, which I had last visited in 1935. At noon, therefore, I had tidied myself up and had been transported to Government House by car UN 1. I cannot resist putting in a quite irrelevant sideline. Since Government House lay between the Jordanian and Israeli zones, security was paramount. I had had to provide in advance my passport number, etc. etc. As we approached in UN 1, the driver spoke into his radio telephone, and reported to me that someone would soon be on the way to the gate with the necessary authorization. We in fact arrived at the gate before the emissary. I held out my passport, and the driver said that the authorization was on its way. But the Jordanian policeman waved everything aside and said 'Ah, Miss Kenyon. I know Miss Kenyon. *Ahlan wa Sahlan* [welcome]'. So I entered Government House on the strength of the fact that I employed various of the policeman's sons as basket-boys.

From this irrelevancy, I return to the finds in Square A XXIV. I returned from Government House about 3 p.m., in the civilized garb required by the occasion, and had hoped for a period of relaxation thereafter. But when I got back there was an urgent message that I was needed on the dig. So all hopes of a siesta (and I confess that this is important on a dig that begins at 4.15 a.m.) disappeared. I shed my party garb and put on dig clothes and went to see what was happening. Andrew Moore, the site supervisor, Doug Tushingham, the photographer Cecil Western, and a number of workmen were closely grouped at the foot of the excavation staircase round the north side of the northernmost wall exposed (on the right in Pl. 46). What was visible was a green object in a little niche or cupboard low in the wall (Pl. 48). Extracting it was not an easy job, for the slab forming the roof of the cupboard had sagged and was resting on the top of the green object. To free it, the stones of the wall beneath the cupboard had carefully to be prised out. Ultimately the object was freed and cautiously lifted out. It is seen in Pl. 49. It proved to consist of a bronze bucket *c.* 6 inches high and *c.* 5 inches in diameter with an iron handle. Inside it was a second bronze bucket, with a bronze handle, and inside that was a bronze jug. The outer bucket was sufficiently intact to contain a basinful of water, accumulated during the winter rains while the area was partially excavated.

The bucket and its contents were relatively intact, but it was quite clear that they had been affected by corrosion during the two and a half millennia or so since they had been placed in the cupboard. We did not dare to try to extricate the inner vessels, and it was certain that once the nest of vessels was exposed to air, decay would accelerate rapidly. Our dig resources, and those of the Amman Museum, did not provide the necessary conservation equipment. It was clear that the objects should reach the British Museum laboratory as soon as possible.

This they did, but the saga is romantic. The Department of Antiquities in Jordan gave rapid permission. I rang up the embassy in Amman. The embassy cabled the Foreign Office, the Foreign Office made contact with B.O.A.C., while I cabled our dig contact in London, Peter Dorrell. B.O.A.C. laid on Operation 'Buckets of Blood'. The bucket travelled in the diplomatic locker. At London Airport, under the supervision of the chief security officer of B.O.A.C., the bucket and its contents went through customs unharmed as 'used domestic utensils', and Peter Dorrell whipped them away to the British Museum.

The skill of the British Museum laboratory extracted from the nest the vessels that are shown on Pls. 50, 51. They have now been returned to the Amman Museum. Corrosion had considerably damaged them. The innermost vessel, the jug, less solid than the buckets, had suffered the most, and the handle cannot be joined to the body with certainty. In no case could the cleaning be carried to the stage at which it was certain that no corrosion remained, for the vessels might have collapsed. It is hoped that the advice given by the British Museum will enable the Amman Museum to preserve the vessels from further deterioration.

The circumstances of the find did of course invest it with a special significance in our eyes. In fact, however, it does have a wide significance. In other countries bronze buckets and jugs of *c.* 800 B.C. might not seem to be of especial importance. In Palestine of this period, however, actual finds of this character have not been made. Moreover, there is an item of evidence that suggests that the vessels were not luxury objects, but belonged to ordinary household equipment. Contained within the buckets was a considerable quantity of miniscule animal bones. They have been identified as those of shrews. They must have been attracted into the buckets by their contents. One can guess that this was corn, and that therefore these containers were associated with the deposit of storage jars in the next room, and were justly described as 'used domestic utensils', and were not part of any exotic equipment.

Square A XXIV was the only area excavated that, though outside the Jebusite-Davidic-Solomonic towns, was within the area enclosed by the wall NA (Pl. 43), the surviving wall to succeed to the original wall which extended the area enclosed on the eastern slopes to the north. The tracing of this later wall, and the establishment of the stratigraphical evidence in connection with it, developed into one of our major objectives. Squares A XXI to A XXII (see fig. 22) were laid out with this purpose. My first effort (Square A XXI) was too ambitious. I tried to jump a distance of *c.* 45 metres to the north of Trench I, and I missed the wall, which we now know from the evidence of Square A XXVI immediately to the south had veered slightly uphill to the west.

Squares A XXI and A XXII did not provide the evidence that they were meant to, but they did in fact provide one of our relatively few dramatic finds. The first season of excavation in this area revealed an upper rock scarp disappearing out of the excavated area to the west, which proved to be associated with wall NA. Lower on the slope was another scarp, 2·75 metres to the east. As we uncovered this, it was clear that there were masonry walls built up against the face of the rock. Walls one metre wide enclosed an area 1·90 metres broad, the enclosed area projecting only 0·50 metres from the face of the rock scarp (Pl. 52). On the most superficial view, there was nothing to do with domestic architecture in this complex. An additional fact was that the walls, and the space between them and the rock scarp, were covered with a filling of mud plaster, apparently on occasion renewed; this last observation I made in the field, and I hope it is exact, but I have not yet found the drawn sections to support the observation.

Having located these walls against the scarp, our next step was to excavate the area between the walls and the scarp. In it was a considerable deposit of pottery vessels. After two seasons of excavations in Jerusalem, I had ceased to expect to find any intact vessels. My mind was thrown back to Jericho, where we had excavated over 400 tombs, in most of which there were deposits of intact pots, though on the tell at Jericho, as at Jerusalem, one found only broken sherds. This find of intact vessels (Pl. 53) could indeed fit well into the general Jericho tomb picture. When each new burial was made, the offerings placed with the earlier burials were pushed to the rear, or thrown out into the tomb-shaft. Given that the steep slope of extra-mural Jerusalem might require a built tomb-shaft instead of a rock-cut one, the deposit of vessels could very reasonably be interpreted in this way.

As excavation proceeded, however, two things became clear: there was no cave, natural or artificial, that would have served as a tomb, only a shallow recess in the rock face, and secondly there were no remains of human skeletons. The latter point was not necessarily conclusive, since in some soil conditions bone does not survive. But in the deposit there were bones, animal bones and objects made of bones. On both grounds I had to accept that the deposit in this embryonic cave did not give us the evidence of a tomb.

The assessment of this evidence following the 1962 season made it clear that the interpretation of this obviously important structure against the rock scarp, with the associated pottery deposit, required further excavation to the north, in which direction the walls were continuing. It was one of the facts of life in excavating Jerusalem that if one made an interesting discovery, to link it with adjacent areas meant that the next stage was two years hence. The intervening year had to be spent in the standard stratigraphical excavation of the overlying deposits. I have virtually come to the conclusion that mechanical removal of *wash* (and I emphasize my italics) is justifiable. Nevertheless, it is only justifiable if the archaeologists concerned know their stuff, know what the wash debris, legitimately removed by mechanical means, consists of, and know how to interpret it. It also means that finance is adequate to make use of complicated machines, and I am not all that sure that most of the standard earth-moving machines could cope with this slope of Ophel.

One can certainly make a case for someone who takes a short cut towards the archaeological evidence fitting in with historical evidence. But my approach remains strictly that in which my archaeological evidence and that of the historical record must be reconciled. The limitations on the archaeological side are that the fairly rapid succession of political events, the succession of one king by another, the stages of Josiah's reforms, and so on cannot be reflected in the archaeological evidence.

In this instance, we did not take a short cut, so we only came to grips again with the interesting structure late in 1963. Plate 54 shows the next stage of clearance, with an area of 9·50 metres by 10·25 metres exposed, part on an upper rock terrace and part at the foot of the scarp into which the original cave had been scooped. Immediately to the north of the walls enclosing the cave was a small room in which there were two oblong monoliths, standing 1·70 metres high (Pl. 55). Such monoliths can be roof supports. But the room in which they stood was only 3·35 metres from north to south (the opposite dimension is uncertain) and these two roof supports would not be required. The monoliths are not structural, and one can therefore legitimately deduce that they were ceremonial, that is to say cult objects. They must be interpreted as the *mazzeboth* of the Canaanite religion, the 'stones' of the stocks and stones condemned by Jeremiah.[1] The use of such pillars by the Israelites is illustrated by the fact that Absalom set up such a memorial to himself during his lifetime.[2] The heathen bowing down to stocks and stones is a familiar component of the Anglican hymnal.

The *mazzeboth* gave reasonable ground for interpreting the complex as a cult centre. In such a context, the pottery deposit in the cave could be satisfactorily interpreted. It was a *favissa*, the classical name for a repository of vessels and other objects offered in a sanctuary which could not thereafter be returned to profane use. An example in Palestine some eight hundred years earlier is the pits surrounding the Late Bronze Age Temple at Tell Duweir, identified as Biblical Lachish.[3]

Further features fitted this cult-centre interpretation. In the west wall of the *mazzeboth* room was a blocked doorway, seen blocked in Pl. 55, and with the blocking removed in Pl. 54. Between this west wall and the rock scarp behind it there was a gap of only *c*. 0·30 metres (Pl. 56). One could look through the doorway, but one really cannot think of anyone passing through it to squeeze along the narrow slot at the foot of the scarp. We did our best to find the reason for the doorway. Plate 56 shows the wall built on top of a large boulder. We wondered whether the boulder masked the entrance into some imposing cave cut into the rock scarp. With enormous effort we shifted the boulder. The answer was that it hid nothing.

One must therefore return to accepting that the door was symbolic, not functional. That being so, I think that one must accept that it was related in function to the higher terrace to the west. Plates 54 and 56 show that at this point there was a rectangular structure. Too little survives, a bare two courses of masonry, to prove its use, but its dimensions, only *c*. one metre square, show that it was not a room. I therefore interpret it with some confidence as an altar. The doorway leads exactly to the

[1] Jeremiah 2:27.
[2] II Samuel 18:18.
[3] *Lachish II*.

foot of the point in the scarp on which the so-interpreted structure is built. Worshippers in the lower room could lean through the doorway, and pour libations at the foot of the altar.

I therefore take the plunge, and claim that we have a cult centre, built on two levels. On the lower level is a cult room, with two standing stones, on the upper level is an altar, the two being connected by an access to pour libations from the lower level. Adjacent to the cult room in the lower level was a repository, part cave, part enclosed by walls, for dedicated vessels that could not be thrown away.

To this evidence from Squares A XXI–XXII and XXVII we have endeavoured to add the evidence from the areas to the north and south. That from the area to the north did not add very much, though it was clear that the same complex extended in that direction.

To the south, however, there was a dramatic addition. Up to this point, we could still trace wall NA; I explained above (p. 135) that for the area A XXI–XXII I made a jump which proved to be off-line for its objective of tracing wall NA, but was *ex post facto* justified by the discovery of the cult centre. The filling-in of the gap between the original Trench I complex and the junction of the tracing of wall NA, the successor of the Jebusite-Davidic-Solomonic wall of Jerusalem, came later. It was only in our final season of 1967 that we completed the excavation of Square A XXV, immediately to the south of A XIX, where the first *favissa* deposit of pottery was found. The excavation of Square A XXV showed again a number of buildings against a scarp below that on which the wall of the period, wall NA, was built. They are seen on Pl. 57 There is nothing that demands any special interpretation, in relation to ordinary domestic structures, except that the carefully cobbled room to the left in Pl. 57 is unusual. The unusual feature is the cave shown in the centre of the view. From the entrance here seen, it extended back for a distance of 8·12 metres, with a roughly rectangular plan, of which the maximum width was 4·20 metres; the rear section had a wall, pierced by a window, dividing it into two bays. The form of this cave could be that of

an Iron Age tomb, and it could well be that this was its original
purpose. It is absolutely certain that this was not its final use,
and it was the evidence of this final use that we found.

As we penetrated through the narrow entrance, we encountered a veritable tumble of pottery (Pl. 140), where there was a
slight admixture of other objects. Since the complete excavation
of the cave showed that there was no trace of burials, or indeed of
bones, it was clear that we had again a *favissa*. This could be
related to the cult complex close to the north, or it could be
associated with a separate cult centre, for which the architectural
remains did not provide clear indications.

The contents of this *favissa* amounted to some 1,300 objects.
For the Jerusalem excavators, starved of intact objects from the
general excavation areas, and supported by a number of museums
in Britain, Canada, the United States, New Zealand, and quite a
lot of other countries, intact objects were of great importance, for
with them we could, from the proportion of the finds allocated to
us by the Department of Antiquities, recompense our supporters
with museum-worthy objects. It was the irony that afflicts so
many excavations (I think virtually all of those with which I
have been associated) that major finds come so late in the
planned excavation season (and a planned excavation season is
based on the most exigent finance) as to create enormous embarrassment. We welcomed this find enthusiastically, for it was the
richest deposit of material of the Old Testament period that we
found. But it came within a fortnight of the planned end of the
final season of the excavation. The field and headquarters staff
did magnificently to excavate, plan, and photograph the cave and
its finds within the fortnight of the main dig period. But beyond
that remained the sorting, mending, drawing, and photographing
of the finds. To cover the costs of assistants to do this work
absorbed the whole of our contingency reserve for site-filling,
transport of finds to England and elsewhere, and so on. Such is
the fate of careful planning for archaeological contingencies.

The catalogue of the finds consisted very largely of pottery
vessels, for the most part ordinary domestic vessels: jugs, bowls,

cooking pots, and lamps, the latter no doubt to illuminate the place of offering, the others probably as containers of solid or liquid food. A pottery vessel certainly not for domestic use was a fine incense-burner, for which an illustration in black and white does not do justice, for it is covered by a finely burnished red slip. In addition to the vessels, there were a large number of pottery figurines and miniatures of furniture. The latter were in the minority – a few chairs or thrones and tables. The great proportion (429 registered objects and very many fragments) consisted of human or animal figurines. Most of the human figurines were female of the type known as pillar figurines, the lower part being simply a slighter splaying stump. The torso, with well-accentuated breasts, usually the hands beneath them (Pl 59), are characteristic of fertility figurines in western Asia since as long ago as the seventh-millennium B.C. Neolithic Jericho.[1] So seldom do the heads of these figurines survive attached to them that one is tempted to think that they may have been purposely broken off when they were consigned to the repository, but a more prosaic explanation may be that it can be seen they were made in separate moulds, and the junction between the two parts may therefore have been easily broken. The association of these female figurines with a fertility cult, abhorrent to the worshippers of Yahweh, is very obvious.

The animal figurines were even more numerous than the human ones. The modelling is crude, and when only the torso or legs survive one cannot be dogmatic as to whether a horse or a dog is intended. Even some of the heads are ambiguous. Nevertheless, we have a number of certain horses, and no certain dogs (or other animals), so it may be that all the fragments belong to horses. Some can be identified by a certainly horsy face, and some have riders. A very interesting feature is that several of the horses have a disk on the forehead, between the ears.

The cult association of the human figures would seem to be clear. The interpretation of the animal figurines is much less certain. A very great number of fragments have been found in the

[1] *Digging up Jericho*, Pl. 19A.

main excavation area at Jerusalem and at all Iron Age II sites. I have been inclined to consider that it was at least possible that some of the animal figurines were children's toys. This is less probable if it is accepted, as I believe it must be, that these two cave deposits are associated with a cult centre. The best evidence of a cult connection is probably the disk on the forehead of the horses, which is unusual, and perhaps unique to this deposit. In western Asia and in Egypt such a disk represents the sun. It seems a perfectly reasonable assumption that horses with a disk on the forehead are miniature models of the Horses of the Sun. In II Kings 23:11 it is described how Josiah, in connection with his great purification of the religion of Judah, and the restoration of the true worship of Yahweh, 'took away the horses that the kings of Judah had given to the sun, at the entering in of the house of the Lord'. The whole of II Kings 23 is a vivid indication of the degree of idolatry and of the worshipping of strange gods that existed in Judah in the seventh century B.C. Much of this was due to the absorption by the infiltrating Israelites of the culture of the Canaanite occupants of the land; the fertility figurines just described can with very great probability be attributed to this influence. Another aspect was the insistence of the super-power in the background, in the seventh century B.C. Assyria, that homage should be given to her gods. Josiah's cleansing of the Temple of symbols such as those of the horses of the sun was an indication of political revolt as well as of religious purification.

A reasonable interpretation of the deposits in the two caves is that they are derived from a sanctuary, or possibly two sanctuaries, of a cult associated with fertility worship and with the allied worship of the sun; the threads of the various cults flourishing in western Asia at this time are so interwoven that one would be rash to define it more closely. It is a salutary lesson that the centuries-long struggles of the supporters of the pure worship of Yahweh were so far from establishing a national religion that such a cult centre should exist almost within a stone's throw, at least within 300 metres, from the south-east corner of the enclosure of Yahweh's Temple.

It has been suggested to me that the deposits in the cave are actually associated with Josiah's purification of the Temple and destruction of the centres of heathen and unorthodox arts (II Kings 23), *c.* 620 B.C. For two reasons I think that this is unlikely. The date of the pottery vessels seems to me to be nearer 700 B.C. than 620 B.C.; this is an impression only, and it will not be until the final analysis of the pottery has been completed that one can claim with precision where this find fits into the history of Jerusalem. Secondly, the agents appointed by the king to root out the evil cults would not have deposited, with some considerable care, complete vessels in a protective repository. The deposits are not associated with a destruction; they belong to a time when the cult with which they were associated was flourishing, and the central date is *c.* 700 B.C.

★

CHAPTER EIGHT

The Last Century of the Kingdom of Judah

MENTION HAS BEEN MADE in the preceding chapter of events in the reign of Josiah, in the middle of the seventh century B.C. It has, however, been suggested that the final stage of the cult centre belonged to about 700 B.C.

It was outside the original east wall NB, which was probably still in existence. It was also outside the only surviving successor of that wall, wall NA. Wall NA, however, did not immediately succeed NB. The latter was sealed by a number of surfaces, of which the uppermost was a cobbled road running north-south (Pl. 63). This road and the underlying surfaces were very clearly cut by the foundation trench of wall NA (fig. 25). The outer eastern edge of these surfaces is cut by the steep erosion line, and erosion must have completely removed the retaining wall, presumably the town wall which would have been necessary to support the surfaces. Surfaces belonging to this vanished inter-mediate wall overlay the structures associated with the cult centre.

The total disappearance of this wall is probably due to the fact that its foundations were not carried down to rock. It may have been hurriedly built. In due course, it was succeeded by wall NA, firmly founded on rock. This wall certainly, if not its pre-decessor, was on a line extending along the slope of the hill to the north of the original limits. The difficulties of dating this wall by archaeological evidence are described above (pp. 130–1). It is probable that when it was built, a whole new area on the eastern

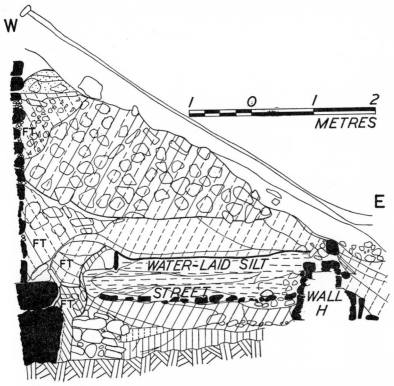

FIG 25   Section against town wall NA on east side of Jerusalem, showing its foundation trench cutting deposits which ran to a vanished town wall farther east

slope was enclosed within the walls; to this period belong the structures in Square A XXIV described above (p. 132). The plan (fig. 26) suggests that the wall runs to the south-east corner of Solomon's temple platform. This is a reasonable guess, but it could be that the inclusion of the eastern slopes continued below the walls of the temple platform, and that the massive wall found by Warren 46 feet east of the temple platform was the continuation of our wall NA. To establish this would be most laborious, a step-by-step affair, with no jumps, as my efforts at jumps showed, and I very willingly leave this to my successors.

It can, however, be accepted that wall NA provides evidence,

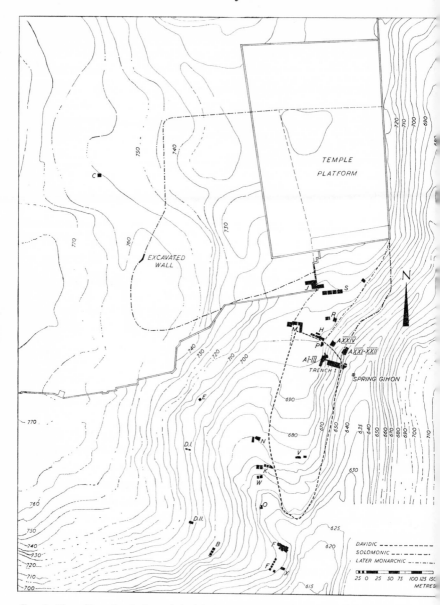

FIG 26   Plan of Jerusalem in the period of the later monarchy

with the supporting evidence of Square A XXIV, of a considerable extension of the area enclosed within the walls. Archaeologically I would not like to be dogmatic about the date within the eighth–seventh centuries B.C. The Biblical evidence makes many references to the rebuilding of walls, but the written records lack the precision that can enable one to establish what was happening in geographical terms. A very important point of interpretation is the *mishneh*, which is to be translated as 'the Second Quarter', which appears in II Kings 22:14, with reference to Huldah the Prophetess and her prophecy of woe from which Josiah was to be excluded. At some stage an additional area had been added to the Solomonic city. The Biblical record is not sufficiently precise to enable one to say when this took place.

Previous discussion of the situation of the *mishneh* lacked the necessary basis of adequate archaeological evidence. For long it has been accepted on the basis of the Bliss and Dickie exploration (see above, p. 21 ff.) that within the period of the monarchy of Judah (if not in that of the United Monarchy) there had been an expansion onto the western ridge from the original site on the eastern ridge. The excavations in 1961 clearly proved that this could not be substantiated for the southern part of the western ridge.

The excavations of our 1961–67 expedition did not provide any firm evidence of expansion onto the western ridge during the period of the monarchy of Judah. As just mentioned, it was certain that there was nothing of this period on the eastern flank of the southern part of the ridge; the summit of the ridge was at the time of our excavations inaccessible, as it was in no man's land. Our excavations in the area in the south-west corner of the Old City, belonging to the Armenian Patriarchate, also produced no evidence of buildings within the period of the monarchy. There was plenty of Iron Age II pottery, but this was either associated with quarrying or with dumped deposits. This evidence from within the walls of the Old City has recently been confirmed by Israeli excavations outside the walls, immediately to the south. One can say very firmly that the present evidence is that on the summit of the western ridge there was no occupation within the period of the monarchy of Judah.

An intriguing new possibility has been introduced by Israeli excavations in the area of the Jewish Quarter on the eastern slope of the western ridge. Here houses were located, assigned by the excavators to the eighth century B.C., built on bedrock. The second stage is a wall (Pl. 62) which from its massiveness and width, 3 metres, can reasonably be interpreted as a town wall. The 1971 excavations have not yet made its direction clear. A surprising bend uphill, to the west, may turn out to be part of a gateway, for the evidence described in the last paragraph shows that it cannot have curved round to enclose the summit of the ridge. Its line is indeed mysterious. On the evidence that the summit of the hill was not occupied, it must have enclosed an area to the east, representing an extension across the central valley from the wall of the temple platform. But to build the wall on a slope commanded by the summit of the ridge some 15 metres higher and only 285 metres away seems a very odd policy. There is also the mystery of what the wall did to the south. Professor Avigad, the excavator, suggests[1] that it continued south along the flank of the western ridge to enclose the Pool of Siloam (see below, p. 158). This it certainly did not, for this is the area which was adequately tested in 1961–62 (fig. 11), and the evidence was firm that there was no occupation here until the first century A.D. The evidence at the moment suggests strongly that, unless it enclosed an area on the western ridge so restricted that our site L was outside it, it must have curved back to join the town on the eastern ridge somewhere north of Site M (fig. 26), where on the slope there was no occupation prior to the post-Exilic-Hellenistic period. The line might be approximately that of the south wall of the present Old City. A possible line is suggested on fig. 26, but with the lack of any evidence this is quite hypothetical. This extension to the west is, therefore, a possible competitor as the location of the *mishneh*.

It is certain that the wall on the new line on the eastern slope

[1] *IEJ* 20.3–4.

received a great deal of attention during the final century in which Jerusalem was the capital of the kingdom of Judah. In addition to the vanished wall, wall NA was rebuilt, in places almost to its foundations, four and possibly five times (see fig. 25). The earliest of these walls is not likely to be appreciably earlier than 700 B.C.

The last quarter of the eighth century and the seventh century were periods of peril for the Israelite kingdoms. Warfare amongst the states of western Asia, between Judah and Israel themselves, and each of them at intervals with their neighbours, Assyria, Ammon, Moab, and Edom, was endemic, and at earlier stages there were incursions from Egypt. The threat in the eighth century was much more serious, with the rise to power of Assyria in Mesopotamia, and the development of great territorial ambitions by its rulers. The threat came in a series of waves, for as each new ruler succeeded, he needed a period to establish himself and dispose of competitors, but the tide, though spasmodic, was steadily more engulfing. The climax for Syria came with the accession to the throne of Tiglath-pileser III in 745 B.C., and the threat to the kingdoms of Palestine and Transjordan followed rapidly. At first, the lesser powers thought that they could retain their identity by paying tribute, but this gave them only temporary respite. The first disastrous impact on the northern kingdom of Israel was in 743–33 B.C. The great cities of Megiddo and Hazor were destroyed, and the kingdom of Israel was truncated of its northern part.

The capital of Israel, Samaria, survived briefly. Its capture by Sargon II in 722–21 B.C. was followed by the end of the kingdom of Israel, which was completely annexed by Assyria. This brought the threat very close to Jerusalem, for the southern boundary of Israel was only about 20 miles north of Jerusalem. For the moment Jerusalem and Judah survived owing to one of the periodical ebbs in the ebb and flow of Assyrian advance. The next flow came in the reign of Hezekiah. We know of the campaigns of Sennacherib from the Assyrian records. The capture of Lachish, one of the most important towns of southern Palestine, is illustrated in reliefs found at Nineveh.[1] There is archaeological evidence of the destruction at this time of Beth Shemesh, Gibeah, and Tell Jemmeh.

The threat to Jerusalem *c.* 700 B.C. is described in II Chronicles 32 and II Kings 18–19. The city was in the end saved when the Assyrian army was withdrawn because it had been smitten by plague (II Kings 19:35–36). But it could justly be claimed that the great defensive efforts of Hezekiah had so prolonged the siege as to create the conditions in which disease could strike the attacking force disastrously. Hezekiah did not, in fact, confine himself to prayer and diplomacy, though his fervent reliance on prayer and hopes in the use of diplomacy are very clear from the Biblical record. In II Chronicles 32:5, it is recorded that 'he strengthened himself, and built up all the wall that was broken . . . and another wall without' (archaeological evidence on this other wall is indecisive). The defence of the city was thus part of Hezekiah's activities. On the basis of the general impressions gained from the 1961–67 excavations, it seems that the evidence obtained on the eastern slope is likely to be more detailed than elsewhere. On the western slope of the eastern ridge there is radical destruction caused by centuries of occupation; on the eastern slope there is destruction and erosion, but not quite so radical. For the evidence at Jerusalem of this period of Hezekiah's attempt to stem the advance of Assyria, one has, in the area excavated between 1961 and 1967 low on the eastern slope, an original wall of Jebusite-Davidic period, surrounded by a wall that has completely vanished (see above, p. 144) and wall NA (above, p. 135 and Pl. 43) of substantial appearance but on visual evidence rebuilt to a low level several times (fig. 25). Each of these walls was on a line that was new in relation to the Davidic-Solomonic *enceinte*, and certainly enclosed a new quarter, whether or not this was the *mishneh*. The levels associated with the earliest, vanished wall sealed the cult centre and its caves, and the pottery evidence from the caves shows that too early a date cannot be given to this wall. It and all its successors are likely to

[1] Now in the British Museum; see A. H. Layard, *Nineveh and Babylon*, p. 148.

belong to the century and a quarter or so between the last quarter of the eighth century B.C. and the final Babylonian destruction in 587 B.C. One of the walls or rebuilds must have been the work of Hezekiah. It would fit well that he was the builder of the vanished wall, for its lack of firmly based foundations suggests haste. On the other hand, it could be argued that Hezekiah would be unlikely to increase the area of the walled city at a time of acute menace, though against this it might be that he felt the need to defend a built-up area hitherto outside the walls. If the vanished wall is not to be attributed to Hezekiah, wall NA or an early rebuild must be. It is not very likely that archaeological evidence will provide a conclusive answer. In the first two centuries of Roman Britain one can date assemblages of pottery within decades, for one can associate the different elements with sites precisely dated by the historical record. In Palestine, the precisely dated deposits are usually separated by centuries rather than decades. I doubt whether, when the analysis of the pottery is complete, one will be able to identify features that one can say should be attributed to Hezekiah or his predecessors or successors *in the present state of our knowledge.* The italics are to emphasize the fact that we have recorded, and shall publish, the pottery forms that can be associated with the vanished wall and the various stages of wall NA. In the present state of knowledge, there may not appear to be significant differences in the pottery that can be assigned to each stage. Greater definition may come with further investigation and additional scientific aids, and one hopes that the publication of our excavation evidence will enable this definition to be applied to our finds. Meanwhile, all that one can say is that one of the archaeologically recorded stages in the defences is likely to be attributed to Hezekiah's activities described in II Chronicles 32:5.

Hezekiah's repairs to the defences of Jerusalem were sufficient to hold the attacking Assyrians at bay until the fatal disease struck them. The chronicler, however, did not give these measures priority. Work on the walls is described in II Chronicles 32, verse 5, but verses 3 and 4 are concerned with Hezekiah's measures to prevent access by the Assyrians to the city water-supply. The leaders of the inhabitants of Jerusalem supported the king 'saying, why should the kings of Assyria come, and find much water'. 'So there were gathered much people together, who stopped all the fountains, and the brook that ran through the midst of the land'.

On present evidence, the only perennial source of running water adjacent to the Jerusalem of this period was the Spring Gihon, running into the Kedron Valley. Bir Eyub, 250 metres south of the tip of the eastern ridge, was too far away to be of use in time of war. No permanent spring fed the central valley, down which water only ran in the rainy season. The other source of water for the inhabitants of Jerusalem was their cisterns. Once lime mortar had been discovered about the beginning of the first millennium B.C., winter rains could be conserved in cisterns and it is highly probable that each house had its cistern, as was in fact customary down to recent times and compulsory during the British Mandate. Cisterns do not provide a water-supply to attackers until the town falls. Hezekiah's defensive measures were therefore concerned 'to stop the waters of the fountains that were without the city', and his concern was therefore with the Spring Gihon.

The importance of the spring in the Jebusite-Davidic periods has been described (above, pp. 38, 84). The evidence for the relation of this to other rock-cuttings connected with the spring was recorded by Père Hugues Vincent.

The clearance of the accumulated deposits in the Siloam Tunnel was the work of the Parker expedition in 1911 (see above, p. 30). It was a very considerable undertaking, and it was to the advantage of the villagers of Siloam as regards the use of the water-supply. The archaeological results of the Parker expedition were salvaged by Père Vincent (see above, p. 30).[1] In addition to his investigation of the earliest access to the spring and the stages in the use of the water that can be ascribed to the earlier periods of the Jewish monarchy, he established, in his analysis of

[1] *Jérusalem sous Terre.*

the Parker discoveries, that channels, carrying the waters of the Spring Gihon down the Kedron Valley, were later than the complex providing the water-supply of the original city on the eastern ridge, and earlier than the Siloam Tunnel. It would seem that, in the centuries immediately following the capture of Jerusalem in c. 1000 B.C., control of the water-supply from within the city became less important. This could be due to greater confidence that the power of the kingdom centred on Jerusalem, the United Monarchy first, then the kingdom of Judah, was sufficient to keep enemies at a distance from the source of the Spring Gihon and from any other connections with a more distant source which Solomon, in his expansion to the north of the original town, may have tapped. On the other hand, it could be due to an increasing confidence in the conservation of rain-water, with the invention c. 1000 B.C. of lime mortar to serve, among other purposes, as a lining to cisterns, infinitely superior to the previous mud mortar. The somewhat unreliable rain-water of upland Palestine could therefore be safely stored. I would not like to place too much weight on this explanation, since I doubt whether, when Professor Albright made this nice distinction about the chronological appearance of lime mortar, an adequate number of field archaeologists had made available to the scientists evidence upon which the scientists could come to a conclusion for which the basis was sound for the archaeologists. Nevertheless, I am prepared to accept that at a certain stage (with all my reservations just expressed) efficient cisterns rendered the internal control of the water-supply less important.

The intervention of the super powers created a different situation, and Hezekiah therefore was impelled to protect the water and make it accessible only from within the walls.

Today, any tourist can visit the Spring Gihon, usually known as the Virgin's Fountain. Steep, and rather slippery, steps lead down to the water below, up which steps women and boys carry jars filled from the spring. Tourists can also visit the southern end, where the waters emerge in a pool which in its present state has a faintly classical appearance, and is certainly the remnants of the New Testament Pool of Siloam. It is also the successor of the place where Hezekiah considered that the waters of the spring would be safe (see below, pp. 156–9).

Between the Spring Gihon and the Pool of Siloam is the Siloam Tunnel, sinuous in plan (fig. 27), cut through the solid rock of the southern end of the eastern ridge. When Warren explored the tunnel in 1867, it had silted up to the extent that he and Birtles had to wallow through on their stomachs (see above, p. 18). Today one can walk through easily, knee or thigh deep in water, with ample head clearance (Pls. 65–6), but even those who, like myself, do not suffer from claustrophobia, must have a sensation of plunging into the unknown, committing one-self to fate, on embarking on this walk of 533 metres in the bowels of the earth. *We* know that the route is uncomplicated and that we can arrive safely at the other end. Warren did not know this. At any point he and Birtles might have been pinned in the narrow space through which they wallowed, and overwhelmed by a higher flow of water which would have given them no chance to escape.

Today one may not appreciate the labour and perils of the first explorers. One must also spare a thought for those who first constructed the tunnel. One aspect of their achievement was the sheer physical labour of boring their way through solid rock, rock that had relatively soft strata at intervals, but some very hard strata as well. The man at the sap-head (and from the width of the tunnel there could have been only one) carved his way into the rock with, presumably, an iron pick or adze; not many iron tools have survived in Palestine, but it is reasonable to suppose that by *c.* 700 B.C. there was an adequate supply of such tools. A man behind him must have gathered up the dis-lodged fragments, probably from between his legs, for there was no room for the pickman to stand aside. The second man would have filled the containers, very probably woven baskets, for which the nearest English equivalent is an old-fashioned fish-basket, which we still used at Jericho, but which at Jerusalem had been superseded by containers of similar shape made of old

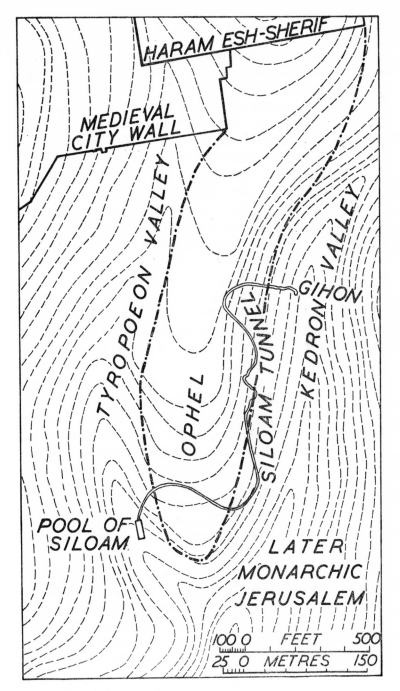

FIG 27   Plan of Siloam Tunnel

motor-tyres. These containers must have been passed back from
hand to hand to the point of approach. We know that the tunnel
was dug from each end, for this is implicit in the inscription
found near the sound end of the tunnel, cut in its wall, which
records the excitement when the gangs from north and south met.
The point of junction is nearer to the northern end than the
southern, and a rough estimate is that up to the point of junction
between the northern and southern gangs, the former had had to
carry out the rock spoil for a distance of 300 metres.

The second aspect of the achievement of the men who excavated the Siloam Tunnel is that they arrived at the intended
destination. It is no mean feat to burrow through the heart of a
hill without the aid of a compass. If it had been possible to lay
out a direct line on the surface on which to align the start of the
tunnel, and then keep a straight line, it would not have been too
complicated. The men who planned the tunnel probably felt
that this left the first length of the tunnel too close to the surface
along the eastern flank, and also they had available the tunnels
connected with the first, Jebusite, system (see above, pp. 84–9).
The tunnel therefore plunges back into the heart of the hill
(fig. 27), and then manages to find its way along the eastern
flank of the hill to meet the southern gang which had started
from the intended destination of the water. The plan in fact
shows a considerable number of meanderings. Particularly
surprising is the S-curve between the southern section crossing
the hill and the section running (rather erratically) along the
eastern side. The great bulge to the south-east takes place beneath
the area excavated by Weill in 1913–14, where he claimed
to have identified the Royal Tombs of the House of David, and
it has been suggested that the bulge was to avoid passing beneath
this sacred area. This interpretation does not appeal to me at all.
In the first place, I regard the evidence for identifying the rock
cutting as the Royal Tombs as non-existent; I believe that they
are cisterns, of rather unusual form, but a form which has far
less connection with tombs of the period in question. Secondly,
I do very much doubt whether the excavators, some 60 feet

down in the rock, knew that they were in the vicinity of the spot of the suggested Royal Tombs. I hesitate to add a third reason, for one must admit that religious taboos in a devout population can go to great lengths, but it does to modern comprehension seem improbable that the military would waste vital time (think of the plugging away involved in digging the tunnel just described) when there was an appalling threat from the greatest power in western Asia. My explanation of the curves, the wiggles, the sinuosity, is quite simply that there was a considerable degree of trial and error; divergences had to be corrected and the right direction resumed. What I do not attempt to explain is how the correct direction *was* resumed. I leave this to engineers, surveyors, geomorphologists, who may add to the archaeologists' interpretation the facts from which we might hope ultimately to be able to interpret ancient records. Anyhow, the result was that contact was made between the spring and the place to which Hezekiah planned to divert the waters of the Spring Gihon.

Involved in this exercise was not only the direction but the level of the flow of water. In this, as in the line of the tunnel, it seems that there was a degree of trial and error. At the north end, where the water-level of the spring indicated the necessary level for the base of the channel, the height of the tunnel is 1·94 metres. The party starting from the south end had to make an estimate of the level required. Had this been accurate, it would have been a miracle, unless the engineers had available far more accurate levelling instruments than we have any reason to suppose. In fact, one may reasonably conclude that they were *c.* 2 metres out. This was the conclusion of Père Vincent to account for the fact that at the south end the tunnel had the completely unnecessary height of 3·96 metres, and a little to the north as much as 5·08 metres, and he supported his conclusion by observations of technique of the cutting of the tunnel. One can accept with some confidence the suggestion that it was necessary to lower the southern section by 2 to 3 metres, an amazingly small amount in view of the circumstances, though that does conflict with the

Siloam inscription that states that the water started to flow as
soon as the northern and southern parties achieved junction.
This would in any case have been impossible, for the waters
must have been diverted while the excavation of the tunnel was
proceeding. Anyhow, the gangs from the opposite end did meet,
and the levels were adjusted so that the waters could flow from
the Spring Gihon in the Kedron Valley to the Siloam Pool in
the Tyropoeon, or central, valley.

Hezekiah's success in transferring the waters of the Spring
Gihon from the eastern to the western valley was complete, and
even today no water from the spring flows down the Kedron (or
Siloam) Valley along the flanks of the eastern ridge. Today,
the Pool of Siloam is an open pool near the south end of the
valley that bounds the western side of the eastern ridge, from
which the overflow eventually returns the water to the Kedron.
Hezekiah's objective in depriving an army of access to water by
transferring it to a pool in the valley to the west of the eastern
ridge seemed comprehensible and to have been satisfactorily
achieved when it was accepted that the walls enclosing the western
ridge belonged to the period of the monarchy of Judah, or
even earlier. As has been seen (above, p. 93), the 1961–67
excavations have shown quite conclusively that the area of the
western ridge adjacent to the Pool of Siloam was not enclosed
within the walls of the city until the first century A.D. In whatever
way one has to interpret the most recent evidence concerning
expansion on to the northern end of the western ridge within the
period of the monarchy (see above, p. 148), the evidence of the
excavated sites shown on fig. 11 makes it entirely clear that the
slopes of the western ridge above the Pool of Siloam were
undefended and could thus have been accessible to an enemy.[1]

This problem that our finds created, to explain why after
enormous labour Hezekiah brought the water to a position
outside the walls, only slightly less exposed than at the original
source, caused me a lot of worry. I admit I wasted quite a lot of

[1] The possible reservation that has to be considered for the Hellenistic period
(see below, pp. 200–1) does not apply to the eighth–seventh centuries B.C.

our inadequate financial resources in looking in improbable positions for a wall that could have protected the pool. In fact, any wall that did not carry the defences well up the slope of the western ridge would not have served this purpose, and our excavations showed that at this stage the area was outside the walls (see above, p. 93).

The solution dawned on me in a blinding glimpse of the obvious. As just said, the Pool of Siloam is today an open pool in the valley between the eastern and western ridges, its present walls perhaps deriving something from the Roman period. From this pool there is an outflow, which today one can see beneath an overhanging rock curve (Pl. 69). It cannot be doubted that this rock curve is a rock-cut channel that has been truncated on its outer edge. One can in fact see clearly that the whole tip of the eastern ridge has been truncated by an artificial scarp (Pl. 68), perhaps of the post-Exilic period. The natural line for the outflow would have been down the centre of the valley. It would seem, however, that Hezekiah's engineers wished to conceal the line of the outflow until the water was dissipated on the slopes of the Kedron. This only makes sense if the reservoir into which the waters flowed from the Siloam Tunnel was concealed, and it was essential not to give a clue to its position by an obvious outflow channel. One must therefore conclude that the original reservoir was a rock-cut cistern, lying outside the line of the walls defending the eastern ridge, but accessible from within them by a shaft or staircase of the type so familiar at an earlier date in Jerusalem, and also at sites such as Megiddo, Hazor, and Gezer. I can produce no archaeological evidence to prove this interpretation, and I have not been able to observe any supporting evidence in the remains of the present pool, except that there is a bay in the contours of the west side of the eastern ridge at this point, which could have been caused by the collapse of a roof-cut approach to a rock-cut cistern. Nevertheless I shall remain convinced (and I have convinced most of my colleagues whose opinion I respect) that this is the correct interpretation unless very clear evidence to the contrary is produced.

As already stated (above, p. 150), the reason that the siege was raised was because the Assyrian army was smitten with plague (II Kings 19:35–36). It is obvious that the delay imposed on the attackers by Hezekiah's defensive measures gave time for the plague to assume serious dimensions. Yahweh may have intervened in support of his chosen people, but the chosen people had nobly supported the intervention.

The undeniable fact is that the kingdom of Judah did survive for more than a hundred years after the recession of the wave of Assyrian expansion that had threatened to overwhelm Hezekiah. There are some grounds for believing that this century, the seventh century B.C., was a period of reasonable material prosperity in Jerusalem. As will be seen, we have terribly little in the way of structures that can be ascribed to this period. This is due to the ensuing destructions. But in fills that can be ascribed to the Babylonian destruction, and in other deposits which in date of deposition belong to a much later period (for instance the second century A.D.; see below, pp. 228–38), there is an enormous amount of pottery and other objects which (with my usual cautionary reservation 'in the present state of our knowledge') seem to belong to this period.

Buildings that may well belong to this final period of the monarchy of Judah have been excavated by Professor Avigad on the eastern slope of the western ridge (see above, p. 148). I write at a time when Professor Avigad has not yet reached the point where he can state with confidence the date and area of the expansion during the period of the monarchy of Judah onto the western ridge. I am very prepared to accept that there was some expansion from the eastern ridge onto the western ridge at *its northern end*. All the evidence of the 1961–67 excavation goes to show that this expansion did not reach the summit of the western ridge.

At this point I begin to feel apologetic to the general reader. At a time when much work is going on and new finds are suggesting new theories, it is necessary to consider these theories in a way which may seem rather confusing to him. Professor Avigad is entirely professionally cautious in his interpretations of the evidence that his excavations, in the area of the Jewish Quarter of the Old City, have produced. My belief is that the expansion from the Davidic-Solomonic town on the eastern ridge took place in the eighth-seventh centuries B.C. (or perhaps one should say at a period during the history of the monarchy of Judah, as yet undefined). The evidence at present seems to me to be that this expansion enclosed only the eastern, lower, slopes of the western ridge within the defences; the improbability of such a line of defences is referred to above (p. 148).

The evidence for the history of the area of Jerusalem on the western ridge during the later years of the monarchy of Judah is controversial. That concerning the eastern ridge is factual but rather pedestrian. I have already referred to the evidence that there were several rebuilds to the eastern wall NA that succeeded the original Jebusite-Davidic wall. They were in the same adequate but uninspiring dry-stone masonry as the first wall on this line. Behind them, up the slope of the hill, the massive sub-structures of the terraces seen in Pl. 64 certainly were in use during the seventh century B.C., and may in part have been built now as reconstructions of earlier phases. At the foot of the terraces are strongly built walls or rooms which again probably supported an upper storey. The clearest evidence of the dependence of the houses on the eastern slopes upon the terraces built in the Jebusite, Late Bronze Age, period is seen at the top of the slope, immediately east of Macalister's so-called Davidic Tower, Square A I–III on the plan (fig. 18). In the view shown in Pl. 32, the massive stone fills belong to the Late Bronze Age. Above can be seen several floors, upon the uppermost of which a man is standing. On the pottery evidence, all these floors belong to Iron Age II, the period of the monarchy of Judah. Successive collapses and denudations had therefore removed the Late Bronze Age houses which the terraces had been planned to support. The fate of the earlier Iron Age, Israelite, houses was almost as absolute, though at least some floors and foundations of walls survived.

The final stage in the life of the terraces belongs, on the evidence of finds, without doubt to the seventh century B.C. A strip only 7·50 metres wide survives between the town wall on the crest of the ridge, of which the post-Exilic date has already been mentioned (above, p. 77) and will be discussed below (pp. 191 ff.), and the steep erosion slope that sheered away the outer edge of the upper terrace and the complete superstructures of the lower terraces, an erosion that took place after the Babylonian destruction of 587 B.C.

Even within the area exposed, the degree of destruction of the seventh-century buildings varies. At the southern end, almost nothing above the foundations survives. In this area there was, however, a find of special importance, that of at least thirty-four beautifully shaped limestone weights (Pl. 72). The 'at least' is required since, in spite of our strict system of site supervision, some similar weights did appear in a Jerusalem shop; the answer, of course, was to take great care that one did not employ a member of the numerous family of the antique dealer concerned on any site where finds of marketable value might be made. Certainly in Jerusalem we were much more at risk in such matters than we had been in Jericho. I remain convinced that we did not lose very much, and that a *bakshish* system both invites the planting of objects and is quite absolutely destructive of the accurate record by exact layers of finds. We have, at any rate, the exact record of provenance of a far larger number of weights than has ever been found in controlled circumstances before. All the weights are fairly small, the heaviest 24 shekels = 268·24 grammes, the smallest a $\frac{1}{4}$ *n-ṣ-p* = 2·63 grammes. It would probably be reasonable to deduce that the man inhabiting this much denuded house at the crest of the eastern ridge was a merchant in fine goods, a jeweller, a silversmith, or a craftsman at a similar level. Twenty-two (or possibly twenty-four) are inscribed with their weights, sixteen (or possibly eighteen) in shekels, the standard most often referred to in the Bible, two in *p-y-m.*, two-thirds of a shekel, and two in *n-ṣ-p.*, a standard not easy to relate to a shekel, but in the neighbourhood of 85 per cent. This collection of contemporary (for they all come from the final use of these houses on the east of the hill) inscribed weights has in fact enabled Professor R. B. Y. Scott to make a most valuable study[1] of the system of weights in use in the last stage of the monarchy of Judah. In assessing the intended value of a weight, it is necessary to take into account its state, for a much-used weight in this rather soft limestone has obviously lost an appreciable amount of its volume. Professor Scott therefore carefully classified the weights into four categories by degree of wear. The surprising point to emerge is that the weight of 4 shekels in absolutely mint condition gave a shekel value of 11·34 grammes, and this can be taken as the standard in use in Jerusalem in the reign of Zedekiah, immediately before the Babylonian destruction of the city. On the other hand, the mass of some of the worn specimens was as much as 2·2 per cent greater. Professor Scott suggests that among the reforms of Josiah was that of the standardization of weights, which extant examples show to have varied much in different areas. In the production of new standard weights, copies would have been made from specimens preserved in the royal chancery or the temple treasury. In so doing, allowance might not have been made for reduction in weight through wear, and the new standard would have emerged as slightly lighter than the original.

The rest of the buildings produced no such interesting objects. At the northern end of the excavated strip, walls were preserved rather better, though the maximum height was only 2 metres. The evidence for both the plan and the masonry technique was clear. The masonry technique was crude. It produced virtually uncoursed, dry-stone walls, of sufficient width to provide stability, which were given additional cohesion and acceptable appearance by a thick coating of mud mortar on the faces. The photographs (Pls. 70, 71) show little of this surface treatment, for in periods of destruction it rapidly disappears; but there were sufficient traces to prove that it originally existed. The main

[1] *PEQ*, 1965, pp. 128–39.

element in the plan was a tripartite room at the northern end of the excavated strip, incompletely excavated, and very considerably destroyed. Enough is, however, known of the houses of seventh-century Judah to allow the plan to be interpreted. These tripartite rooms can be described as having a central nave divided from side aisles by piers, usually monolithic, that is to say a single slab of rock, standing, as normally uncovered, to the height of about 4 feet. The Jerusalem examples are seen on Pl. 71. It has always rather worried me how these structures could work. To the best of my belief, the monoliths, found, for example, in many buildings at Tell Nasbeh,[1] are never high enough to support a ceiling that gave adequate head room on the ground floor; the Jerusalem examples certainly would not do so. One would have thought that it was structurally impossible to balance other stones on top of the monoliths to provide a firm support for the ceiling. One has to choose between this improbable structural method and a conclusion that what survives for the archaeologist to discover is a storage or perhaps stable substructure with a ceiling only about 4 feet high. So far archaeology has not given us the answer, and it will be great good fortune if it does. Meanwhile, I incline to believe that substructure interpretation is the most likely one.

The interpretation of the plan of these Jerusalem buildings is therefore uncertain, even though it has many parallels in the buildings of seventh-century B.C. Judah. To the south of the main tripartite room are some smaller ones. One contained the base of an oven with a domed roof of clay, of the type of domestic oven usual in the Iron Age. Between the room with the oven and the tripartite room to the north was a staircase (Pl. 70), in its surviving form certainly secondary to the main lay-out; amongst the evidence for this was the fact that it blocked the doorway leading into the room with the oven. This staircase is a reminder that all these buildings had to be accommodated to a steep slope. The view on Pl. 29 shows how the Iron Age build-

[1] C. C. McCown, *Tell en-Nasbeh*, pp. 206 ff.

ings incorporated the skeletal structure of the Late Bronze Age terraces. The strip of surviving Iron Age buildings is at *c.* 686 metres above sea-level. Above the level of this strip no above-surface walls survive. The staircase shown in Pl. 70 is absolute confirmation of the reasonable supposition that the terraced buildings continued up to the crest of the ridge.

★

CHAPTER NINE

The Destruction of Jerusalem and the End of the Monarchy of Judah

BY ONE MEANS or another, the Assyrian threat *c.* 700 B.C. in the reign of Hezekiah was averted. A pseudo-autonomous kingdom of Judah lasted for another century. The pressure on the petty states of the Mediterranean coast from the great powers of Mesopotamia was relaxed during the process in which Assyria succumbed to the new Babylonian power, with a climax in 626 B.C. Thereafter the Mediterranean states had to face the fresh power of Babylon.

The kings of Judah tried, with the revival of Egypt at the end of the seventh century B.C., to play off one great power against another. Egypt had in fact reasserted itself under Necho, and Josiah of Judah paid the penalty of an attempt to resist the re-imposition of Egyptian power when he was killed in a battle with Necho at Megiddo in 609 B.C. The Babylonians in due course defeated Necho in 604 B.C. In the next fifteen years or so, the kings of Judah tried to assess the relative strengths of Babylon and Egypt. Their ultimate judgement, or hope, was wrong, and Judah succumbed to Babylon. Jehoiakim's revolt against Nebuchadnezzar in 598 B.C. was followed by the siege and destruction of Jerusalem in 597 B.C., after Jehoiakim's son Jehoiachin had reigned only three months. Jehoiachin was taken as a prisoner to Babylon with most of the leaders and craftsmen of Judah – according to II Kings 24:14, ten thousand captives in all. Jerusalem was thoroughly plundered. In II Kings 24:13 it is said that the king of Babylon 'carried off all the treasures of the house of the

Lord, and the treasures of the king's house and cut in pieces all the vessels of gold in the temple of the Lord, which Solomon king of Israel had made'.

It is clear that Jerusalem, though captured and sacked, was not destroyed. The exiled Jehoiachin was succeeded by his uncle Zedekiah. When he in turn rebelled against Babylon, Jerusalem was able to withstand a quite considerable siege, until it alone survived of all the walled towns of Judah. Jeremiah (34:7) refers to the stage when only Lachish and Azekah were left in addition to Jerusalem. One of the letters written on potsherds found at Tell Duweir, the site of Lachish, comes at a stage when Azekah had apparently fallen,[1] and next must have come the destruction of Lachish, leaving the ruins uncovered in the excavations.[2] Zedekiah made a last despairing effort to get help from Egypt.[3] Even though the defeat of Necho by Nebuchadnezzar in 604 B.C. had effectively ended Egyptian interference in Palestine, according to Jeremiah,[4] Egypt did respond to the plea, and the advance of the Egyptian army did cause the Babylonians to withdraw from Jerusalem. This must have prolonged the siege, to the extent that the defenders were enabled to replenish their supplies.

There is no evidence of the length of the intermission in the siege. The city eventually fell in the ninth day of the fourth month of the eleventh year of the reign of Zedekiah,[5] eighteen months after the beginning of the siege. It was apparent from the sequence in the account in II Kings 25 that famine was the main factor in the fall of the city. Only when the inhabitants were reduced by famine was a breach made in the walls. Zedekiah and his army fled, but were overtaken near Jericho. Zedekiah was blinded, and ended his days as a prisoner in Babylon.

A siege of eighteen months, even with a temporary reprieve,

[1] *Lachish I*, pp. 79–87.
[2] *Lachish III*, pp. 103–58.
[3] *Lachish I*, p. 51.
[4] Jeremiah 37:5.
[5] Jeremiah 39:2; II Kings 25:3.

is a clear tribute to the strength of the walls of Jerusalem. It is, of course, very possible that Nebuchadnezzar did not bother to deploy a great number of troops against it. Having overrun the rest of Judah, he could afford to encompass the city with siege-works[1] and wait for famine to do its work. Nebuchadnezzar himself did not direct the operation, for when the city fell, he was in Syria, in the kingdom of Hamath, Nevertheless, the walls were clearly strong enough to be a formidable obstacle to a normal field force. The only surviving evidence of the wall of the period is the length of 24 metres exposed at the base of Trench I and the extensions to the north (Pls. 20, 43, plan, fig. 26). It is probably typical of the wall along the eastern side of the town where both the original wall and that of the subsequent extension (see above, p. 89) were built well down the slope. Its great strength lay in its position with relation to the very steep slope. It has already been pointed out (above, p. 89) that it was so situated as not to be commanded by projectiles from the other side of the Siloam Valley. It could therefore only be attacked up the slope. The total surviving height of the wall as seen in Pl. 43 was below the internal level, built against the pre-existing fill and, with this solid packing, impervious to battering rams. Above the surviving portion, even a modest superstructure would have provided ample protection to the houses within, since the attackers had to approach from so much lower a level. On the east side, the wall probably stood on the crest of a scarp above the central valley (see above, p. 93), and thus again towered to an impressive height above the attackers, with again protection against battering rams in the solid rock basis. Physiographically, only the north side was weak, and it was very likely that the attack came from that direction, as it did in the Roman destruction in the first century A.D. Certainly, Zedekiah and his followers escaped from the south end of the city,[2] which would support this suggestion. There is, however, no archaeological evidence; in the very limited area of the wall

[1] II Kings 25:1.
[2] II Kings 25:4.

exposed, the destruction of the wall to the interior ground-level is more likely to have been caused by erosion than by enemy destruction.

After the capture of Jerusalem in 598 B.C., the city was plundered, but the Biblical account does not say that it was destroyed. Even the plundering was not apparently complete. The account in II Kings 24:13 says that the treasures of the Temple and palace were carried off, but only the gold vessels were specifically mentioned. After the capture in 587 B.C., the loot is described in II Kings 25:13–14 in much more detail, with special emphasis on the bronze fittings rather than on the gold, presumably already vanished.

> And the pillars of bronze that were in the house of the Lord, and the stands and the bronze sea that were in the house of the Lord, the Chaldeans broke in pieces, and carried the bronze to Babylon. And they took away the pots, and the shovels, and the snuffers, and the dishes for incense and all the vessels of bronze used in the temple service, the firepans also, and the bowls. What was of gold the captain of the guard took away as gold, and what was of silver, as silver. As for the two pillars, the one sea, and the stands, which Solomon had made for the house of the Lord, the bronze of all these vessels was beyond weight.

All the riches of the Temple were thus ruthlessly stripped off and carried away. It is strange that no mention is made of the Ark which had presumably been in the Holy of Holies since placed there by Solomon, though not thereafter mentioned. Perhaps its loss could never be explicitly admitted, but it is never heard of again.

The sacking of Jerusalem was this time followed by fire.[1] Nebuzaradan, the captain of the bodyguard, 'burned the house of the Lord, and the king's house and all the houses of Jerusalem; every great house he burned down'. More disastrously still, 'And all the army of the Chaldeans, who were with the captain of the

[1] II Kings 25:9.

guard, broke down the walls around Jerusalem' (II Kings 25:10). All the inhabitants save the poorest in the land were carried into exile.

The walls of the capital of a country that had revolted twice in ten years had obviously to be destroyed for political and military reasons. The effect on Jerusalem was much more disastrous and far-reaching than merely to render the city defenceless. The artificial substructure of the whole of that part of the city on the eastern slopes has already been described (above, p. 95). The whole system of terraces down the slope, dependent on retaining walls buttressed in turn by the fill of the next lower terrace, was ultimately dependent on the town wall at the base, forming the lowest and most substantial of the retaining walls. A breach in the town wall would let down the fill behind it, and the rains of a winter or so would spread the destruction far up the fill and on either side of the original breach. A vivid impression of this is given by the erosion channels produced on the slope today after a winter of heavy rains (Pl. 75), and every now and again during the excavations disconcerting finds of Roman pottery beneath intact Iron Age levels could in due course be traced to underground erosion tunnels through the loose tumble, such as can be seen in the modern erosion.

Within the area excavated, which at its base was a band *c.* 50 metres long, this erosion process brought down the whole of the east side of the town in the tumble of stones that is seen in Pl. 64. Since the contours of the rest of the eastern slope are similar, the erosion was probably universal. In all the lower part of the slope only the lower parts of the very substantial walls survived. The most dramatic evidence of the collapse process is seen in Squares A I–III just below the crest of the ridge. Here the tripartite house seen on Pl. 71 was found buried in rubble up to the top of the monoliths described above (p. 164). In fact, only half the house survives. The view in Pl. 71 shows that at the point where the second line of monoliths should have stood, the floor breaks away, and the steep tip-lines over its broken edge echo the resultant cascade down the slope, which followed the collapse of the retaining wall, originally Late Bronze Age, seen on the right in Pl. 30. The destruction of which this collapse is an example obliterated the whole eastern quarter of Jerusalem, and the eastern slope was never again included within the town.

CHAPTER TEN

★

The Post-Exilic Period

THE ACCOUNT IN II KINGS 25 is explicit that almost the entire population of Jerusalem was carried away into captivity in Babylon. In Jeremiah 52:28–30 the number given is, however, only a total of four thousand six hundred, which would, of course, be in addition to the number of the armed force that escaped with Zedekiah, many of whom were probably killed when the Babylonians overtook them in the Jordan Valley. The excavation evidence from many sites, for instance Tell Beit Mirsim, Beth Shemesh, and Tell Duweir, is that town and village life was severely disrupted. Tell Beit Mirsim, for instance, was abandoned, and on all other sites occupation was on a much-reduced scale. Judah was not, however, depopulated as Israel had been by the Assyrians, with the replacement of the northern tribes by exiles from other parts of the empire. Nebuchadnezzar appointed a Jew, Gedaliah, to be governor, with his headquarters at Mizpah, probably Tell Nasbeh, 6 miles north of Jerusalem. Jerusalem was therefore left in ruins, inhabited by some of the poorest of the land, left to be vinedressers and ploughmen.[1]

For the next seventy years, life in Palestine was uneasy and, on archaeological evidence, poverty-stricken. Gedaliah was murdered by Ishmael, leading a group opposed to collaboration with the Babylonians and backed by the king of the Ammonites. Many of those who had gathered round Gedaliah at Mizpah fled to Egypt for fear of Babylonian vengeance, in spite of the adjurations of Jeremiah, and were roundly denounced by him (Jeremiah 42–44). The Biblical record is blank thereafter until the

[1] II Kings 25:11.

seventy years of exile prophesied by Jeremiah had been completed.

Relief for the exiles in Babylon came with the achievement of empire by a new power in Mesopotamia. Babylon fell to Persia in *c.* 538 B.C., and Cyrus the Great became the ruler of the wide-flung Babylonian empire without, apparently, any opposition from the satellite petty states on the Mediterranean littoral. There is ample evidence that the Persians ruled the races subject to them in an enlightened way, with an intelligent assessment that you have less trouble from subject races if you do not interfere with, and even give support to, the beliefs which to the group concerned are of very great importance. An element of syncretism is certainly involved, but an element that was acceptable to both parties.

Ezra 1:1-4 gives the Jewish version of the instructions of Cyrus to the Jewish exiles in Babylon to return to Jerusalem:

> Thus says Cyrus king of Persia: The Lord, the God of heaven, has given me all the kingdoms of the earth, and he has charged me to build him a house at Jerusalem, which is in Judah. Whoever is among you of all his people, may his God be with him, and let him go up to Jerusalem, which is in Judah, and rebuild the house of the Lord, the God of Israel – he is the God, who is in Jerusalem.

The account suggested that all those of the Jewish exiles who did not return to Jerusalem should give material support to the more ardent members of the community who did return. The contributions of the Persian ruler were of almost unbelievable generosity: the presentation of the vessels looted from Jerusalem by Nebuchadnezzar (Ezra 1:7-11).

The subsequent chapters of the book of Ezra indicate the response of the exiles to the challenge of a return to their homeland (Ezra 1:5-11), involving a hard life in comparison with the luxuries and civilization of Babylon. If the lists in Ezra 2 can be relied upon, people from a very wide tribal, village, and town background took the opportunity to return; exact numbers, giving a total adding up to 42,360, cannot be relied upon too greatly, but the overall impression is probably correct. One can therefore accept a position that in the last third of the sixth century B.C. the inhabitants who had remained after the Babylonians had carried off all except the poorest in the land (II Kings 25:12), and after the flight of a large group to Egypt as described in Jeremiah 42–44, received a very great stimulus from the return of the descendants of the élite that had been carried away into exile.

It was of very great importance for the history of the Jews and of the Jewish religion that the nucleus of the exiles had continued to live as a group, people for whom their religion remained the most important thing surviving to them in their life by the 'waters of Babylon' where they 'sat down and wept when we remembered Zion' (Psalm 137.1) in a strange and unclean land (Ezekiel 5:13). The observance of the Sabbath and and maintenance of the circumcision took on importance as distinguishing the Israelites from the races amongst which they lived. But above all for their religion a return to Jerusalem was necessary, for in the reforms of Josiah in the seventh century and the teaching enshrined in the Book of Deuteronomy, Yahweh could only be worshipped in Jerusalem. The return of the exiles from Babylon not only brought back to Judah the descendants of the literate upper class, but provided to that part of the population, no doubt numerically much larger, that had remained in the land, a great religious stimulus.

As far as public buildings were concerned, the exiles returning to Jerusalem concentrated first on the rebuilding of the Temple. This was Cyrus's mandate to them, and one cannot doubt that the devoted band that returned to a hard life in Jerusalem was inspired by religious motives. Moreover, it is improbable that, tolerant as were the Persians, they would encourage such a recalcitrant subject race as the Jews to rebuild the defences of their old royal capital.

The efforts of the returned exiles to rebuild the Temple had to overcome many obstacles. The first step was to resume sacrifices at 'the altar of the God of Israel' (Ezra 3:2). In the second year after the return from exile, the rebuilding of the foundations of the Temple was begun (Ezra 3:8ff). It is interesting to note that the new builders had recourse to 'the Sidonians and the Tyrians to bring cedar trees from Lebanon to the sea, to Joppa' (Ezra 3:7) just as had Solomon in building the first Temple.

At this stage, the Biblical record (Ezra 4:1–3) brings into prominence the sense of exclusiveness of the returned exiles. They believed that they alone had maintained unsullied the true religion of Yahweh. They refused to allow the inhabitants of the old northern kingdom of Israel, racially contaminated by the immigrants transplanted after the Assyrian absorption of Israel at the end of the eighth century B.C., to have any share in the rebuilding of the Temple. Ideologically, this narrow attitude is comprehensible, but it laid up a lot of trouble for the struggling revival of a Jewish state. Ezra 4:4–24 describes the complaints and warnings sent by the northerners down to the time of Ahasuerus (Xerxes) and Artaxerces, which hindered the work on the Temple. No doubt there was also the competing need for families to build their own houses which may have militated against complete zeal to rebuild the Temple. Only after the accession of Darius in 522 B.C. did the returned exiles in Jerusalem succeed in persuading the Persian chancery to search for the document by which Cyrus authorized the rebuilding of the Temple. The document, found in Ecbatana, one of the Persian capitals, is quoted in Ezra 6:2–5.[1] Darius gave emphatic orders that the decree of Cyrus was to be honoured (Ezra 6:6–12), and the rebuilding of the Temple was resumed, spurred on by the words of the prophet Haggai, who referred scathingly to the diversion of the activities of the inhabitants to building their own houses (Haggai 1:3–6).

Impelled by the persistence of Haggai, work on the Temple was resumed in 520 B.C. The man in charge of the work was

[1] For a discussion of Cyrus's edict see Roland de Vaux, *The Bible and the Ancient Near East*, 'The Decrees of Cyrus and Darius on the Rebuilding of the Temple', pp. 63–96.

Zerubbabel, a man of royal Davidic lineage, the grandson of Jehoiachin, the penultimate king of Judah. His status was that of a Persian official, governor in Jerusalem, and possibly in Judah, but subordinate to the governor of the main Persian province of the lands that once comprised the kingdom of Israel and Judah, which was centred in the province of Samaria. It can readily be inferred from the writings of the prophets Haggai and Zechariah that the hope was stirring that this descendant of the royal house of David would be a Messiah to re-establish the kingdom of Yahweh on earth and a temporal kingdom of Israel.

There is nothing in the Biblical record to suggest that Zerubbabel saw himself in such a light, and it is quite certain that after an initial year of putting down threats from competitors for power, the recurrent theme of all ancient empires, Darius was far too firmly in charge for the Israelites, a minuscule group in the scale of the Persian empire, to have the slightest chance of re-establishing a temporal power. Zerubbabel's place in history is simply that of the man who achieved the rebuilding of the Temple, a second Temple of rather humble character (Haggai 2:3) that intervened, with many changes of fortune, between the Solomonic Temple and the third Temple built by Herod the Great in the last third of the first century B.C. The rebuilding was completed in the sixth year of the reign of Darius, 515 B.C.

In Chapter 6, the only structural evidence concerning Zerubbabel's rebuilding of the Temple has been described. This is the straight joint that separates the Herodian addition to the south end of the temple platform (see above, p. 111) from an earlier wall to the north of masonry with much heavier bosses. This wall of the platform that preceded that of Herod can reasonably be taken to be that built by Zerubbabel, for no reconstruction of the Temple could have been attempted without making good the platform that converted the narrow top of the ridge into a level area adequate for the building and its courts (see above, p. 111) and fig. 21). Zerubbabel was probably faced by a situation in which the Babylonian destruction of the Temple by fire had largely destroyed the actual building, vulnerable because of the great amount of timber it contained, and the destruction of the walls of Jerusalem (II Kings 25:10) is likely to have involved those of the temple platform, at least on the east side, for the probability is that they formed also the eastern wall of the city (see above, p. 145). Breaches in the platform wall would, in the years of poverty following the exile of the leaders to Babylon, have resulted in erosion and spreading collapse, as elsewhere on the east side of the city (see above, p. 170), and it was this that Zerubbabel had to repair before even the foundations of the Temple itself could be relaid.

One can nevertheless take it as certain that Zerubbabel's work was based on Solomon's foundations. Ruined as it was, the Temple had remained in existence. In the sixty years of the exile it was still the religious centre of the 'poorest in the land', probably in fact the larger part of the population of the former kingdom of Judah. Still more striking is the fact that inhabitants of the former kingdom of Israel, racially mixed though they were, also came there to offer sacrifices, as recorded in Jeremiah 41:4:

> On the day after the murder of Gedaliah, before anyone knew of it, eighty men arrived from Shechem and Shiloh and Samaria, with their beards shaved and their clothes torn, and their bodies gashed, bringing cereal offerings and incense to present at the temple of the Lord.

The task of Zerubbabel was therefore that of putting this Temple in order again. In the account of the Solomonic Temple in Chapter 6, the assumption is made that Zerubbabel made use of the surviving Solomonic walls. This is likely, on grounds both of piety and of economy of effort. It is therefore assumed that the ground plan of the supporting platform was that described above (pp. 112–14). The surviving masonry, to the right of the straight joint in Pl. 35, is likely to be in origin that of Zerubbabel, though an analysis of the courses visible suggests that there may be about three styles possibly representing rebuilds during the stormy life of Zerubbabel's Temple. The link of this masonry style, characterized by largish stones with heavy, irregular bosses, with that current in Phoenicia to the north from the sixth to the fourth centuries B.C. is illustrated in the surviving remains of the great platform of the Temple at Eshmoun, dated to the late sixth century B.C.[1] The account of the building of the post-Exilic Temple does not record that recourse was had to artisans from Phoenicia, as had been the case for the Solomonic Temple. It is, however, specifically stated (Ezra 3:7) that the wood was brought from Tyre and Sidon, and it is very probable that the necessary artisans were also sought there, for no other scrap of wall surviving from post-Exilic Jerusalem suggests any comparable skill in stonework. The resemblance between the walls of the temple platform at Jerusalem and those of the Persian period in Phoenicia is easily comprehensible on these grounds.

The lack of any archaeological evidence of Zerubbabel's actual temple building merely echoes that concerning Solomon's Temple and is repeated by that concerning Herod's Temple. Not a stone survives that can be attributed to any of the successive Temples. Even the literary evidence for that of Zerubbabel is scanty. In Ezra 6:4 it is stated that the rebuilt Temple was to be sixty cubits (c. 30 metres) long, which was the length of the Solomonic Temple (I Kings 6:2), and sixty cubits wide, whereas the Solomonic Temple was only twenty cubits wide. This substitution of a square building for a relatively narrow rectangle, with its build-up of successive halls to the Holy of Holies, is improbable, and likely to be a scribal error; but this is the only record we have. Since the Ark had disappeared without mention, it might be claimed that the Holy of Holies had no function, but it is certain that it still played a part in the rebuild. The description noticeably lacks the exotic appurtenances of the pillars and basins of bronze of its predecessor, recorded in II Kings 25:13 as having been cut to pieces in 587 B.C. Only the gold and silver vessels returned by Cyrus (Ezra 1:7–11; 5:14–15, a gift confirmed by Darius; Ezra 6:5) are mentioned as fittings. Some impression

[1] Maurice Dunand, Supplement to *Vetus Testamentum*, VII. 'Byblos, Sidon, Jerusalem', pp. 64–70. The relationship with the Jerusalem wall is discussed here and in Kenyon, *Mélanges Université Saint-Joseph*, XLVI, pp. 140 ff.

of the relative poverty of the rebuilt Temple is implicit in the tears of those who remembered the first Temple when they saw the first stages of its successor (Ezra 3 :12).

There is little evidence, either archaeological or literary, concerning what else was done in rebuilding Jerusalem, nor indeed any evidence of either sort concerning the next sixty years or so. There was, of course, no question of rebuilding the palace, for there was no longer a king. This must in fact have added stature to the Temple, for it was no longer part of a complex which included the abode of the king, with a certain element in its conception of a royal chapel, as the combined and interlocked description of Solomon's building operations might imply. The priests in the Temple had been royal officials, and it is only now that the 'High Priest' becomes the leader of the nation.

One can certainly take it that the returned exiles rebuilt the dwellings in Jerusalem, an operation that can well be compared with the 'post-Blitz' restoration of London in the 1940s and 1950s. The ruins of Jerusalem were less devastated than those of London, since fire and not high explosives was involved. In most cases, roofs, floors, and contents provided the combustible elements. In the chief centres of destruction, the walls of stone may have been so calcined that they could no longer support the weight of superstructures. Elsewhere, all that was required is likely to have been new roofs and floors. In any case, it was only the houses of the rich that had been burnt; in II Kings 25:9 it is said of Nebuchadnezzar's captain of the bodyguard that 'every great house he burned down'. This suggests a selective destruction rather than a wide-sweeping 'Fire of London' (in the A.D. 1666 sense), which involved a far more combustible town. One can therefore accept as probable that quite a lot of the domestic buildings of Jerusalem survived (except those on the eastern slope): the hovels and the least important possibly completely, the medium-scale houses probably capable of easy repairs, only the grand houses seriously destroyed. Quite apart from the inherent probabilities, there are two Biblical references in support; in Haggai 1:4 is the complaint that the returned exiles are living in 'panelled houses' and in Haggai 1:9 the prophet denounces the people: that while the House of the Lord still lay in ruins 'you busy yourselves each with his own house'. Still more important, for it bears on one's interpretation of the next stage, is the recognition that certain houses owned by well-known men provided topographical landmarks for the ultimate rebuilding of the city walls.

The suspicions of the neighbouring groups, already referred to in connection with the rebuilding of the Temple, would have made the Persians hesitate to permit the rebuilding of the walls of Jerusalem in the sixth century even if they had been to that degree complaisant. There is no clear evidence why, seventy years later (see below), they allowed this to be done. The rebuilding of the walls was the work of Nehemiah, sent as governor to Jerusalem in the twentieth year of Artaxerxes (Nehemiah 2:1), Nehemiah being a Jew whose family had remained at the Persian Court till that point, but who was in touch with the Jews in Jerusalem. The date of Nehemiah's mission can be disputed, for the reigns of Artaxerxes I, Artaxerxes II, and Artaxerxes III were of sufficient length to provide a twentieth year. There is also the complication of the chronological relationship of Nehemiah and Ezra. The strong probability is that it was during the reign of Artaxerxes I that Nehemiah was sent to Jerusalem, the date of his arrival being thus c. 445 B.C., and that his activities must be placed before those of Ezra.[1] It can be suggested that stresses in maintaining Persian rule in Egypt made it advisable to make friendly gestures to the minor groups fringing the routes to Egypt.[2]

There has been a gap of something like 140 years during which Digging up Jerusalem has had little to contribute to the history of the city, apart from the single fact of the straight joint in the foundations of the temple platform. The story of the intervening period has had to be built up from the interlocking Biblical records, II Kings, Jeremiah, Haggai, Ezra; most of them written, or at least edited, during this and later

[1] *Noth*, pp. 318–20.
[2] ibid., p. 313.

periods. With the activities of Nehemiah, archaeology can again establish a link with, and contribute to, the literary evidence.

Nehemiah's activities are recorded in the Book of Nehemiah, which in the first six chapters, concerned with rebuilding the wall of Jerusalem, is written in the first person. The resulting record gives a vivid impression of actuality. Nehemiah's first act was to survey the state of the walls of Jerusalem, which he did with very little delay:

> So I came to Jerusalem and was there three days. Then I arose in the night, I and a few men with me; and I told no one what my God had put into my heart to do for Jerusalem. There was no beast with me but the beast on which I rode. I went out by night by the Valley Gate to the Jackal's well and to the Dung Gate; and I inspected the walls of Jerusalem which were broken down and its gates which had been destroyed by fire. (Nehemiah 2:11–13)

This whole procedure is so eminently realistic that one must accept it as a factual record in an historical document. For those who have to try to relate the literary evidence to the archaeological evidence, the problem is that the landmarks listed in the description of the account (Nehemiah 2:13–15) cannot be securely identified. There is one point of which one may be reasonably certain, and that is the King's Pool. There is little doubt that this is the Pool of Siloam, constructed by King Hezekiah, and lying beside the tip of the eastern ridge. It was at that point that Nehemiah ran into difficulties.

> Then I went on to the Fountain Gate and to the King's Pool; but there was no place for the beast that was under me to pass. Then I went up in the night by the valley and inspected the wall; and I turned back and entered by the Valley Gate, and so returned. (Nehemiah 2:14–16)

The account is somewhat elliptical. It was presumably *after* he reached the King's Pool, and therefore at the point at which the circuit of the walls turned northward up the Kedron Valley that his way was barred. At this point, archaeology can throw very revealing light. The complex nature of the buildings of Jerusalem on the east side, and their vulnerability to enemy attacks, natural disasters, and decay have been sufficiently described (see above, p. 95). The tumble of stones uncovered by our Trench 1 (Pl. 64; p. 170) is a vivid sample of the ruinous state of the eastern side of Jerusalem that baulked Nehemiah's donkey. The event shows that the sight of this cascade of stones persuaded Nehemiah that he could not attempt to restore the quarter of Jerusalem on the eastern slope of the eastern ridge, or the wall that had enclosed it.

Nehemiah's next step was to persuade the whole community to play its part in rebuilding the walls of Jerusalem (Nehemiah 2:17–20), and the success of his persuasion is recorded in Nehemiah 3. Defined lengths and the associated gates were assigned to family groups, resident in Jerusalem or recruited from the rest of Judah, or to professions such as the priests, the goldsmiths, or the merchants. In spite of threats from hostile neighbours to the north and east, the work of rebuilding was completed in fifty-two days (Nehemiah 6:15). It has hitherto been taken that this remarkable achievement shows that Nehemiah was able to base his work on very considerable surviving elements of the wall of the period of the monarchy. The references in Nehemiah 3 defining lengths of wall built by references to named gates, presumably pre-existing gates and therefore belonging to the period of the monarchy, support this theory. The archaeological evidence from the excavations on the eastern side of the eastern ridge makes it clear that this interpretation does not apply to the wall low on the eastern slope. It is absolutely certain that no buildings on the slope, post-Exilic, Hellenistic, or Roman, succeeded the great tumble of stones that marked the final collapse of the Jebusite-Israelite terraces. Indeed, the whole reason for including the eastern slope, unattractively steep, had disappeared when the Spring Gihon in the Kedron Valley ceased to be vital as a water-supply; the Gihon waters themselves were now conveyed by Hezekiah's tunnel to the central valley, aqueducts may have brought in water from the south-west, and the construction of efficient cisterns was an easy matter with the use of lime mortar. A further reason to accept a limitation in area was shortage of population. In Nehemiah 7:4 it is said: 'The city is wide and large but the people within it were few and no houses had been built'. Nehemiah had to bring into the city inhabitants of all the districts of Judah, chosen by lot (Nehemiah 11:1–2).

Our excavations have in fact identified a wall that can be attributed to Nehemiah. I have already referred to the walls and towers on the crest of the eastern ridge found by our predecessors in the area covered by our Squares A I–III, and XXIII (fig. 28). The most prominent and most famous is the so-called Davidic Tower, dismissed on p. 77 above as centuries post-David, and still not reached at our present chronological stage. North of this tower is the so-called 'Jebusite ramp' (Pl. 76),[1] which visual observation shows is later than the tower (Pl. 41; see below, p. 192). To the north again is a smaller tower, built against a wall of roughly trimmed masonry founded on the summit of a rock scarp (Pl. 79). The structural succession makes it clear that this wall is the earliest of those on the crest of the eastern slope. Our trench A XVIII (opposite P on fig. 28) showed that against the scarp upon which this wall was built, and overlying tumbled masonry derived from the Babylonian destruction of important buildings of the period of the monarchy,[2] was a series of midden tip-lines, lapping up against the foot of the wall on top of the scarp, material that must have been tipped over the wall. The finds in this midden material belong to one of the rather dim periods for which archaeologists in Palestine have not yet produced precise dating criteria. My provisional conclusion based on the evidence (and firm conclusion that this interpretation is right, for it fits in with the rest of the historical evidence) is that the chronological bracket is fifth to early third centuries B.C., and I am very content

1 Macalister, *APEF* IV, facing p. 40.
2 *PEQ*, 1963, p. 16, Pl. VIII B.

to accept that this material represents refuse thrown over the wall built by Nehemiah *c.* 440 B.C.

This evidence that on the eastern side Nehemiah's wall did not follow the line of the wall of the period of the monarchy does, in fact, receive support from the Biblical record. In the 1962 season, in which these facts concerning the wall on the crest of the eastern slope were emerging, we had by good luck as one of our site supervisors a student of the Ecole Biblique, Roger Dieny, whose thesis for the Ecole was the Jerusalem of Nehemiah. He was very much intrigued by the new evidence, and gave it careful consideration. His conclusion was so obvious that it seems incredible that no one had thought of it before. A long catalogue of the sections built by individuals, leaders, towns, is based on lengths of the wall defined by gates with recognizable location. For instance

> Hanum and the inhabitants of Zanoah repaired the Valley Gate; they rebuilt it and set its doors, its bolts and its bars, and repaired a thousand cubits of the wall as far as the Dung Gate. Malchiazah the son of Rechab, ruler of the district of Beth-haccherem repaired the Dung Gate; he rebuilt it and set up its doors, its bolts and its bars. (Nehemiah 3:13–14)

There is then a clear break. Such defining points thereafter as are given are the houses of individual householders:

> After him their brethren repaired: Bavvai the son of Henadad, ruler of half the district of Keilah; next to him Ezer the son of Jeshua, ruler of Mizpah, repaired another section opposite the ascent to the armoury at the Angle. After him Baruch the son of Zabbai repaired another section from the Angle to the door of the house of Eliasib the high priest. After him Meremoth the son of Uriah, son of Hakkoz repaired another section from the door of the house of Eliasib to the end of the house of Eliasib. After him, the priests, the men of the Plain, repaired. After them Benjamin and Hashub repaired opposite their house. After them Azariah the son of

Maseiah, son of Ananiah repaired beside his own house . . . .
(Nehemiah 3:18–23)

and so on. I have quoted at some length, both to emphasize the
efficient gang system employed by Nehemiah and to show how
the record delimits in this second stretch the sections assigned to
the various groups.

Roger Dieny was quite satisfied that the sections just mentioned
come on the eastern side of the town. The archaeological evidence
therefore fits the literary evidence very well. The ruinous terraces on the eastern slope were abandoned and the eastern wall
built along the crest of the ridge to the north of the north wall
of the Jebusite-Davidic town, using the line established by
Solomon's extension which joined the Davidic town to the
Temple. To the west side of the eastern ridge belongs the length
of the wall where the earlier gates were still identifiable; the
account in fact suggests that most of the building concerned the
gates, which is very probable, since enemy destruction would be
particularly concentrated upon them. It is suggested above
(p. 93) that the Jebusite-Davidic wall followed the western crest
of the eastern ridge, and the archaeological evidence is clear that
this was the line that the post-Exilic wall followed. A point of
uncertainty is what happened to the late expansion onto the
lower slopes of the western ridge, revealed by excavations still
in progress (see above, p. 148). I have not heard of any evidence
that the seventh-century B.C. occupation here was followed by
anything belonging to the earlier post-Exilic periods, fifth to
early third centuries B.C. It seems quite possible that this excres-
cence from the enlarged Jerusalem of Solomon was abandoned,
as were the eastern slopes, in Nehemiah's rebuilding, taking place
in great haste owing to the hostility of neighbours (Nehemiah
4:7–23), and needing to provide for a much reduced population
(see above, p. 183). I have not therefore seen any reason as yet to
revise my plan of post-Exilic Jerusalem, produced on the evidence
of the 1961–67 excavations (fig. 28).

This plan represents what I believe to be the evidence for the

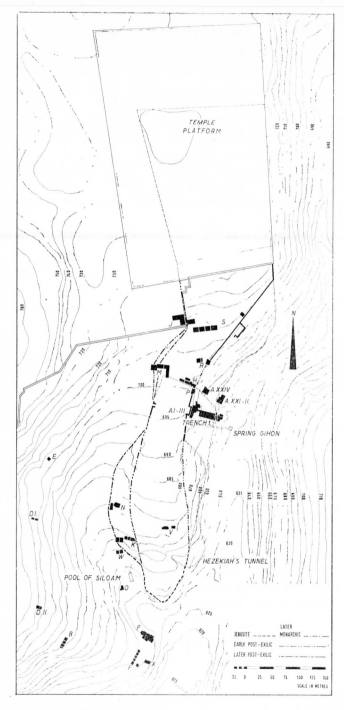

FIG 28   Plan of Post-Exilic Jerusalem

first walled city of Jerusalem in the period succeeding the Babylonian exile, a Jerusalem dominated by the Temple, re-created in its original dimensions; materially it was impoverished, but politically the Temple and the priests had grown vastly in stature. On the material plane, there was no longer a king's palace. Regrettably, we have no archaeological evidence owing to quarrying as to the buildings that took the place in later periods of those that I have suggested (above, p. 127) were administrative buildings of a Solomonic Royal Quarter.

Nehemiah's rebuilding of the walls of Jerusalem comes at a halfway point in the history of the Persian rule of the great Mesopotamian-based empire of western Asia. Palestine had no particular importance at this period, save as fringing the route to Egypt. Within the province that included Judah there were no important events. The period for Palestine is an historical blank and as far as Jerusalem is concerned, it is also an archaeological blank. It was a period of very great importance in the development of Israelite law and religion,[1] but archaeology has no contribution to make on this subject. The next archaeological evidence concerns the Maccabean period.

[1] *Noth*, pp. 338–43.

★

CHAPTER ELEVEN

Jerusalem in the Hellenistic Period and the Time of the Maccabees

AFTER THE DEFEAT of the Persians by Alexander at the battle of Issus in 333 B.C., Palestine fell into Alexander's hands with little opposition, and until the first century B.C. officially formed part of one of the Hellenistic empires. In the third century B.C., Jerusalem and Judah were within the sphere of the Egyptian Ptolemaic empire, with its capital at Alexandria. Alexandria in fact became a centre of Judaism second only to Jerusalem, and the centre where the translation of the accepted books of the Old Testament into Greek, known as the Septuagint, took place at this time. It was still recognized, however, that Jerusalem was the cult centre, and there was no foreign interference in the cult of Yahweh there. The scanty archaeological evidence gives no indication that Greek culture had any influence there at this time. Palestine-Syria was, however, an area of conflict and dispute between the Ptolemies of Egypt and the Seleucids who ruled northern Syria and Mesopotamia from their capital of Antioch-on-the-Orontes, and in 198 B.C. Palestine passed finally into the sphere of Seleucid influence. The material evidence suggests that there was no great change. Jerusalem pursued its own way, little influenced by outside cultures.

This last sentence is the essence of my conclusion concerning the culture of Jerusalem during the fifth to second centuries B.C. When we embarked on the excavation of Jerusalem, we knew that we ought to find remains of the periods in which it was certain from the evidence of, for instance, the books of

Nehemiah, Ezra, and Maccabees and the works of Josephus that there was full occupation and activity in Jerusalem. I felt confident that I could assess the evidence for this period without much difficulty, for my first introduction to Palestinian archaeology had been at Samaria, and I had a large share in the study and publication of the pottery and other finds. I could not have been more wrong. There is barely any connection between the pottery and other material remains of Jerusalem and Samaria. The latter site was rapidly Hellenized. One's interpretation of the pottery can be founded on the pottery of the Greek mainland, though many vessels were certainly local copies. These Greek-based vessels barely occur in Jerusalem; the few black-glazed or black-washed vessels were always worthy of special comment. Jerusalem remained right down to the first century B.C. quite firmly outside the material culture of the Hellenistic world. A sole, very curious, exception is that we found a considerable number of Rhodian jar handles; the xenophobic population of Jerusalem was apparently not averse to drinking Rhodian wine.

This difference between Jerusalem and Samaria to the north has its roots far back in history, and more immediately in the Assyrian introduction into the northern kingdom of elements from elsewhere to replace the population carried into exile. The inhabitants of Jerusalem and Judah, who had suffered a less disruptive exile, refused to accept as equals the mixed groups inhabiting the northern kingdom. The break between those worshipping Yahweh at the Temple in Jerusalem and the inhabitants of the northern area became acute with the establishment of the Samaritan sanctuary on Mount Gerizim as a rival centre for the worship of Yahweh, probably early in the third century B.C.[1] The religious break has a strong foundation in the cultural break, for which the archaeological evidence is clear.

On p. 187 above I said that the next archaeological evidence concerned the period of the Maccabees, but I have digressed to emphasize the extent to which during this whole period, post-Exilic to (in general Near Eastern terms) Hellenistic, the material

[1] On the chronology of this foundation, see *Noth*, pp. 351–6.

culture of Jerusalem was self-centred, not incorporating or accepting much from adjacent areas and, regrettably, not producing anything that can be recognized as an indigenous material culture.

Archaeology can thus offer very little to illustrate the way of life in Jerusalem during the post-Exilic-Hellenistic period. Historically, however, the second century B.C. marks a new stage in the history of Jerusalem and Judah, with the advent of the native Maccabean rulers, and for this stage excavations have produced some structural evidence.

There were two main elements in the emergence of Maccabean rule in Jerusalem: the decline in power of the Seleucid empire and the conflict in Jerusalem between Hellenizing influences and the orthodox followers of Yahweh. Antiochus IV Epiphanes, who seized power in 175 B.C., was induced to interfere in the quarrels between the opposing groups and in due course carried his interference, in 169 B.C., to the extent of attacking Jerusalem, destroying its walls, and establishing a fortress, the Akra, to dominate the town. In 167 B.C. he took the still more drastic step of abolishing the worship of Yahweh and setting up a cult of Zeus Olympius. The revolt against this terrible sacrilege was led by the Hasmonean family, first by Mattathias and then by his son Judas, whose nickname Maccabeus came to be applied to the whole movement. His remarkable military success against the weakened Seleucid power established the Maccabean rule of Jerusalem, and eventually of Judah.

The next twenty-five years or so constitute a period of intrigue and counter-intrigue, with, on the whole, a gradual build-up of Maccabean power. In 141 B.C. Simon, another of the sons of Mattathias, at last reduced the fortress of the Akra, and foreign military interference was thus removed from Jerusalem, and Jerusalem was refortified. The heyday of Maccabean rule was the reigns of Simon (142–134 B.C.), John Hyrcanus (134–104 B.C.), Alexander Jannaeus (103–76 B.C.), and Salome Alexandra (76–67 B.C.). For about eighty years, the Maccabees tried to build up a new kingdom that could rival that of David and Solomon. The successive rulers fought many wars, and at times, due to the weakness of the imperial powers, their conquests brought many parts of the ancient kingdom under their control. The whole basis of their position was, however, shaky, for a number of reasons: the fluctuations in the strength and policy of the imperial powers; the fratricidal struggle for power that is one of the least attractive features of the period to modern eyes; and the fact that there was a hard core of conservative followers of the religion of Yahweh, of which the adherents disapproved of temporal power and, in the increasingly apocalyptic vision of the period, wished to wait the institution of divine rule.

As far as the history of Jerusalem is concerned, we have, therefore, from the period from 167 B.C. a strong growth of opposition to foreign rule and from 141 B.C. the firm establishment of native rule, with a relatively strong native rule lasting until the advent of the Romans in 63 B.C. It is likely that to this period all the structures that the 1961–67 excavations have traced as additions to the first post-Exilic town fortified by Nehemiah in c. 440 B.C. belong. I cannot yet be as precise as I hope that ultimately I shall be as to the dating of the additions to Nehemiah's town, for this depends on the detailed analysis of the finds.[1] The evidence concerning the defences of the eastern ridge is relatively clear. Nehemiah's wall along the crest was strengthened and repaired in a number of places, there being three examples of this in the distance of 50 metres cleared at the top of Trench I.

The earliest was a small tower seen in Pl. 77, built over the partly ruined top of Nehemiah's wall, in the area where Nehemiah's wall was first identified securely (see above, p. 183). It was built, as can be seen on the left of Pl 79, on top of a midden deposit containing pottery of the fifth-fourth centuries B.C., but

---

[1] I have said this so often that I feel some apologia is required. I should have had a gap of, say, seven years instead of three between Jericho and Jerusalem. As it is, I am still (1972) finishing off Jericho before starting on the Jerusalem finds. In an ideal situation, one would have innumerable stooges (or one could upgrade them to Research Assistants), but British archaeology does not provide the finance. Therefore Jerusalem must wait until I have finished Jericho.

cannot be more precisely dated, since the earlier excavations had cleared the fill against its face.

The second is the massive tower considered by Macalister in the 1923–25 excavations to have been added to the Jebusite wall after the capture of the city by David. Plate 78 shows how it was in fact constructed on top of the seventh-century B.C. houses destroyed in 587 B.C. (see above, p. 170). Macalister had trenched along the face of the wall, thus cutting the levels associated with it and removing the foundation trench that must have cut into the layer of debris sloping up against the wall on the crest of the hill. The line of the slope can, however, be deduced from the character of the masonry on the north face of the tower, seen in Pl. 81, about half-way up the surviving height of the wall.[1] The level of pre-existing debris seems to have sloped down somewhat to the south. It is therefore clear that much of what survives was foundational, and that the formidable task of building out from the crest of the hill involved sinking foundations down to the first solid fill, in this case the seventh-century ruins. Though Macalister's trench cut most of the contemporary surface, and removed the foundation trench, the line of the surface could be traced at one point. Beneath it were coins and pottery down to the second century B.C. The tower is therefore certainly Maccabean, and a suitable context would be the activities of Jonathan who, c. 143 B.C., according to I Maccabees XII, gave orders 'to make the walls of Jerusalem higher'.

The third structure is that called by Macalister 'the Jebusite Ramp'. Seen today, it is a most curious structure, seeming to provide a convenient staircase up to the top of the wall for any attacker from the east. This is an illusion, for most of the regularity and step-like structure is due to restoration work carried out by the Department of Antiquities in an attempt to preserve Macalister's discoveries. Secondly, the whole of the structure was certainly below ground-level. This can be seen in Pl. 81, on

---

[1] It should be noted that the top course at the angle and up to three courses further south were rebuilt by the Department of Antiquities after the excavation.

which the line on the north face of the tower indicating the ground-level has already been pointed out; the 'ramp' starts just at that point. The 'ramp' can in fact be interpreted as a buttressing of a weak point in the defences, at which probably a wash-out of the type so familiar in this area of ancient Jerusalem (see above, p. 170) had occurred. A collapse caused by such a wash-out could well be referred to in the same passage in I Maccabees XII: 'and there fell down part of the wall of the brook that is on the east side'. If the building of the tower can in fact be ascribed to Jonathan, this could be the actual collapse described, for, as can be seen on Pl. 81, the structure is certainly later than the tower; it is curious that Macalister reversed this order.

The building operations of the Maccabean rulers that have been identified on the east side were confined to repairing Nehemiah's defences. On the west side they included some extension of the area of the city. The main evidence for this comes from Site K, supported by that of Site N immediately to the north (see plan, fig. 29). The central valley is here very much silted up. On Pl. 82, its line is joined by the path leading down the hill which in the foreground is marked by the trees. This line can also be seen in the air photograph (Pl. 12) above the small dark patch indicating the area of the Pool of Siloam. In Pl. 82, the line of the summit scarp is beneath the upper house just to the right of the cypress and behind the lower house farther right. In front of this line, the modern contours suggest a terrace bulging out into the valley, to a point between the cypress and the electric-light pole. Excavation in fact proved this terrace to be ancient, and to belong to the Maccabean period. In front of the lower house, rock was only about a metre below the modern surface. On the western side of the area it was at 10·75 metres below that surface. The terrace had been created by the construction of a massive wall on the west side. A width of 3·50 metres of its top was uncovered (Pl. 83), but it was impossible to expose its outer face, since it ran beneath the road down the valley. There is little doubt that it was both the town wall and the retaining wall of a considerable new area added to the town. Within it was a series of massive foundations, carried *c.* 5·25 metres below floor-level. One can conclude that there was a building of importance, perhaps public, in this new area; the deepness of the foundations was required by the fact that the whole area was made ground. The date of this building was late second–early first centuries B.C. The plan on fig. 29 gives the suggested curve of this addition to the city which at this point reaches a width of 37 metres; its curve round to the south to rejoin the main ridge north of the Pool of Siloam is suggested by the modern contours. Only in a few pockets in the rock was any Iron Age pottery found in the whole of Site K, up to the summit scarp; this is one of the points showing that on the west side the Iron Age town did not extend down the slope of the valley. Above the original walls was another series of very deep foundations, dating to the first century B.C., which like their predecessors had been destroyed by a collapse of the outer retaining wall.

The next point to the north at which there is an indication of the line of the Maccabean wall is in the area 75 metres south of Site M on fig. 29, in which J. W. Crowfoot in 1927 identified a gate built in massive but rough masonry.[1] Because of the character of the masonry, Crowfoot considered that the gate must have been in origin Bronze Age, and therefore Jebusite. The identification as Maccabean of the walls on the eastern crest shows that this criterion does not apply, and therefore makes comprehensible the find of a hoard of coins of Alexander Jannaeus (103–76 B.C.), which Crowfoot had to explain away by assuming that the gateway was kept clear and there was no rise in surface for twelve hundred years or more. One can in fact interpret it as a gate in use in the Maccabean period. There is not adequate evidence to say whether it was built in that period. From the style of masonry, it could have belonged to the time of Nehemiah, but it is suggested above (p. 185) that on the west side Nehemiah followed the line of the wall of the period of the monarchy, which

[1] *APEF* V, 1927, pp. 12–13.

should be further up the slope; there is certainly no indication
of an Israelite wall at this point.

Site M, 75 metres to the north, provided confirmatory evidence.
At the east end of the site was found a fill of tenth-century B.C.
date associated with Solomon's enlargement of the city (see above,
p. 116). This was cut by a wall of first-century B.C. date, but
beneath it and to the west were walls of the second–first centuries
B.C. which ran up to a wall 9 metres farther west, based on rock
8·85 metres lower than that at the east end of the trench. We
have therefore here an indication of the line of the Maccabean
wall.

Up to this point it is possible to say with some confidence that
the Tyropoeon Valley was not included within the city. There
is no further definite evidence in the area between Site M and the
walls of the Old City. I have already mentioned (above, p. 116)
my hypothesis that the line of Solomon's extension is that followed
by the section of the south wall of the Old City that forms a
salient from the wall of Herod's temple platform; the stratigraphical reasons for this suggestion are described below (pp.
221–2). The line of the post-Exilic wall could well have run to
join this earlier wall.

The evidence of a Maccabean town wall on the western side
of the eastern ridge at least as far north as Site M (plan, fig. 29)
fits in well with the evidence from Sites E, D I, D II, B, and F
(fig. 29) that there was no trace of occupation on the eastern
slopes of the western ridge until the first century A.D. It seems
certain that the Tyropoeon Valley at least as far north as site M
was outside the city.

There remains the problem of the extension of the town onto
the western ridge. Herod's buildings there, in the area of the
present Citadel, succeeded fortifications of the Maccabean period.
As will be seen, the second building phase there is dated to c. 100
B.C., during the rule of either John Hyrcanus (134–104 B.C.) or
Alexander Jannaeus (103–76 B.C.). A slightly doubtful earlier
stage is assigned to Jonathan Maccabeus (c. 153–143 B.C.).

In considering the problem of the extension to the western

ridge, it is necessary to take into account the Akra, built as a
fortress to dominate the Temple by Antiochus IV Epiphanes in
169 B.C., occupied by a foreign garrison and by Jews disaffected
to the Maccabees, until it was captured by Simon in 141 B.C.
There is no adequate evidence to identify the site of the Akra.

The general tenour of the references is that it was a fortress
dominating Jerusalem and especially the Temple. The only at all
specific localization is given in I Maccabees 1:29 ff., in which it is
said that the foreign attackers, having destroyed houses and taken
captive women and children and cattle, 'builded the city of
David with a great and strong wall, with strong towers, and it
became unto them a citadel'. In this citadel were located both the
foreign garrison of the Syrian rulers and a place for the 'sinful
nation, transgressors of the law', with the subsequent passage
emphasizing the threat to the Temple and orthodox religion.

The crux of the identification of the Akra is the Maccabees I
statement that this fortress controlled by foreigners was based
on the city of David. At this point there emerges a difficult point
of interpretation between the important Jewish historian Flavius
Josephus and modern evidence. As has been seen, the excavation
evidence is definite that the city of David was on the eastern
ridge. In Josephus's day Jerusalem included both the eastern and
western ridges. In *Antiquities*, VII. iii. 61 ff., he interprets the
Biblical account of the Israelite capture of Jerusalem as involving
two stages, the capture of the lower city and the capture of the
Citadel, and it is to this stage he assigns the events of II Samuel 5:6
leading to Joab's success (see above, pp. 98–9). This is probably to be
interpreted as meaning that he located the Citadel on the higher
western ridge, and he quite clearly includes the western ridge in
the city of David, referred to in II Samuel 5:7 as the stronghold
of Zion. Thus by the time of Josephus, in the first century A.D.,
the name Zion appears to have been transferred to the western
ridge, where it was firmly established in pilgrims' accounts in
the fourth century A.D.

The problem is to decide whether the site of the city of David
was still correctly identified when I Maccabees was written.

The book covers the period down to 134 B.C., and drew upon an earlier source. It could therefore have been written no earlier than the late second century B.C., so it is possible that error had already arisen.

There are three main reasons why I find it hard to believe that this Akra occupied by a foreign garrison for thirty years was on the eastern ridge. The first is that if one follows A. D. Tushingham's suggestion[1] that a massive wall found in Site H (see fig. 29), for which there was inadequate stratigraphical evidence, was part of the 'great and strong wall' of Akra referred to in I Maccabees 1:33, the implication would be that the whole of original Jerusalem was occupied by the foreigners, leaving only the little neck of the ridge between that point and the temple platform as the area occupied by the supporters of the Maccabees. This seems to fit neither the picture that the Maccabees controlled all Jerusalem except Akra, nor the implications of its name as the Citadel, which should imply a relatively small fortified place.

The second reason is the implications in I Maccabees and Josephus that the Akra dominated the Temple. The 'sinful nation' established there 'became a sore snare: and it became a place to lie in wait in against the sanctuary' (I Maccabees 1:35–36). The point is especially emphasized when at last the Akra was captured by Simon in 141 B.C. According to Josephus (*Antiquities*, XIII. vi. 215), Simon then proceeded 'to level the very mountain itself upon which the citadel happened to stand, so that the temple might be higher than it'. The task took three years, 'After which the temple was the highest of all the buildings, now the citadel, as well as the mountain on which it stood, were demolished' (ibid., 217). This cannot conceivably apply to the site of original Jerusalem, where the rock at Site H, where there are deposits of the tenth century B.C., is at c. 702 metres, while the rock on the site of the Temple is at 740 metres. Though there has been quarrying on the crest of the ridge within the original city, it is impossible to accept that the crest originally stood up over 40 metres above the houses at the head of the slope described

[1] *Atlas of the Biblical World*, pp. 166–9.

above (pp. 161 ff.). On the other hand, if the Akra had been on the western ridge, representing the first spread to that area since the destruction of the seventh-century B.C. town, rock at a level of 740 metres is reached within a distance of *c*. 150 metres from the estimated western line of the temple platform, and quarrying to throw back the dominating area farther away from the Temple would be a possible undertaking.

A third reason for my preference for a site for the Akra on the western ridge is that Jonathan, though he could not capture the Citadel, put the occupants to great straits by a siege wall, 'so that it might be all alone, that men could neither buy nor sell' (I Maccabees VI:36). To have enclosed the whole site of the original city, with walls built either at the bottom of the valleys or on the steep, debris-encumbered slopes, would have been a terrific undertaking.

It must be admitted that there are other passages both in I Maccabees and in Josephus which appear to conflict with those that I have quoted, for instance the statement in I Maccabees XIV:37 that Simon converted the Akra into a Jewish fortress. But if one has to pick and choose between conflicting statements in our two historical sources, I would prefer to accept those passages which seem to me to make better topographical sense. I recognize, however, that there is a formidable weight of opinion against me.[1] I doubt whether there will ever be any conclusive evidence recovered.

The localization of the Akra which I prefer would therefore make it the first building stage on the western ridge during the post-Exilic period. According to whichever localization one prefers, one can interpret the fortifications in the area of the present Citadel in three different ways: firstly as undertaken after the Akra was captured, secondly as an attempt to extend the area of the city to make up for what had been occupied by the

---

[1] e.g. *Noth*, p. 365; J. Simons, *Jerusalem in the Old Testament*, pp. 144 ff.; A. D. Tushingham, *Atlas of the Biblical World*. On the other hand, F. M. Abel, *Histoire de la Palestine* I, p. 122, and Vincent, *Jérusalem de l'A.T.*, pp. 175 ff., place the Akra on the western ridge.

Akra, or thirdly as an expansion marking the growing power and prosperity of the Maccabees after the final expulsion of Seleucid dominance. The area of the Citadel was excavated by C. N. Johns,[1] who found four building phases in the defensive structures. Johns suggested that the first dated to the time of Jonathan Maccabeus (c. 153–143 B.C.). It has already been suggested (above, p. 192) that Jonathan could have been responsible for the tower at the head of our Trench I. As the first securely established Maccabean ruler of Jerusalem, it would be quite possible that he extended the defended area on to the western ridge. I retain some doubt that the walls of the first building stage may be only the rougher foundations of the second building stage, and Johns's description[2] supports that interpretation. If my hesitation is justified, the expansion on to the western ridge may only have taken place c. 100 B.C. Further excavation, if meticulously carried out, might decide this problem.

The second building phase Johns dated to c. 100 B.C., thus the work either of John Hyrcanus (134–104 B.C.) or Alexander Jannaeus (103–76 B.C.). With the third stage, Herodian, and the fourth stage, Roman, we are not concerned at this point. A probable continuation of the wall at the Citadel was found in Site L, in the Armenian Garden area in the south-west corner of the Old City (see fig. 29).[3]

These two points, at the Citadel and in the south-west corner of the Old City, are the only two points upon which we can be certain for the area included in the Maccabean extension on to the western ridge. The first plan that I published of the extension to the western ridge as existing in the Herodian period[4] tentatively placed the southern boundary of the extension on the line of the present south wall of the Old City, solely for the reason that the earlier wall might have created a configuration of the ground followed by the later wall, probably Roman in origin.

[1] QDAP XIV.
[2] QDAP XIV, p. 128.
[3] PEQ, 1968, pp. 110–11.
[4] PEQ, 1966, p. 86; Jerusalem, fig. 11.

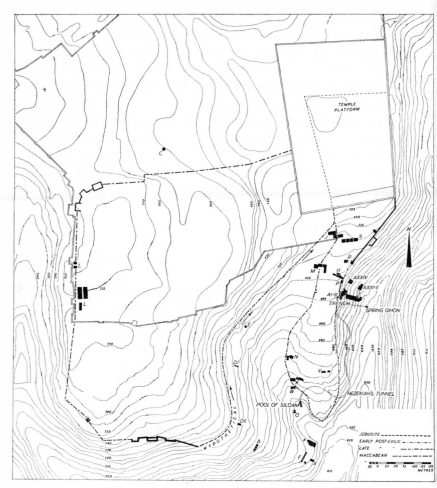

Fig 29   Plan of Maccabean Jerusalem

It is, however, virtually certain on strategic grounds that by the
Maccabean period a considerable part of the crest of the western
wall must have been defended. The subject of Hellenistic defences
has recently been studied in a doctoral thesis by A. W. McNicoll,
and I gladly accept some but not all of his conclusions about
Jerusalem. The new factor that by Maccabean times made

demands on the plan of the walls of Jerusalem was the invention of the catapult about 400 B.C. in Syracuse and the development of the torsion projectile engine *c.* 350 B.C.[1] The range of Hellenistic artillery was probably about 350–400 metres,[2] and would obviously be greater if firing from a higher elevation. This means that hostile artillery placed just below the flattish top of the western ridge, at, say, the 750 metre contour, could dominate the town on the eastern ridge, which only reaches an altitude of 725 metres immediately south of the temple platform, and slopes down to 640 metres at the southern tip. The contacts of the Maccabean rulers with the Seleucids would have made them well aware of the artillery potential of the day, even if they did not possess torsion engines themselves. One must accept the probability that they would have been obliged to fortify enough of the western ridge to protect the original town on the eastern ridge.

The assumption must therefore be that, continuing the known line from the Citadel to Site L, some part at least of the line of wall traced by Bliss and Dickie (fig. 29) following the curve of the Hinnom Valley round the west and south sides of the ridge represents the Maccabean fortifications. It will be remembered that our trenches at Sites E, D I, D II, and B provided no evidence for occupation earlier than the first century A.D. These sites represent the limit of the area available to us between 1961 and 1967, for the summit of the hill was in no man's land between Jordan and Israel. In his thesis, McNicoll discounts this evidence, and considers that the whole of the Bliss and Dickie circuit, crossing the Tyropoeon to the top of the eastern ridge, is Maccabean, since he points out that Hellenistic defences often included areas not built up simply from the necessity of protection from artillery. As he shows, this is certainly true in Asia Minor, but it is not a conception for which there is so far evidence in Palestine. It might be acceptable for Jerusalem if confirmed by other evidence, which I do not believe is the fact.

[1] E. W. Marsden, *Greek and Roman Artillery* I. *Historical Development*, pp. 48 ff.
[2] ibid., p. 91.

The main reason for accepting that part of the Bliss and Dickie line is Maccabean, and for McNicoll's claim that the whole of it is, is Johns's observation[1] that the masonry of his style 2, with heavily bossed stones, laid mainly with courses of headers alternating with courses of stretchers, closely resembles portions of wall discovered by Bliss and Dickie. As the plan (fig. 6) shows, the first stretch of the circuit was traced by a rock scarp only. Just west of south from the Coenaculum, part of a tower was found, and for the next 300 metres or so a continuous line was traced, mostly with evidence of two periods. The uppermost was shown to be Byzantine at earliest, from its relation to Roman and Byzantine structures. The lower included a tower which was certainly Herodian (see below, p. 235) and also some sections with bossed masonry to which Johns compares his style 2 at the Citadel. The first section is a fragment just where the gap indicated by dotted lines on fig. 6 occurs, a gap caused by the existence of an old Jewish cemetery which prevented any excavations. This fragment, Y on Bliss and Dickie's General Plan (see also *B. and D.*, p. 39), here reproduced as fig. 30, certainly compares well both in bossing and coursing with Johns's masonry[2] (Pl. 84). I am less happy about the piece of wall picked up beyond the cemetery.[3] Bossed stones are included, but also a number of flat-dressed stones, and the coursing is not the same. Our Site B was close to this point. The wall had not survived there, but the deposits inside the line were very clearly only of the first century A.D. The third section to which Johns makes a comparison is between the two gates in the south-east corner of the circuit. The drawing of this[4] looks very much closer to Y and to Johns's walls except that the joints are less close. The reason for doubting that this is *c.* 100 B.C. is that it was almost exactly against the inner side of this that our trench located a foundation trench to the wall that dated it to the first century A.D. The gate

[1] *QDAP* XIV, pp. 150–2.
[2] *QDAP* XIV, Pl. LIII. 1 and 2.
[3] *B. and D.*, p. 84.
[4] ibid., p. 86.

Section.

16¼" 18" 25½" 20½" Scarp

SPECIMEN AT Y.

FIG 30   Bliss and Dickie's drawing of Maccabean masonry at Y

immediately to the east was almost certainly an insertion in this wall (see below, p. 269).

My inclination therefore is to believe that the Maccabean wall enclosed only the higher area of the western ridge. Tushingham[1] adopts the line of scarp and wall found by Bliss and Dickie running north-east from the tower south-west of the Coenaculum (fig. 6). This would be an acceptable line, but the surviving fragments are no earlier than Crusader or later.[2] It also takes no account of the section of wall for which Johns's comparison seems justified. The plan that I suggest (fig. 29) turns north at about the point that the wall disappears beneath the Jewish cemetery and follows approximately the 710 metres contour. The exact line is entirely hypothetical. I am very ready to accept evidence for another line, but I shall require a lot of convincing to believe that at this stage the Tyropoeon Valley was included. Tushingham, in fact, in his reconstruction suggests that the eastern and western ridges were joined only by a bridge from the temple platform. It would seem to me surprising that all intra-mural traffic should be directed via the sacred enclosure, and it would

[1] *Atlas of the Biblical World*, map 32.
[2] *B. and D.*, pp. 68–75. See below, p. 268.

also make communications between the two sections highly vulnerable in time of war. There is certainly no evidence, literary or archaeological, that the two areas were joined. I find it easier to believe that they were approximately as shown on fig. 29, but am prepared to be proved wrong.

The Maccabean period, so vividly portrayed by the literary sources, is infuriatingly dim archaeologically. It is for this reason that this chapter, with the need to discuss conflicting evidence and hypotheses, has been so tediously long.

★

CHAPTER TWELVE

Jerusalem of Herod the Great and of the New Testament

INHERENT IN THE SUCCESS of the Maccabean rulers in achieving virtual autonomy was the decay of the Hellenistic Seleucid empire. This decay was accelerated by the expansion of Roman influence into the eastern Mediterranean. The climax came under the rule of Pompey, whose defeat of Mithridates and Tigranes in Asia Minor led on to the decision to eliminate Seleucid rule in Syria. His legate, sent to Damascus in 65 B.C., was apprised of endemic struggles in Jerusalem between members of the Hasmonean (Maccabean) ruling family, and both competitors endeavoured to get Rome on their side. In the event, Pompey swept the competing factions aside and firmly occupied Jerusalem, with considerable slaughter and destruction, in 63 B.C.

At this stage, Pompey had finally broken up the Seleucid empire, and consequently he was able to reorganize his conquests. In Palestine and Syria, a number of districts were established, which very sensibly took account of the religious and cultural entities involved. The fairly widespread expansion of the Maccabean rule was cut back to the area in which the religious centre of the inhabitants was Jerusalem, thus excluding, for instance, the area to the north, for the inhabitants of which the cult centre was on Mount Gerizim (see above, p. 189). The stage was therefore one of considerable setback for a temporal power centred on Jerusalem.

Nevertheless, instability in Rome offered very adequate opportunities for the factions in Jerusalem, mainly amongst the

Hasmonean contenders for power, to engage in prolonged and unsavoury intrigues. When Caesar in 48 B.C. defeated Pompey, the Jerusalem contenders rapidly turned to him, each in an attempt to gain power for his faction. One can only summarize the succeeding period as 'intrigue continues'. The strong man who emerged as the supporter of one of the Hasmonean claimants was Antipater, an Idumean (or Edomite), who had married Mariamne, a member of the Hasmonean family, and who was supported by Caesar. Out of a welter of intrigue, war, and murder, Antipater's son Herod emerged, and in a visit to Rome he secured the support of Antony and Octavian, and in 40 B.C. the Senate appointed him king of Judea. With Roman support Herod was able to conquer his kingdom, and when Jerusalem fell to him in 37 B.C. his position was secure. On the defeat of Antony at Acteum in 31 B.C., Herod shrewdly changed sides and became an ardent supporter of Octavian, or Augustus as he then became known. Herod's support of Augustus was well rewarded by extensions of territory.

There was great political adroitness in Herod's subservience to Augustus. It is nevertheless true to say that Herod genuinely admired Roman culture and its material representation in art and architecture. He did his best to build or adapt cities in his kingdom to the Roman standard that he admired. This can be seen best at Samaria, which he renamed Sebaste, the Greek equivalent of Augusta; at Caesaria, which he built as a new town, both described in laudatory terms by Josephus; in his incredible fortress at Masada; and in his Roman-style villa at Jericho.[1] In Jerusalem, Hellenization had been anathema to the orthodox since the struggles against Antiochus Epiphanes early in the second century B.C. The barely different Romanization (for in Asia Roman culture was firmly founded on the Hellenistic) was equally suspect. Herod therefore had to proceed very cautiously.

For Herod's building activities in Jerusalem, we have some

[1] A summary of Herod's work is given in Kenyon, 'Some Aspects of the Impact of Rome on Palestine', in *Journal of the Royal Asiatic Society*, 1970, pp. 181-91.

archaeological evidence and literary evidence in the description of Herod's work by Josephus. From the order in Josephus's account, it might appear (though one would be rash to base too much on this owing to his somewhat discursive method) that Herod did in fact first build those foreign elements, a theatre and an amphitheatre,[1] and the disapproval of the inhabitants is fully recorded in the ensuing section of Josephus. For these structures, there is no archaeological evidence at all. Amphitheatres customarily lie outside the city walls. Theatres are ordinarily within them. It is improbable that Herod would have been so confident of his power (the Josephus XV.viii passage in fact shows how closely he watched public reactions) as to obliterate (I almost wrote bulldoze) a part of the built-up area of the existing city in order to make place for his alien public buildings, though for the glory of the Temple he apparently did (see below, pp. 221-2). It is reasonable to conclude that we must look outside the walls for Herod's amphitheatre and theatre.

The next mention in Josephus[2] is that 'Since, therefore, he had now fortified the palace in which he lived, and the temple by a strong fortress Antonia'; he then proceeded to his *magnum opus*, the rebuilding of the Temple.

The most important surviving work of Herod is the platform of the rebuilt Temple. The Temple is described in detail by Josephus,[3] for it was the Temple that Josephus himself knew. Of the Temple itself not a stone survives the Roman destruction and the subsequent Moslem buildings. It is clear that in rebuilding it Herod kept close to the traditional plan, merely restoring to it the magnificence that the builders of the post-Exilic period could not achieve. The constituent elements were the same, but his dimensions exceeded those of the Solomonic Temple. A great portico, one hundred cubits (50 metres) wide and one hundred cubits high (*War*, V.v.4(207)), was the successor to the Solomonic

---

[1] *Antiquities*, XV. viii. 1.

[2] ibid., XV. viii. 5.

[3] A brief account is given in *Antiquities*, XV. xi. 3; the more detailed account is in *War*, V. v. 1-6.

portico sixty cubits wide.[1] Behind this grandiose portico, there were the stark chambers of the Holy Place and the Holy of Holies, surrounded, as was the Solomonic sanctuary, by three tiers of small rooms. The internal dimensions of the Holy Place and the Holy of Holies, respectively forty and twenty cubits in length, seem to have remained the same. In the main hall were the table for shew-bread, the seven-branched candlestick, and the altar for incense.[2] Between this main hall[3] and the portico were curtains. In the Holy of Holies 'there was nothing at all'. In Solomon's Temple this innermost sanctuary had housed the Ark of the Covenant (see above, p. 120). Josephus seems almost to have forgotten that this was the function of the Holy of Holies. As suggested above (p. 169), the Ark must have disappeared in the Babylonian destruction, if not earlier.

The magnificence and luxuriance of Solomon's Temple has been described above. The opulence of Herod's Temple is not in doubt, but the appearance as described has a suggestion of monotony in comparison with its Solomonic predecessor. The great emphasis was on gold – sheets and sheets of gold.

> Now the outward face of the temple in its front wanted nothing that was likely to surprise either men's minds or their eyes; for it was covered all over with plates of gold of great weight, and at the first rising of the sun, reflected back a very fiery splendour, and made those who forced themselves to look upon it, to turn their eyes away, just as they would have done at the sun's own rays.[4]

We have here the record of an eyewitness, for Josephus was of a priestly family, and he would have frequented Herod's Temple, which was only destroyed in his lifetime. The only elaboration of the golden decoration described by Josephus was that the door

---

[1] The Biblical account is in I Kings 6:2–3; a plan interpreting the Biblical evidence is given in *Jérusalem de l'A.T.*, Pl. CI.

[2] *War*, V.v.5 (216–18).

[3] *War*, V.v.5 (219).

[4] *War*, V.v.6 (222).

into the first hall from the portico was 'all covered with gold, as was its whole wall about it: it had also golden vines above it, from which clusters of grapes hung as tall as a man's height'.[1] Within the Temple, little is described except the 'Babylonian curtain' which was 'truly wonderful'.[2] It would seem that it was on the exterior that Herod lavished most of his attention, perhaps comprehensibly, for he, not being a member of a priestly family, could not enter the inner court or the Temple itself. The final touch in the description of the exterior is Herod's version of a bird-repellent: 'On its top it had golden spikes with sharp points, to prevent any pollution of it by birds sitting on it'.[3] To use gold for such a purpose suggests the extremes of ostentation.

Outside the Temple was the court of the priests. Beyond was the court to which males of pure Jewish blood were admitted, beyond again the court to which Jewish women were admitted. All these courts were linked by elaborate gates, decorated with gold, silver, and 'brass'. Admission to this area was guarded by a barrier, with tablets in Greek and Latin warning all foreigners that they could not penetrate further on penalty of death. The lay-out of the whole complex is shown on fig. 31, which represents the considered view of Père Vincent.[4]

All of this one must take from the description of Josephus. There are some uncertainties, for instance, as to inside and outside dimensions, but the general plan is certain, and it is only reasonable to accept Josephus's picture of the appearance of the Temple.

It is when we come to the platform upon which the Temple stood that archaeology can begin to make a contribution. Josephus in his description of the exterior of the Temple itself makes a distinction between the façade of the porch and the rest of the building, 'for as for those parts that were not gilt, they

[1] *War*, V.v.4 (210).
[2] *War*, V.v.4 (224).
[3] *War*, V.v.0, V.v.6 (224).
[4] *Jérusalem de l'A.T.*, Pl. III.

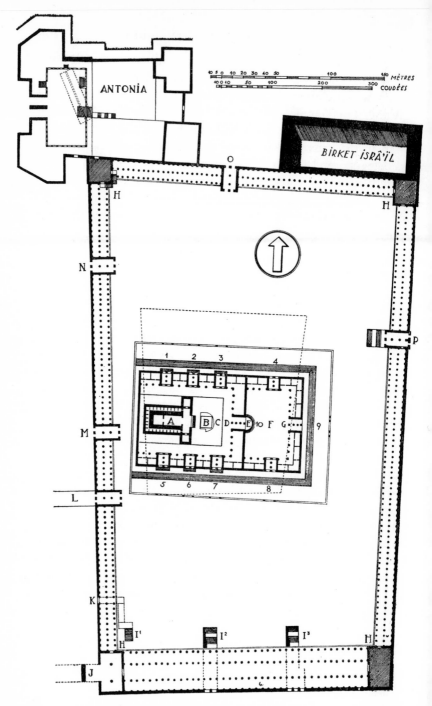

FIG 31   Reconstruction of plan of the Temple of Herod the Great

were exceeding white';[1] 'Of its stones some of them were forty-five cubits in length, five in height, and six in breadth'.[2] None of this 'exceeding white' masonry of the Temple itself survives. But we can recognize its description in the masonry of the Herodian addition to the temple platform. Herod doubled the size of the platform.[3] The necessity of massive retaining walls to create a flat area on top of a steep ridge has been emphasized in connection with the Solomonic Temple (see above, p. 111). The tremendous impression created by Herod's new platform walls is vividly described:

> And this cloister deserves to be mentioned better than any other under the sun; for while the valley was very deep, and its bottom could not be seen, if you looked from above into the depth, this vastly high elevation of the cloister stood upon that height, insomuch that if any one looked down from the top of the battlements, or down both those altitudes, he would be giddy, while his sight could not reach to such an immense depth[4].

There is hyperbole in this, but the surviving height of the Herodian wall is *c.* 40 metres, and one cannot estimate the amount of superstructure that has disappeared. The south-east angle of Herod's temple platform is today sufficiently impressive (Pl. 80). Its real dimensions are best conveyed by the section of Warren's sounding (fig. 32).

Herod's extension of the temple platform demanded, like the work of all his predecessors, a strong retaining wall to a fill supporting the platform above. The internal faces of these successive walls were never visible, and in fact we know nothing about them. At each successive build or rebuild of the platform, the external face of the retaining wall was very prominent. That of the Herodian rebuild was magnificent (Pls. 85 and 87).

---

[1] *War*, V.v.6 (223).
[2] ibid., (224).
[3] *War*, I. xxi. 1 (410).
[4] *Antiquities*, XV. xi. 5 (412).

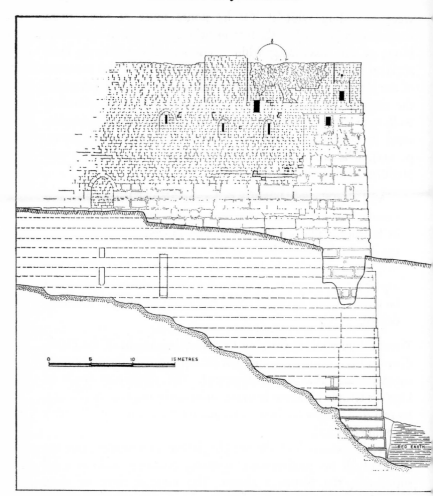

FIG 32   Warren's shaft against the south-east angle of the platform of the Haram esh-Sherif. The large ashlar blocks from 7 metres from the top of the wall to bedrock are Herodian

In the superstructure, the stones were of great size, a point emphasized by Josephus. They have a narrow, slightly sunk, margin, and the centres of the stones are beautifully dressed to a flat finish. This style of stonework is completely alien to Palestine. One must suspect that Herod, like his predecessors, imported craftsmen from elsewhere, possibly like them from Syria, though no exact parallels are known. Foreign craftsmen could not, of course, have worked on the Temple itself, for anything to do with that was reserved to the priests, whose training in stone-cutting, expressly mentioned by Josephus,[1] could have been by foreign craftsmen.

Herod's doubling of the size of the Temple was achieved by his addition of a width 32·72 metres at the south end, from the straight joint described above (p. 111) and illustrated on Pl. 35. Herodian masonry can be traced all along the southern front and on the west for a distance of 185 metres, here, therefore, completely enclosing the earlier platform (see above, p. 112). To make this extension, Herod had to carry his platform right across the central valley and some 27 metres up the slope of the western ridge (fig. 20). The new walls would have been backed by a fill of earth for most of their height, but along the south side vaulted corridors were used to provide the uppermost 13 metres of the required height. These vaulted corridors are today known as Solomon's Stables. This attribution is purely legendary, and the lower parts of the piers are of the stonework typical of smaller-scale Herodian work, in which a flat-dressed margin surrounds a flat, pick-dressed central area (Pl. 66). The upper parts of the arches are of Crusader work.

Surrounding the Court of the Gentiles on the summit of the platform were cloisters with roofs supported on columns, on three sides engaged columns and two free-standing rows, on the south side, the Royal Cloister, a similar row of engaged columns on the outer side and three other rows, forming a higher nave and two lower aisles. The scale of construction of the Royal

[1] *Antiquities*, XV. xi. 2 (390).

Cloister much impressed Josephus, and he described the circumference of the columns thus: 'and the thickness of each pillar was such, that three men might, with their arms extended, fathom it round, and join their hands again'.[1] The height of the column was 27 feet, which sounds rather squat in comparison with the circumference, and the capitals were Corinthian.

Josephus describes the temple platform as approached by four gates on the west side.[2] The south front is simply described as having gates, and the north and east were not mentioned. Certainly those to the west and south were the more important, for they gave access from within the city. The sole eastern gate, the Golden Gate, is visible today, though modified by later rebuildings. It nevertheless remains as a fine monument of the Hellenistic-Roman classical style in which Herod's Temple was built, to the extent to which Herod could overcome xenophobic prejudices. For the northern gates there is no archaeological evidence.

Of Josephus's four gates on the western side of the temple enclosure he says:[3]

> The first led to the king's palace, and went to a passage over the intermediate valley, two more led to the suburbs of the city, and the last led to the other city, where the road descended down into the valley by a great number of steps, and thence up again by the ascent, for the city lay over against the temple in the manner of a theatre, and was encompassed by a deep valley along the entire south quarter.

The description is unambiguous that right down to the time of Herod the western ridge was divided from the eastern ridge on which the Temple was situated by a deep valley. One gate, the first mentioned, seems to lead to a crossing of the valley to Herod's palace, which was certainly on the western ridge, by a 'passage'

[1] *Antiquities*, XV. xi. 5 (413).
[2] *Antiquities*, XV. xi. 5 (410).
[3] ibid.

and this may be the bridge[1] referred to elsewhere by Josephus.[2]

There are two possible candidates for this 'bridge', neither of them completely satisfactory. The basis of the first is Wilson's Arch, discovered by Captain Wilson in 1867 and further explored in the following year by Warren (fig. 33). The arch has a span of 12·80 metres, the whole span being completely preserved over the greatest depth of the central valley, the level of the rock being 23 metres below the crown of the arch, and it supports the street running to the main entrance on the west side of the Haram, the Bab el-Silsileh (see fig. 44). It is certain that the arch belongs to the Herodian period. The spring of the vault is integral with the east wall of the Haram and its masonry is typically Herodian. The difficulty in interpreting it as part of a bridge is that immediately adjacent to it to the west is a complicated maze of vaults, some certainly later, some possibly earlier. The problem is also complicated by the suggestion that the line of the vaults represents the first north wall to join the new city on the western ridge to the old one on the eastern ridge. The disentangling of all these problems would be an intriguing plunge into underground Jerusalem. Apparently the vaults and chambers are now (1972) being cleared, but unfortunately by the Jewish religious authorities and not by the Department of Antiquities, so it is improbable that we shall learn any firm archaeological facts. I had hoped to visit the vaults, which I had penetrated in 1966 as described above (p. 16), but the only access open in 1972 was through the Wailing Wall area, which by Jewish religious precepts was not open to a woman.

The other candidate for the gate leading by a bridge to the western hill is that connected with Robinson's Arch (see above, p. 14). No trace of the gate in fact survives, for the upper part of the Haram wall is a late rebuilding, but the spring of the arch, in Herodian masonry and from the Herodian wall (Pls. 5 and

[1] My own view is that all these interpretations are so uncertain that I shall have no hesitation in supporting a variant interpretation if adequate evidence is produced.

[2] *War*, II. xvi. 4 (354); VI. vi. 2 (325).

FIG 33   The excavation of Wilson's Arch. The masonry of the arch, seen in the foreground, is Herodian

87), is clear evidence that a gate must have existed. Warren devoted a considerable amount of effort to trace the connections of the arch to the west. He located the western pier of the arch, giving a span of 12·80 metres, identical with that of Wilson's Arch, and believed that he had found the implacement of another pier to the west again.

The area of the south-west corner of the temple platform has been stripped by Professor Mazar in excavations that began in 1967,[1] when the objections of the Islamic authorities to any excavations adjacent to the wall of the Haram, which had limited our excavation area, no longer carried any weight. The new excavations fully exposed the pier, located by Warren. At the level of the paved street that represents the Herodian ground-level, the pier had in it recesses that apparently housed bazaar-like booths.[2] The most important new evidence was that adjacent to this pier to the west were the remnants of a series of barrel vaults leading up from the south. One must accept Professor Mazar's conclusion that these represent the support of a flight of stairs leading up from the south to reach the level of the entrance to the Temple carried on Robinson's Arch. This seems perfectly reasonable as providing a means of entry to the Temple from the lower area of the eastern and western ridges. Nevertheless, if this had been the sole purpose, a straight flight of steps along the western wall of the temple platform would have been a much simpler solution. If the primary object of the Robinson's Arch system had been to span the valley, a cross-connection to the south would be entirely sensible. The present excavations have found no trace of a continuing series of arches to the west, but the complete lack of stratigraphical evidence has the result that

[1] *Eretz Israel* 9, in Hebrew, with English version as a separate monograph on first season; *Eretz Israel* 10, on 1969–70 seasons, published in English as a separate monograph.

[2] In this description of the finds round the south-west angle of the Haram I am indebted to Professor Mazar's courtesy in showing me his finds, and it is dependent on my recollection of what was visible and my interpretation thereof.

one can place no weight on negative evidence. My reservations at this stage may be resolved in due course.

Warren's shafts showed that 12 metres below the spring of Robinson's Arch from the wall of the Herodian temple platform there was a paved street. Beneath the paving of the street was a large-scale drain, which apparently ran the whole length of the Herodian city. Its impressive plan and construction are described by Warren and fully explored and illustrated by the 1969–70 excavations.

This paved street is joined at the south-west corner of the temple platform by another, also recorded by Warren, and further traced by Mazar's excavation. This street rises steadily to the east, sometimes in a slope, sometimes with two or three steps. Mazar's excavations have shown that the street, as it extended to the east, was supported on a series of underlying vaults. The problem of whether the vaults were in fact subterranean would require more precise stratigraphical evidence than we have so far had available. Warren's excavations had shown that beneath this level the Haram walls were constructed of roughly bossed stones. Above the level of the street the stones are of the accepted standard of Herodian masonry. The street clearly belongs to the Herodian period.

The south wall of the Haram provides evidence of two ancient gates, the Double Gate and the Triple Gate (fig. 2). The paving of the street running along the south wall of the Haram has largely been robbed towards the east, but it is clear that the street was leading to the Double Gate. Excavations in this area are proceeding apace. I can only record my 1972 appreciation of the results. This appreciation was that the street along the southern wall provided access to the Double Gate and the Triple Gate. Each of these gates was also approached by steps from the south. At this point I must make a reservation concerning Mazar's interpretation. Excavation in such terribly complicated areas of successive destruction, building stages, and occupation levels requires a detailed and very patient excavation technique that he did not employ. There is no doubt that associated with Herod's building operations there was quarrying on a large scale in the whole area to the south of the Haram (see below, p. 221). I think that the evidence suggests that all the rock-cuttings adjacent to the revealed stairs belong to an earlier period, and are not associated with the Herodian temple.

Josephus does not describe these gates on the south side of the temple platform; he simply says that there were gates.[1] Since Josephus does not describe the gates, and nothing of the superstructure survives, we have no data concerning them beyond the visible plan. Both must have provided entrance into the temple area by sloping passages. The level at the base of the Triple Gate is 725·60 metres, that of the courtyard to which it led was probably near that of the present courtyard at 738 metres. These sloping passages still exist, and were in part explored by Warren but are today inaccessible.

Though gates on the east side are not mentioned by Josephus, there is a very impressive gate there, the Golden Gate (Pl. 4). In its present form it is Byzantine, but its origin is probably Herodian, with a general plan similar to that of the Double Gate in the south wall, and entrance into the interior was by sloping passages.

Herod's reconstruction of the Temple was his outstanding achievement in Jerusalem, outstanding in the assessment of Josephus and presumably his contemporaries, and visibly outstanding today. Modern taste might find his temple building, and also that of Solomon, unbearably luxurious and ostentatious. The sheer majesty of the supporting walls of his temple platform and the technical perfection of the masonry are much more impressive today.

When Herod built the Temple and his various other buildings he clearly had a great need of building stone. Much, no doubt, would have come from quarries outside the town. But he seems surprisingly to have gone to the extent of razing the area immediately to the south of the Temple and to have quarried the rock beneath it. Outside the Haram is an area bounded on the north

[1] *Antiquities*, XV. xi. 5 (411).

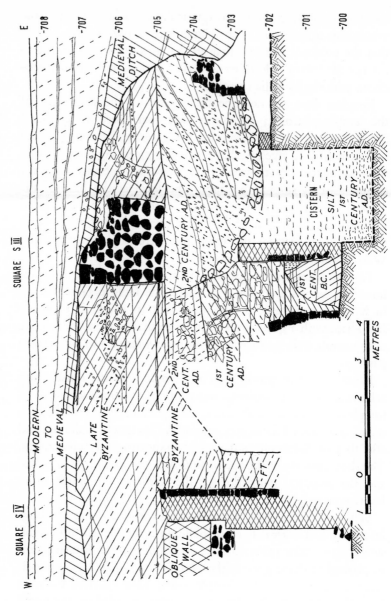

FIG 34 Section in Site s, showing, on right, 1st century A.D. cistern cut into quarrying sealed by 1st century B.C. fill

by the south wall of the Haram, on the west by the salient of the present wall of the Old City, and on the south and east by the modern road to the Dung Gate (Pl. 88), our Site s. We had started excavations here with great expectations. It was a nice, unencumbered, relatively level area (Pl. 89), where there should have been evidence of the Solomonic period and everything thereafter. Some bearing on the Solomonic expansion was provided by Square s II on the east side. (Work is seen in progress in the foreground in Pl. 88.) In the rest of the area excavated, seen in Pl. 89, a deep layer of uninteresting soil, mainly agricultural, covered a Byzantine building (see below, p. 271), and beneath it nothing but quarrying. When we first exposed this, we took it that the quarrying belonged to the time of the construction of the Roman city of Aelia Capitolina. Some of it did belong to this period. But there was clear evidence that quarrying on a big scale had taken place before buildings of the first century A.D. were erected. Figure 34 in Square s III shows a cistern of a house of that period constructed on already quarried rock, cut into a fill dated by pottery to the Herodian period.[1] The most striking evidence of this quarrying is to be seen in Square s I against the foot of the town-wall salient (Pls. 91, 94 and fig. 35). The quarrying has cut into two cisterns, and it has ended in a vertical scarp beneath the town wall. The town wall here is certainly post-Herodian, for it is built against the Herodian temple platform, and its masonry, in enormous blocks with heavy bosses, visible in Pl. 89, is certainly not Herodian. A reasonable conclusion is that it belongs to the time of Aelia Capitolina. Quarrying of that period to the foot of the wall was therefore reasonable. There was no dating evidence here, as in medieval times an erosion gulley had washed away all earlier deposits. The quarrying, however, must be linked with that at Square s III, only 7·50 metres to the south, with quarrying to an almost identical level, and it must therefore be dated to the

[1] I use the term 'Herodian' for the period of Herod the Great. Professor Mazar uses it more generally for the whole period down to the destruction in A.D. 70.

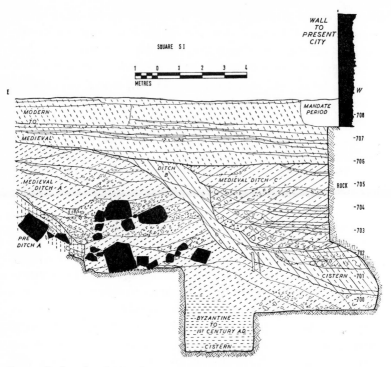

FIG 35   Section of south side of Trench s 1, showing quarrying at base of salient in present south wall of Old City

Herodian period. There must have been some reason for the Herodian quarries to stop on that line and my suggestion is that it represents the original line of the Solomonic extension; I have explained above (p. 114) how this fits well with the probable plan of the temple platform. When in Maccabean times the town expanded onto the western ridge, either the point at which the wall of the western ridge joined the eastern defences was farther north, or the original wall was retained in existence within the city.

Herod would certainly have wished to clear some of the buildings in this area, in order to provide a dignified approach to the Temple from the south. As already described, Professor

Mazar's excavations have revealed flights of steps leading up to the Double and Triple Gates, and there may have been an open plaza over most of the area, which was built up during the first century A.D. Herodian quarrying was, however, not limited to this area, but extended to Site R, 50 metres to the south. His expropriation of land and houses must have been ruthless.

Josephus pays little attention to anything that Herod may have done for the defence of Jerusalem. There are two points upon which one can base theories concerning the north and west walls; to the south walls I shall return below. The first point is the fortress Antonia, built by Herod as a successor to the Maccabean fort Baris at the north-west corner of the temple enclosure. The researches of Père Vincent[1] into the horribly complicated problems of scarps, fosses, quarries, suggest a plan as shown on fig. 36. Père Benoit[2] shows good grounds for querying the earlier conclusions concerning the plan of the Antonia. It probably lay completely south of the road leading in from the present St Stephen's Gate, but we are left with no indications as to its plan other than its description by Josephus. One can certainly accept that it was on the rock summit bounded by the scarp south of the present street of Bab Sitti Miriam leading in from St Stephen's Gate. This high area of rock is today bounded on the south by the rock scarp at the north end of the Haram. The date of this scarp is not proved, and it could be that it was cut in Roman or Moslem times. This would make it easier to find space for the grandiose construction with four towers which is described by Josephus.

The second point is the existence of undoubted Herodian masonry at the Citadel, the main medieval structure that dominates the western ridge today, beside the Jaffa Gate (Pl. 90). The tower today known as the Tower of David (on right on Pl. 90) can be identified as the tower Phasael, one of three built by Herod as the nucleus of his palace, and Herodian masonry survives to two-thirds of the present height. Herod's palace is

[1] *Jérusalem de l'A.T.*, pp. 196–214.
[2] *Harvard Theological Review*, 64, pp. 135–67.

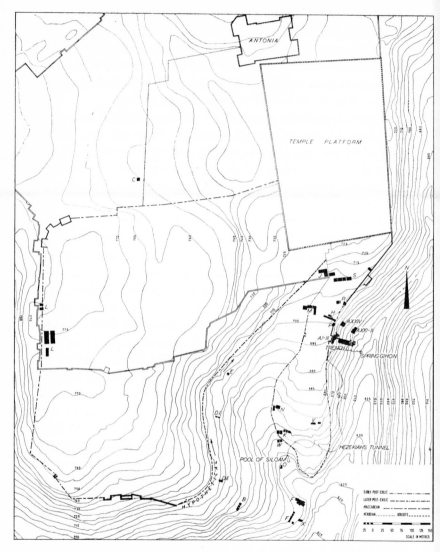

FIG 36   Plan of Herodian Jerusalem

described by Josephus in ecstatic terms.[1] The three towers, Phasael, Hippicus, and Mariamne, were excellently built and furnished, and were part of the north wall of the enclosure, and within was a palace which Josephus says 'exceeds all my ability to describe it'. Towers, houses, porticoes, courts, dove-cotes, canals, groves of trees gave an impression of the greatest luxury and considerable space; indeed a fascinating picture in the context of the area at present. We had hoped to find some part of the ruins of this magnificent complex in our excavations at Site L, but nothing survived there of this period, and it is probable that the palace was farther to the north. In recent excavations at the Citadel, a grid substructure of walls has been suggested as forming a podium 3 to 4 metres high to support buildings belonging to the palace.[2]

We have therefore as points in the northern defences of Jerusalem the fortress Antonia at the north-west corner of the temple enclosure and Herod's towers in the present citadel area. We come now to a crucial historical problem. The life of Christ described in the Gospels belongs to the first three decades of the first century A.D. The Jerusalem of the period of the Gospels is that created by Herod. The building of the Temple may not have been yet completed,[3] but it is certain that the Temple that Christ knew was that built by Herod. Archaeology can do very little to present a general picture of the Jerusalem of the period. In almost every case in the area excavated, all structures have been removed and all evidence destroyed. One must simply visualize the Biblical scenes at the Temple in the light of Josephus's description of the Temple that Herod built. The city of the time one can probably visualize as not at all unlike that shown, for instance, in Pl. 3. One can give very little archaeological support, and in fact in some cases must suggest negative evidence

---

[1] *War*, V. iv. 3-4.

[2] R. Amiran and A. Eitan, 'Excavations at the Citadel, Jerusalem', *IEJ* 20, pp. 9 ff.; and *IEJ* 22, pp. 50-51.

[3] According to *Antiquities*, XX. ix. 7 (219) it was finished during the procuratorship of Albinus (i.e., *c.* A.D. 63).

for some of the sites shown to tourists. The Tomb of David, for example, has nothing at all to do with David nor has the Tomb of Absalom (Pl. 80) anything to do with Absalom. I have much more compunction in denying the authenticity of two other sites, for they are so lovingly portrayed by their guardians. The Sisters of Sion show visitors a pavement within the Antonia as the 'Lithostratos' or pavement where Jesus was judged by Pilate (John 19:13). It is quite possible to argue that Pilate's seat of judgement was in the Antonia, as is persuasively done by Père Vincent,[1] and the Sisters who so eagerly explain things to tourists do so with much conviction. Nevertheless, strong grounds have been produced for associating the pavement with the adjacent Hadrianic Arch.[2] This may be the case of basing too firm certainty on inadequate evidence, but it does not worry me as it does not distort the picture in the way that, for instance, does 'David's Tower' overlying second-century B.C. ruins (see above, p. 77). There is still less basis for the claim of the Assumptionist Fathers of St Peter Gallicantu that they have discovered the prison of St Peter. All our evidence in the immediate neighbourhood suggests that the buildings, stepped streets, and cisterns belong to the Byzantine period. Archaeologically I would say that the claim is very much not proven, but again the interest of the tourists is aroused by a story vividly told which does not conflict too seriously with known facts.

There is one most crucial problem concerning the Gospel story on which our excavations have thrown most unexpectedly clear light. This is the problem of the authenticity of the site of the Church of the Holy Sepulchre, built by Empress Helena in A.D. 320, and believed to cover the site both of the Crucifixion – Calvary – and of the Holy Sepulchre. The Church of the Holy Sepulchre today lies in the very heart of Jerusalem. Everything in the Gospels leads one to expect that the place of Crucifixion was outside the walls, and that of the burial had to be by all Jewish laws. I remember my own puzzlement when I

[1] *Jérusalem de l'A.T.*, pp. 216 ff.
[2] Père P. Benoit, op. cit.

first visited Jerusalem at seeing the Church close-pressed on every side by buildings (Pl. 93), and I am sure this is shared by most visitors.

The answer, of course, is that the walls of the present Old City are not those of the time of the Gospels. The problem is to establish where these walls were, and, in particular, where the north wall was. My original plans of excavation in Jerusalem did not provide for the examination of this problem. Excavation in the very heart of the Old City seemed too out of the question. It did, however, happen that in the area of the Muristan, immediately to the south of the Holy Sepulchre (plan, fig. 2), there was some waste land belonging to the Order of St John of Jerusalem. The officers of the Order, especially Sir Stewart Duke-Elder, most enthusiastically supported the suggestion that we should excavate here. Their initial interest was that we should expose remains of the medieval Hospital of St John, the existence of which on this site being the reason that the land belonged to the Order. We did find remains that probably belonged to the Hospital, but consisting only of very massive foundations of piers; all superstructure had been removed in drastic clearance early in the twentieth century.

Having started the excavation of our Site c, however, we obviously had to carry on down, for the opportunity of digging within the heart of the Old City made it essential that one should extract every bit of information. I confess that though I continued to express enthusiasm about the possibilities of the site, I had not much hope of any very definite evidence concerning the earlier stages of the history of Jerusalem. The problems of excavating a site in the heart of a built-up area with no access for motor traffic (Pl. 92) are very great. The photograph shows the area available, and the top of our sounding. We had first to dig through some eight feet of modern, post-1920, rubbish before we reached intact medieval levels, Ommayad houses with the foundations of the medieval piers of the Hospital of St John cutting through them. Beneath were Byzantine levels, and beneath that we started to go on down and down. As we went down, our area had to contract. By the time we had got rid of the modern dumps on top, it had already contracted to 7 metres by 7 metres. As we went down, all the time we had to leave steps for the basket-carriers who removed the soil. By the time we reached the bottom, the area was *c.* 4 metres by 4 metres. All the time the excavated soil kept piling up around us. At one point I spent £300 on using donkeys to carry out soil to the nearest point to which trucks could come, whence it was carried outside the city. The respite was slight, but did in fact make enough difference to enable us to get to the bottom.

Beneath the Byzantine levels the fill consisted of a continuous series of tips (Pl. 96 and fig. 37). Throughout, the contents, in interlocking layers, produced an enormous assortment of material of two periods, the late seventh century B.C. and the first century A.D. It was clearly a single fill derived from two different sources. At the depth of 2·50 metres below the beginning of this fill there was a break, with the appearance of a massive drain running from west to east (see Pl. 96). Beneath its level there was a change in direction of the tips, but the character of the fill, alternating layers of seventh-century B.C. and first-century A.D. material, continued on down. One can conclude that when an appropriate level in the fill was reached, the drain was constructed, and the tipping was then resumed.

The later content of the tipped material was overwhelmingly that associated with Jerusalem up to the destruction by Titus, material most usefully classified in the Qumran excavations as belonging to the monastery destroyed in A.D. 68.[1] My field assessment, however, was that the pottery found included forms that we did not find in the A.D. 70 Titus destruction levels, and which belonged to the time of the Hadrianic building of Aelia Capitolina. This is a tentative assessment, which can only be confirmed when the detailed classification of the pottery is completed. To a British archaeologist of the mid-twentieth century, it will seem quite shocking that one cannot distinguish with certainty between Flavian and Hadrianic pottery. This is

[1] *Qumran*, pp. 29–33.

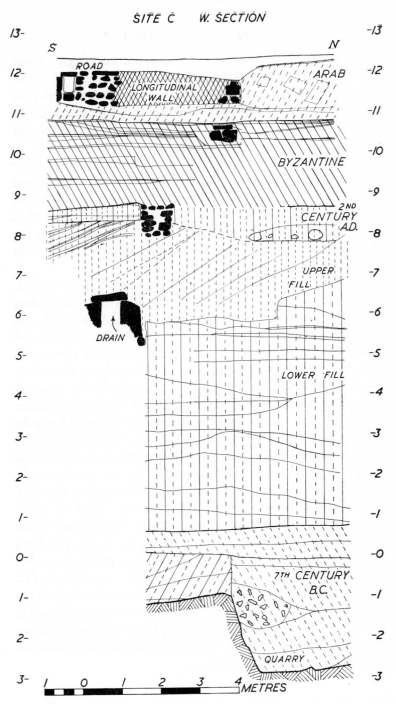

FIG 37 Section of Site C, showing deep filling of 1st–2nd centuries A.D. above 7th-century B.C. quarry

certainly so, for exact stratification has for long been applied even less to Hellenistic-Roman levels than to those of earlier periods. The Qumran excavations[1] provided clear-cut evidence for the pottery of the end of the first century B.C., the period of Herod, and for the time of the Roman conquest and destruction of A.D. 70. No other excavations have provided criteria to differentiate so clearly the characteristics of the pottery and other finds, such as stone vessels. Qumran finishes at A.D. 68. I do not think that a site in Palestine had produced clear evidence for the basic criterion of pottery of the Hadrianic period. I believe that the pottery analysis of Site C will show that an element in the classification of finds must belong to a period later than the Titus destruction.

My assessment of the result is that in our Site C we had, beneath the Byzantine levels, a major fill of material derived from seventh-century B.C. and first-century A.D. deposits, but that there is enough later material to show that the fill contained pottery of the second century A.D. This means that the deposit belongs to the time of the Hadrianic reconstruction of Jerusalem, for it is, of course, dated by the latest material in it. The implications of this concerning the Hadrianic period are discussed below.

This fill went right on down to a depth of 11 metres from the point at which we reached ancient deposits. At that point there was an abrupt change, which is visible in Pl. 96 at the level of the shoulders of the man standing at the bottom of the trench. He stands on bedrock, with the rock to the right in the view scarped down, very obviously by quarrying, detail of which is seen in Pl. 98. This quarrying is sealed by the level which underlies the main fill, and the contents show that this level is pure seventh century B.C. The quarrying is therefore seventh century or earlier. One can say with some confidence that quarrying would not have taken place within the closely built-up confines of an oriental city in the first millennium B.C., though it has been shown above that it could take place under the authority of an autocrat like Herod the Great in circumstances in which he

[1] For a general description, see *Qumran*.

was trying to bring Jerusalem into the Romano-Hellenistic world that he admired. I feel that one can say with confidence that this seventh-century B.C. quarry indicates that the area of our Site C was outside seventh-century B.C. Jerusalem. The fact that nothing intervened between the seventh-century B.C. surface and the second-century A.D. fill creates a strong supposition that throughout this time the area of Site C remained outside the occupied area, and therefore presumably outside the walls. As can be seen from fig. 2, Site C, in the Muristan, lies to the south of the Church of the Holy Sepulchre. Since Site C lay outside the walls of Jerusalem until the second century A.D., it follows that the site of the Church was extra-mural at the date of the Crucifixion. The very limited area of excavations on the property of the Order of St John in the Muristan may have produced only meagre evidence of the Hospital of St John, but it provided evidence clear beyond my greatest hopes (which had been increasingly dimmed as we went on down and down for three years) of finding any definite evidence from the space to which the exigencies of excavation logistics reduce a deep sounding in a limited area.

One can therefore make a suggestion, based on firm archaeological evidence, concerning the north wall of Herod's Jerusalem. All the archaeological arguments for generations concerning the authenticity of the site of the Church of the Holy Sepulchre, on all reasonable and historical grounds outside the walls of the contemporary city, though in the heart of the present Old City, are based on Josephus's descriptions of the state of the north wall at the time of the final attack by Titus in A.D. 70. Josephus[1] says that where the city was not 'encompassed with impassable valleys' it was fortified by three walls; this therefore refers to the north side, for the Kedron and Hinnom enclose the other sides. He describes first the old wall, which he ascribes in origin to David and Solomon. This throws interesting light on the lack of current knowledge of the historical topography of the city, for concerning the situation of the city of David and Solomon we

[1] *War*, V. iv. 1–2.

are on firm ground; it follows that statements concerning the location of Akra and of the Citadel of David, discussed above, may have equally little historical foundation. He describes the old wall running from the tower Hippicus (at the present Citadel), built, of course, only by Herod, but having a Maccabean predecessor, to the Xystus, the exercise ground in the valley, of which the exact site is unknown; then to the council house, again unknown; and ending at the west cloister of the Temple. No part of this wall has been certainly identified, but it is usually assumed that the system of vaults in the neighbourhood of Wilson's Arch (see above, p. 215) is related to it, perhaps built against it or using it as part of a causeway across the valley. It is generally accepted that the line shown on the plan (fig. 38) is approximately correct.

The second north wall ran from the Gate Gennath on the old wall; 'it only encompassed the northern quarter of the city, and reached as far as the tower Antonia'. There is no doubt concerning the situation of Antonia, for it was built by Herod at the north-west corner of the Temple, and would have been well-known to Josephus. Unfortunately, nothing is known about the situation of the Gate Gennath. On this there has been prolonged and often acid controversy. Père Vincent is in his best form in his chapter 'Autour d'un rempart mouvant',[1] when he says, with the utmost courtesy and elegance, that those who support any other theory are idiots. The reason for this passionate argument is that on the question of the line of the second north wall depends the problem of whether the site of the Church of the Holy Sepulchre can be authentic, for Josephus says that the third north wall was built by Herod Agrippa (A.D. 40–44) when Josephus was a boy, so on this there can be no confusion. The Crucifixion took place when the second north wall formed the city boundary.

The most generally held opinion has been that the Gate Genneath was a little north of the Citadel (see map 9, fig. 38). A comfortable line running thence would place the site of the Church well within the city. The second theory, supported by

[1] *Jérusalem de l'A.T.*, pp. 146 ff.

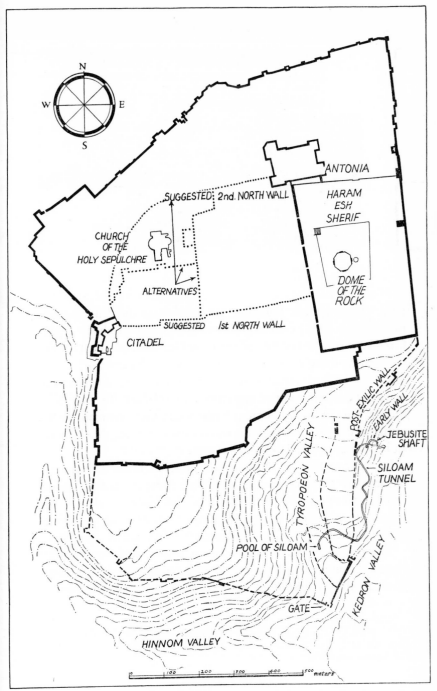

FIG 38 Plan showing alternative lines suggested for second north wall of Jerusalem

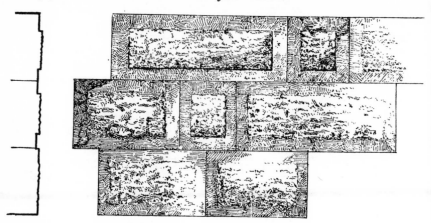

FIG 39   Herodian-style masonry at Bliss and Dickie's point *d*

Père Vincent, made ingenious use of various ancient pieces of
masonry (in fact, of quite uncertain date)[1] and produces a plan
based on a similar position of the Gate Gennath, in which a series
of re-entrant angles left the site of the Church outside. The line
does not look convincing, but one military supporter of this
version produced tactical arguments to support it.[2] The third
theory, supported by Simons,[3] places the Gate Gennath in the
centre of the old wall, with the second wall, running thence north
and west, and enclosing a smaller area.

Our excavations at Site c show that this third theory must
be basically the correct one. The wall must lie east of Site c,
and therefore east of the Church of the Holy Sepulchre. We
have not, of course, proved that the Church *is* on the site of
Calvary and the Sepulchre, but we have shown that it *can* be.

The probability is that the second north wall was built by
Herod to enclose a quarter that had grown up in the angle
between the Temple and the Maccabean 'old wall', though it

[1] ibid., pp. 96 ff.
[2] Captain C. T. Norris, 'New Reasoning concerning the Fortifications of
Jerusalem in the First Century A.D.', *PEQ*, 1946, pp. 19–37.
[3] *Simons*, pp. 282 ff.

could have been the work of one of the later Maccabeans. The interest concerning it derives from its connection with the Gospel story. There is not the same interest concerning the south wall in the time of Herod. It is in fact not likely that he did much here. There is, however, one tower excavated by Bliss on the wall enclosing the southern hill, which, it is suggested above (p. 202), is Maccabean, which is certainly of Herodian-style masonry[1] (fig. 39). It made a great impression on the excavators.

> Here we have the most beautifully-set work we have observed anywhere in our excavations. The fine rubbed jointing is superior to any found in Jerusalem, and is so close that a pin point can hardly be inserted.

It is true that masonry of this type was still being built in the time of Herod Agrippa (see below, p. 242). But since the work on the southern wall ascribed on archaeological grounds to Herod Agrippa (pp. 246 ff.) is quite different, it may be suggested that this tower is the sole surviving trace of repairs made by Herod to the south wall.

[1] *B. and D.*, p. 30 and Pl. V, specimen at *d*.

★

CHAPTER THIRTEEN

Jerusalem in the First Century A.D. down to the End of Jewish Jerusalem

HEROD THE GREAT died in 4 B.C. His intention was to divide his kingdom among three of his sons, and his dispositions were approved by Augustus. Archelaus succeeded to the central area of Judaea, with Jerusalem as its capital, but his misgovernment provoked so much unrest that Augustus deposed and banished him in A.D. 6. Thereafter, Judaea was ruled by Roman procurators until the first Jewish Revolt in A.D. 66, with the exception of the reign of Herod Agrippa (A.D. 40–44). This brief rule of a grandson of Herod the Great and his Hasmonean wife Mariamne followed a period of violent unrest amongst the Jews of Alexandria and Judaea caused by Caligula's attempts to force emperor-worship upon them. Claudius's accession in A.D. 41 brought relief, and with his support Herod Agrippa was able to rule peacefully in Jerusalem, where he posed as a strict supporter of the orthodox religion.

We have literary evidence for the history of Jerusalem during the first half of the first century A.D. in the evidence in the Gospels of Roman rule under the procurator Pontius Pilate. Josephus[1] provides us with a detailed account of the political events. For most of the period up to the time of Herod Agrippa there is little precise archaeological evidence. The city of Herod the Great and Herod Agrippa was brutally destroyed and devas-

[1] *Antiquities*, XVII. xi–XIX. viii; *War*, II. i–xi.

tated after the capture of Jerusalem by Titus in A.D. 70, and its ruins still further overturned by the Hadrianic building operations of the second century A.D. Our excavations have shown that with the exception of a few of the public buildings, quite literally scarcely one stone stands on another. One small exception seems to be in the 1972 excavations, as yet unpublished, of Professor Avigad in the Jewish Quarter, where recognizable remains of a fairly important peristyle building were found.

One can nevertheless infer that the period was one of considerable prosperity in Jerusalem. Pottery of the mid-first century A.D., which we can define fairly precisely from the rich finds of the Qumran monastery destroyed in A.D. 68, is found in enormous quantities. It is found in the actual ruins of A.D. 70, but disturbed deposits are found in even greater quantities. Mention has already been made (above, p. 228) of the enormous tips of material of this period in Site C in the Muristan. Equally large amounts are found in the dumps of soil associated with Hadrianic quarrying in Sites R and S, and in tips down the slope of the eastern ridge and in destruction debris in Site L on the western ridge. The enormous amount of material shows how closely built-up the area was, and one can certainly deduce a prosperous and fully inhabited city.

I have already indicated above that in the case of some public buildings we do have some stones standing one on the other. Herodian work at the temple platform and the tower Phasael at the Citadel has already been mentioned. To these can be added a major addition to Jerusalem by Herod Agrippa which can be identified both archaeologically and in Josephus's record. Josephus describes[1] how Herod Agrippa constructed a new wall, the 'third wall' (see above, p. 232) which ran north from the tower Hippicus, at the present Citadel, and round to reach the original walls on the Kedron, so as to enclose the hitherto undefended extensions of the city to the north, especially the quarter called Bezetha to the north of the Temple.

Like that of every single north wall of Jerusalem, the line of Herod Agrippa's 'third wall' has been disputed. The two main

[1] *War*, V. iv. 2 (147)–(154).

claimants were the line of the present north wall of the Old City and a line of wall some 200 metres to the north (see below, p. 251). The problem has been very firmly settled archaeologically in favour of the line of the present north wall. Excavations against this wall, in which a multitude of structural periods down to Turkish times are clearly visible, were carried out in 1937–38 by R. W. Hamilton, Director of Antiquities under the Mandate. These excavations included a sounding at the Damascus Gate in which remains of the Roman period and earlier were identified immediately beneath the sixteenth-century A.D. gate of Suleiman the Magnificent.[1] In 1964, the municipality of Jerusalem was planning a lay-out along the north wall from the Damascus Gate eastward, and on behalf of the municipality the Jordanian Department of Antiquitie undertook excavations at the Gate, which were directed by the then Deputy Director of the British School, first Mrs Bennett and then Dr Basil Hennessy, between 1964 and 1966.

In a number of areas the excavations[2] penetrated to bedrock, c. 8 metres below the threshold of the present Damascus Gate. Above the natural *terra rossa* was a deposit of field soil giving no evidence of occupation levels, in which there were two cist burials and an infant burial in a jar of the early first century A.D. In the early first century A.D., this was therefore a cemetery area, and *ex-hypothesi* outside the walls. Into these levels were cut the foundations of the magnificent gateway and wall seen in Pl. 99. The first surface of thick plaster, sealing the foundation trench and running through the gateway, contained a coin of Herod Agrippa of the year A.D. 42–43. The pottery from the foundation trench agrees with the construction of the wall in the first half of the first century A.D.

The archaeological evidence fits well with that of Josephus. He describes[3] the line of the 'third wall', and says[4] that 'It was

[1] QDAP X.
[2] Levant II, pp. 22 ff.
[3] War, V. iv. 2 (147).
[4] ibid., (148)–(155).

Agrippa who encompassed the parts added to the old city with this wall, they having been unprotected before; for as the city grew more populous it gradually crept beyond its old limits'. This would apply perfectly to the wall constructed outside any built-up area such as that here described. Josephus also records that the wall was never completed:

> but he left off building it when he had only laid the foundations, out of the fear he was in of Claudius Caesar, that he should suspect that so strong a wall was built in order to make some innovation in public affairs

(a nice euphemism for an attempt to throw off the power of Rome?). Herod Agrippa obviously received a strong intimation from Rome that he should not get above himself.

The excavations revealed what is certainly to be interpreted as the eastern pedestrian entrance (Pl. 99) of a triple-arched gateway of normal Roman plan. The engaged columns flanking the door were largely hacked back when an Ommayad cistern was constructed in the angle. The photograph shows it flanked to the east by a tower in excellent masonry of Herodian type. The line of this tower is exactly followed by that of the existing east tower of the Damascus Gate, which dates from the sixteenth century A.D. Excavations, which could not produce such exact dating evidence as for the east tower, showed that there was a tower in similar masonry beneath the present west tower. On fig. 40, the plan of the present Damascus Gate is shown in solid black (except where it has been interrupted to show the lower pedestrian entrance). Beneath, the hatched outline shows the line of the masonry stratigraphically dated to the reign of Herod Agrippa. The permanence of the plan is remarkable. One can without hesitation infer that directly beneath the present gate was the central arch of the first-century A.D. gate, with another pedestrian entrance to the west.

The stones of the tower shown to the left in Pl. 99 are of the beautifully dressed masonry found in the structures of Herod the Great. The only distinction is that the size of the stones is less.

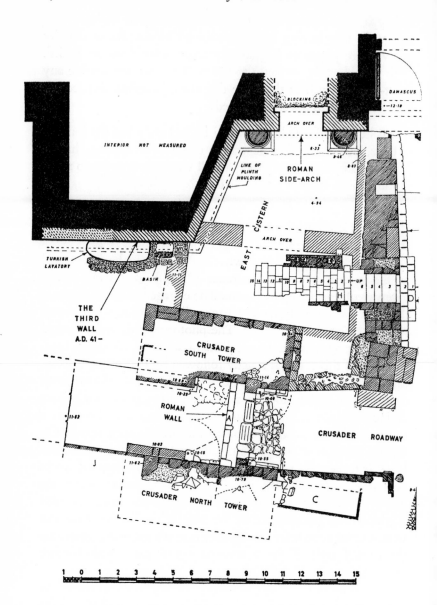

INTERIOR   NOT   MEASURED

BLOCKING

DAMASCUS

ARCH OVER

8·33

9·66

8·63

ROMAN
SIDE-ARCH

LINE OF
PLINTH
MOULDING

4·94

EAST   CISTERN

ARCH OVER

TURKISH
LAVATORY

BASIN

11·11

15 14 13 12 11 10 9 8 7 6 5 4 3 2 1—UP   6   5   3   2   1

THE
THIRD
WALL
A.D. 41 –

H

D

10·91

CRUSADER
SOUTH   TOWER

10·68

11·14

10·25

11·83

ROMAN
WALL

A

10·00

CRUSADER   ROADWAY

10·93

10·15

11·83

J

10·55

10·78

8·2

CRUSADER   NORTH   TOWER

C

1   0   1   2   3   4   5   6   7   8   9   10   11   12   13   14   15

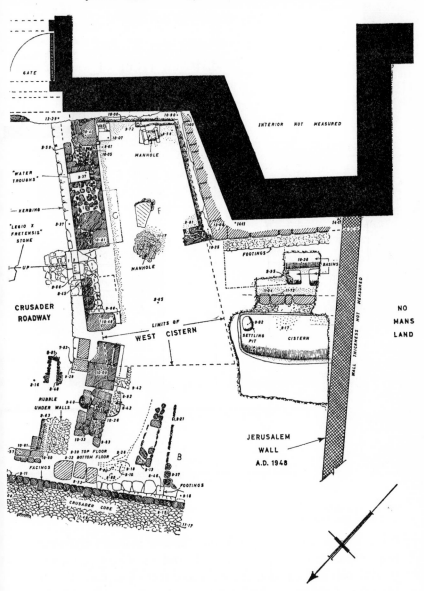

FIG 40 Plan of excavations at the Damascus Gate, showing part of the gates of the period of Herod Agrippa, Hadrian, the Crusaders, and Suleiman the Magnificent

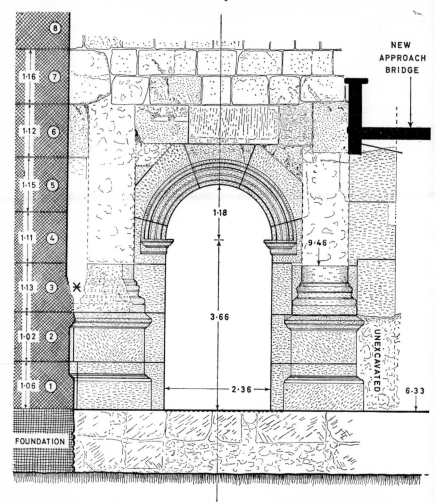

FIG 41 Pedestrian entrance of the Damascus Gate of the period of Herod Agrippa, re-used in the Hadrianic period

It is in fact perfectly reasonable that the new masonry craftsmanship imported into Jerusalem by Herod the Great (see above, p. 213) was still current, for we know from Josephus[1] that the Herodian building of the Temple was barely completed before

[1] *Antiquities*, XX. ix. 7 (219); when the Temple was completed in A.D. 63, 18,000 workmen became unemployed.

the destruction of A.D. 70. The arch of the gateway itself and the pedestals that supported the flanking engaged columns are of the same masonry, and these elements, with those of the plinth mouldings of the tower, provide welcome additions to our knowledge of the architecture of the period. As far as the gateway is concerned, the original structure is complete only as far as the voussoirs of the arch. Fig. 41 shows that above the voussoirs is an entirely different type of masonry. The disregard of the original plan was such that to the right (west) of the elevation the continuation upwards of the engaged column was ignored; only below that point was it necessary for the Ommayad cistern-builders to hack back the column. To the east, the same evidence is seen a course higher. The dating of this upper part of the wall is unambiguously given by a stone, slightly off-centre from the keystone of the arch, on which there is an inscription dating the part of the wall here over the arch to the time of Aelia Capitolina. The inscription is mutilated and incomplete, but can be restored as COL[onia] AEL[ia] CAP[itolina] D[ecurionum] D[ecreto].[1]

The archaeological evidence is therefore clear that in the reign of Herod Agrippa (A.D. 40–44) the construction of a city wall with a grand gateway was begun in an area in which there was no archaeological evidence of previous occupation. This accords with the description of Josephus. It requires a firm determination to ignore the evidence for anyone to refuse to believe that this is the 'third wall', though some such determined people do still exist. Josephus, moreover, suggests that this wall enclosing a large-scale extension to the north was not completed (see above, p. 239) by Herod Agrippa. It could well be that his work here was never carried up higher than it now exists. Alternatively, the upper part, and any completion by the Jews in the face of threatened Roman attack,[2] may have been destroyed by Titus in A.D. 70.

[1] The stone certainly belongs to a public building of Aelia Capitolina. Hamilton (*QDAP* X, p. 23) suggests that it comes from elsewhere. Hennessy (*Levant*, II, p. 24) suggests that it was levered 20 centimetres out of its original position when a relieving arch was constructed in the Crusader period based on the eastern engaged column of the entrance.

[2] *War*, V. iv. 2 (155).

The evidence of these excavations and those of Hamilton some 250 metres farther east[1] show that the north wall of Herod Agrippa's Jerusalem and of Aelia Capitolina corresponds closely with that of the present Old City. On the plan (fig. 42) the complete line of the Old City wall has been followed. For the line west of the Damascus Gate there is no evidence. This must be noted, since the evidence of Site c (see above, p. 231) suggests that there was no occupation in that area until the second century A.D. It does indeed seem very possible that the line of the wall turned south immediately west of the Damascus Gate to join the line suggested for the wall of Herod Agrippa (fig. 42). This would fit the description of Josephus,[2] in which the line of the third wall could be taken as following that of the second wall from the tower Hippicus to the northern quarter specifically associated with the second wall as far as the tower Psephinus (not otherwise known, which on this theory would be at the north-west corner of the second wall) and only *extended* (Josephus's word) from that point. The 'New City' or *Bezetha*, described as enclosed, would be covered by Josephus's description:

> It was Agrippa who encompassed the parts added to the old city with this wall, this having been unprotected before; for as the city grew more populous, it gradually crept beyond its old limits, and those parts of it that stood northward of the temple, and by the hill, being added to the city, made it considerably larger, and occasioned that hill, which is in number the fourth, and is called Bezetha, to be inhabited also. It lies over against the tower Antonia, but is divided from it by a deep valley, which was dug on purpose . . .

This line, suggested tentatively on the map (fig. 42), can only be hypothetical, for there is no supporting evidence; it does seem to fit well the description of Josephus. If, however, the Agrippan line is found to follow the line of the present wall of the north-west corner of the Old City, the absence of first-century occupation

[1] *QDAP* X, pp. 1 ff.
[2] *War*, V. iv. (148)–(152).

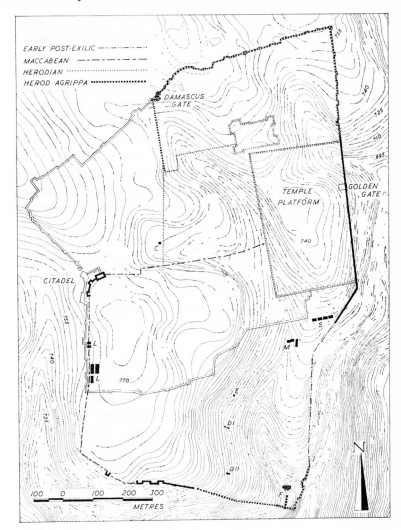

FIG 42   Plan of Jerusalem in the period of Herod Agrippa

in Site C must be due to the fact that the area so recently enclosed had not been completely built up before the destruction of the city in A.D. 70.

Reference has already been made (above, p. 202) to the evidence that it was Herod Agrippa who completed the enclosure of the western ridge by joining the tips of the two ridges across the mouth of the Tyropoeon. This area was explored by Bliss and Dickie. A portion of their exploration of the great buttressed wall across the centre of the valley is shown on fig. 7 to illustrate their excavation methods. The line of this wall was not accessible to us owing to the modern road, so we could not supplement the earlier exploration with any stratigraphically based dating evidence. Some sections of the masonry shown in fig. 7, which obviously represent a series of rebuilds, could be of Maccabean style (see above, p. 202). This need certainly not be taken as implying that the Maccabean town wall ran to this point, for the wall in question forms the dam wall of the Birket el Hamra, the 'Old Pool', seen in Pl. 67. Excavations in the area of Site F showed that there was a succession of dam walls—first century A.D. and Hellenistic and an inferred one of the Israelite period,[1] and this could be one in the same series.

Our evidence, and indeed that of Bliss and Dickie, is against an early date for a town wall running from the south-east corner of Bliss and Dickie's wall (fig. 6) across the dam. We did not obtain any stratigraphical evidence for the gate, which, as described above (p. 22), we re-excavated, but the photograph (Pl. 6) shows that it was of very mixed masonry. This is confirmed by the original excavator's careful record of the masonry. The wall running thence towards the dam is of stones of mixed style and some obviously re-used.[2] The tower which encloses the gate cannot be earlier than Byzantine, since it is built over a wall associated with a Roman bath a little to the south-west.

The area of the gate provided no dating evidence, for we

[1] *PEQ*, 1965, Pls. 15–16.
[2] *B. and D.*, p. 98.

were only clearing late overlying debris and the tunnels of the earlier excavators. Adjacent to the west was, however, one of our main trenches in Site F (map, fig. 11). Here we uncovered the foundations (Pl. 95) of part of the wall investigated by Bliss. Pottery from the foundation trench was quite definitely of the middle to the end of the first century A.D. Within that period the only ruler likely to have enclosed an additional area within the walls is Herod Agrippa. We must therefore accept[1] the conclusion that it was he who closed the gap between the tips of the two ridges, even though here his builders did not use masonry of the excellence of that in the north wall, but were content to employ stones derived from earlier walls.

Buildings in good Herodian masonry are, however, to be found in the newly enclosed area at Site N. As described above (p. 22), this was one of the areas explored by Bliss and Dickie's tunnels. We descended to it from above. The only intact structure that we in fact found was the street that Bliss and Dickie had followed (Pl. 100). Above it, of the total depth of c. 6 metres from the present surface of the level of the street, the uppermost 2 metres consisted of featureless wash, medieval and modern. Beneath there were Byzantine levels to a depth of c. 2 metres and then a tumble of masonry – stones tumbled from walls in the first place, but then still more tumbled by winter torrents down this central valley between the two ridges. Laboriously we traced wash and erosion lines, but the ultimate conclusion was that once the buildings from which the stones had been derived had collapsed, the valley had been given over to the forces of nature and successive winter rains had churned up the ruins.

The date of the initial destruction was very nicely provided by a group of twenty-three coins, probably the slightly dispersed contents of a purse or hoard, of the period of the first Jewish Revolt (A.D. 66–70). The ruined structure along the street was therefore in use in the second half of the first century A.D. The

---

[1] In case this sounds an arrogant assumption, professional colleagues can rest assured that in the full publication they will have available the evidence for this statement.

few stones in position (Pl. 100) and the fallen stones were in the typical Herodian masonry with wide, finely dressed flat margins and flat centres only distinguished from the margins by a bolder style of dressing. The stones in the tumble that we found to the east of the street did not rest on the floors of rooms, but on quite ill-defined surfaces surrounded by no walls with defined faces. The solution to this problem certainly is that the door or gate onto the street seen in Pl. 100 led to a stairway to the higher terrace that the slope of the ridge demanded to the east. When the building was destroyed, the stairway collapsed into the void beneath it. In the collapse were involved three magnificent slabs (1·75 × 1·09 × 0·23 metres; 1·65 × 1·00 × 0·20 metres; and 1·84 × 0·90 × 0·37 metres; Pl. 97), probably derived from an upper roadway as impressive as that still in position.

The masonry at Site N is in Herodian style. The evidence at the Damascus Gate is unambiguous that masons working in the style of those employed by Herod the Great were still employed by Herod Agrippa half a century later. The full analysis of the finds (my recurrent theme) has not yet reached the point at which one can say with certainty whether the Site N lay-out belonged to the time of Herod the Great or his grandson. The stratigraphical evidence (see above, p. 247) that this valley between the western and eastern ridges was only enclosed by Herod Agrippa would lead one to expect that any buildings here belonged to this period. Yet a basic element in the lay-out was probably the street laid out by Herod the Great along the west side of his Temple, a street that passed beneath Wilson's Arch and Robinson's Arch, and extended thence south. The street itself has not yet been traced for any great distance, but beneath it and associated with it was a very fine drain, burrowed along by Warren in his usual indomitable style, and recently exposed in some detail in Professor Mazar's excavations.[1] The earlier excavations traced this with very little doubt to join up with the one that ran beneath the paved street in Site N, to join one that we also exposed in our own Site F on the eastern side of the

[1] *Mazar*, Pls. XII-XIII.

western ridge. One can certainly take it that the general line of the street, as indicated by the associated drain, was part of the lay-out of the time of Herod the Great. We must await the detailed analysis of the finds to decide whether the buildings were added in the time of Herod Agrippa to a street-line of the time of Herod the Great, or whether there was an earlier extra-mural development that was enclosed, in the mid-first century A.D., by Herod Agrippa, as a complement to his enclosures of extra-mural areas to the north.

We can document archaeologically the work of Herod Agrippa at the Damascus Gate on the line of the northern wall, on the line of the southern wall, and perhaps in Site N. I have stressed (above, p. 237) the fact that the sheer bulk of first-century pottery and other finds in Jerusalem shows that for the ordinary people it was a prosperous period. But the record for Herod Agrippa is pitifully slight. Only twenty-six years later, Jewish Jerusalem came to an end, having survived from the period of Jewish rule under David (c. 1000 B.C.) and his successors, and through the successive stages of foreign rule from 587 B.C.; restoration of Jewish influence leading nearly to a new Jewish monarchy from 530 to 63 B.C.; the iron rule of Rome, with Herod the Great, however Romanophil, still ruling by having regard to the strength of the leaders of the orthodox Jewish religion. The three-quarters of a century that followed the death of Herod the Great, the virtual end of an attempt to create an independent Jewish kingdom, is marked, with the short interval of the rule of Herod Agrippa, by increasing Roman authoritarianism, and indeed by unnecessary cruelty and stupidity by the rather inferior officials appointed to this minor part of the Roman Empire. All of this had happened so often in the history of Palestine. The ruthlessness and efficiency of Rome succeeded in obliterating Jerusalem and indeed Palestine as a Jewish state. Today one must, of course, recognize that Rome could not obliterate the concept of Jerusalem and Palestine as the Jewish homeland.

The Jewish revolt against the oppression of Roman officialdom broke out seriously in A.D. 66. The Roman rulers knew that they had to defeat a widely based movement and dealt gradually with the periphery. Only by A.D.70, when Vespasian, originally in control of operations, had left to take up office as emperor in Rome, did Titus, Vespasian's son, mass his forces for the final assault. We have a full account provided by Josephus. It is unedifying. The Jews in Jerusalem were engaged rather more in fighting between the sects than in fighting the foreign power.

Josephus describes in some detail the preparations made by Titus to capture Jerusalem. He had at his disposal the massive force of four legions, the Vth, Xth, XIIth, and XVth. His attack was planned from the north, for through the millennia this was the vulnerable side, the only side of Jerusalem not protected by the bleak topographical features of the delimiting valleys. His headquarters were established on Mount Scopus, the ridge that encircles Jerusalem to the north and east. His troops, to reach the core of the resistance, the Temple, had to penetrate the three north walls of Josephus's description. The wall of Herod Agrippa may not have been completed by its builder (see above, pp. 242–3), but Josephus describes[1] how the Jews, presumably at the time of the Roman attack, built it up to battlements c. 12 metres high. The Roman troops then had to storm the line of the second wall, linked with the fortress Antonia at the north-west corner of the temple precinct; the evidence for the line of this wall has already been given (above, pp. 232–4).Within what one might describe as the suburbs or excrescences, as indeed Josephus recognizes, was the real core, the precinct of the Temple and the area which was 'old' at the time of Josephus, but which in fact (see above, p. 199) probably first became part of the city c. 100 B.C.

It would seem that the 'third' and 'second' walls were penetrated fairly easily by the legions.[2] At this stage, Titus did his best to induce the defenders to surrender.[3] The inhabitants remained defiant, in spite of the barbarities of the various leaders, at war amongst themselves, and of less barbarous, but still cruel,

[1] *War*, V. iv. 2 (155).
[2] *War*, V. vii–viii.
[3] *War*, V. ix.

vengeance by the Romans, and in spite, above all, of the horrors of famine, very vividly described by Josephus. The attacks based on siege-works or 'banks' raised by the Romans were all in turn repelled.

Titus decided to rely for the final capture on the cumulative effect of famine and the really horrible internecine struggles of the sects and parties in Jerusalem. Josephus shows us all too clearly that Titus was fully justified in waiting for the Jews to destroy each other.

His realistic assessment of the position in this respect was matched by his recognition that it would be very bad for morale for the legions to sit outside Jerusalem, doing nothing, while the Jews tore each other to pieces.[1] He was also concerned both to stop completely any foraging for food, and therefore to prevent any lessening of the severity of the siege, and to protect his troops from sudden sallies, of which a number had been very successful. He therefore decided to build a wall of circumvallation. Its line encircling the city with a total length of thirty-nine furlongs (between $8\frac{1}{2}$ and 10 kilometres) is described in detail by Josephus.[2] It was backed by thirteen fortified camps for the attacking troops, from which continuous patrols were maintained.

Our excavations have given good reason to suppose that this circumvallation wall can be recognized in one of the walls that has figured in arguments concerning Josephus's three walls of Jerusalem. Fragments of the wall of massive masonry running roughly parallel to the north wall of the present Old City were first discovered by the pioneer Edward Robinson in 1841.[3] He emphatically identified it as the wall built by Herod Agrippa, the Third Wall of Josephus. As violent an argument as that concerning the course of the Second Wall, with opinions equally dogmatically stated, has gone on about this identification to the present day. Interest in it was greatly revived in the 1920s by excavations along it by Professor Sukenik and Professor

[1] *War*, V. xii. 9 (495).
[2] *War*, V. xii. 2.
[3] *Biblical Researches in Palestine* I, pp. 314-15.

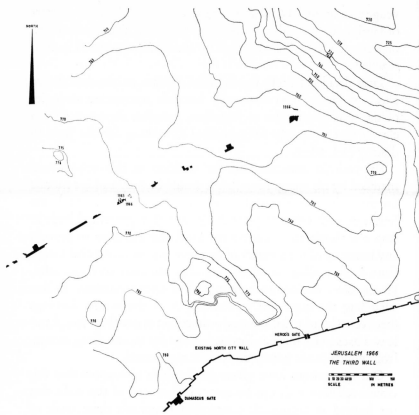

FIG 43   Plan of portions of a wall to the north of the Old City

Mayer of the Hebrew University.[1] The map (fig. 43) shows
the portions of the wall known from their discoveries and those
of their predecessors, with a total length of *c.* 375 metres. Sukenik
and Mayer firmly supported the Herod Agrippa identification.
Even as late as this, however, excavations in Jerusalem were being
carried out by old-fashioned methods without any use of exact
stratification, and these excavations produced no reliable evidence.

The wall is in fact a remarkable one. The stones employed
are enormous, up to 3·65 metres in length, 1·20 metres in height,

[1] *The Third Wall of Jerusalem.*

and 2·30 metres in breadth, with excellent dressing in the Herodian style of a slightly sunk margin surrounding a flat-dressed centre (Pl. 101). The width of the wall is 4·25 metres. The stones, however, are very obviously re-used and had been considerably battered before they were set in their present position. Beneath these massive stones are very inadequate foundations of loose rubble. The wall, for all its size, is in fact a very shoddy affair, with every appearance of hasty construction. On the most superficial grounds it could not possibly be the work of Herod Agrippa. Those who cling to this wall as being the Third Wall can, however, and do, claim that what has been found is the hurried completion by the Jews of the wall begun by Herod Agrippa,[1] presumably as the Roman siege was impending. This might be arguable only if some original work could be found on the line, and were it not that it is disproved by sound archaeological evidence.

In 1965 and 1966 we carried out a number of excavations on the line of this wall.[2] As is the case everywhere, only one course of ashlars survives. One indication that the wall is not a north wall of Jerusalem is that it seems to face south. The south face, seen in Pl. 101, has the re-used ashlars carefully fitted, and was obviously visible above ground. The north face of the same course, seen in Pl. 102, is completely rough, and was obviously foundational. It can be argued, and of course has been argued, for in the discussion of the walls of Jerusalem every argument *has* been used, that the ground-level to the north was higher. As the modern road running east from the Nablus Road to Saladin Road, on the side of which the wall is still visible, has removed all evidence, nothing can be decided about this, and it may be a valid argument.

Fortunately, however, we have some incontrovertible stratigraphical evidence. The Sukenik-Mayer trench along both faces of the wall had removed some of the evidence, but enough survived for a positive conclusion. The wall at the rear was cut

[1] *War*, V. iv. 2 (155).
[2] *PEQ*, 1966, pp. 87–8.

into a fill with a foundation trench at least 1·76 metres deep. In this fill there were a number of coins, of which the latest were two coins of the Roman procurators, dated to A.D. 54 and A.D. 59. The wall was therefore built after that date, and cannot possibly be the work of Herod Agrippa. It was obviously a wall hurriedly built, making use of any available material. If it was a defensive wall built by the Jews, they were not doing what Josephus, a contemporary witness, says that they did, namely completing Herod Agrippa's work. The Roman circumvallation was hurriedly built, according to Josephus in three days.[1] They would have used stones from any structures to hand, such as the tomb of Queen Helena of Adiabene and other rich extra-mural structures that may have existed, or even stones quarried by Herod Agrippa but never used since his work was suspended. The identification of this wall as a part of Titus's circumvallation wall seems to be convincing.

Josephus describes the straits that this complete enclosing of the city brought about, with horrible details of the famine. It was still months before the Romans were able to storm the heart of the city, first the tower Antonia, then the Temple itself, which in the process was destroyed by fire, against the wishes of Titus, and ultimately, in September of A.D. 70, the upper city on the western ridge. The ensuing slaughter and destruction were terrible.

There is ample archaeological evidence of the destruction. The most dramatic was in Site N, where the ruins of the building in fine ashlar masonry of Herodian type have already been described (above, p. 247). In the ruins, churned up by winter torrents, were human bones, including three skulls (Pl. 104), a reminder of the slaughter described by Josephus, which filled the streets with blood. In Site K, on the terrace above, human bones were also found in the drain that ran beneath the first-century A.D. house (Pl. 105). The most striking evidence here, however, is that with the destruction of this house, occupation in this part of Jerusalem comes to an abrupt end. As can be seen

[1] *War*, V. xii. 2 (509).

in the photograph, only the foundations of the walls and the make-up of the floors survive, immediately under the modern top-soil. This part of Jerusalem was left outside the walls of the next stage, part of the Roman Aelia Capitolina. Within the area subsequently covered by Aelia, the destruction was no doubt equally great, but in most cases the evidence is inaccessible beneath modern buildings. The one exception is in Site L. This proved to be a site of incredible difficulty to interpret in excavation, for the fill from almost top to bottom consisted of immense stony washes, intersecting in a most complicated way, and all cutting down steeply to the west. All are undoubtedly caused by successive breaches in the town wall which bounded the area above the steep valley to the west. One such wash, at an angle of *c.* 45 degrees, crosses the stump of a small surviving fragment of what appears to be the town wall of the Maccabean period. The pottery in this wash is first century A.D., and there can be no doubt that the completion of the destruction of buildings in this area resulted from the whole fill in the area being carried away into the valley when the city wall here was destroyed by Titus.

★

CHAPTER FOURTEEN

Aelia Capitolina

WHEN THE SACK OF JERUSALEM in A.D. 70 was completed, Titus left the Xth *Legio Fretensis* to watch over the ruins. Its head-quarters were on the site of Herod's palace on the western ridge, where the three towers of the palace and a part of the west wall were left standing to form part of the defences of the legionary headquarters, which continued there until A.D. 200. We had hoped to find remains of this headquarters in our Site L. Though there were some fragments of buildings that probably belong to the Roman period, nothing looked the least military in lay-out. Probably, like Herod's palace, the headquarters lay further to the north. The only indication that they lay near at hand was the number of fragments of brick, stamped with the legionary mark, LEG X FRE or a number of variants. Some of these are found in most areas of Jerusalem, but the number on Site L were very much greater.

Some Jews continued to live in Jerusalem, but the tragic difference was that there was no longer a Temple in which the full ceremonial of the worship of Yahweh could be carried out. Religious ceremonies continued, but in synagogues, with the forms of observance suitable for those who had no access to the Temple. A new form of Judaism grew up, under the guidance of the priestly Sanhedrin, now established at Jamnia in the coastal plain, concerned with the interpretation of the Scriptures. The Jews of the Diaspora accepted the leadership of the reconstituted Sanhedrin, and the Roman rulers acquiesced in its administration of religious affairs.

The Jews of the Diaspora and the remaining population in

Jerusalem and Judaea all the time must have treasured the hope that just as there had, after the destruction of 587 B.C., been a rebuilding of the Temple and a restoration of something that could be called Judah, so there would be again. We have in fact little historical evidence for the late first and early second centuries A.D., since after the end of the accounts of Josephus no detailed chronicles have survived. Discontent may have been rumbling for a long time, and under Trajan active Jewish rebellion broke out, culminating in A.D. 115 in serious risings in Egypt, Cyrene, Cyprus, and Mesopotamia.[1] Trajan suppressed these risings, but this was only a temporary suppression. Under Hadrian, who became emperor in A.D. 117, discontent came to a head so violent that it is probably to be compared with that of A.D. 66–70. But since we have not a Josephus to chronicle it, we do not have the vivid (and terrible) details. The reason for the ultimate revolt is by no means clear. There are hints that a law against circumcision was suspected to be impending. It is possible that the Jews believed that Hadrian was proposing to establish a Roman city at Jerusalem, with as its centre a temple of Jupiter, for Dio Cassius gives evidence that Hadrian, in the course of his journey in the East in A.D. 130–31, did establish a number of such Roman cities. There is no evidence that he visited Jerusalem, but he was as near as Jerash.

At all events, the revolt broke out, culminating in A.D. 132, under the leadership of a man called Simon Bar-Kochba. Coins bearing the inscriptions Year 1 and Year 2 show that the rebels maintained the struggle for a considerable period. The final quelling of the rebellion was only achieved in A.D. 135.

It was at this point that the decisive step of establishing a Roman city, Aelia Capitolina, to obliterate Jewish Jerusalem, was taken. There is no conclusive evidence of whether the planning of such a Roman city was or was not a ground for the revolt. It is certain that it took place as its result. There is little literary evidence concerning the building of Aelia Capitolina.

[1] The only evidence is from scanty references in Dio Cassius (*Romaika*, LXVIII. 32) and Eusebius (*Historia Ecclesiastica*, IV. 2).

Indeed, here, the archaeological evidence, though scanty, gives the greater help.

The Roman decision was apparently to base their city on the north end of the city of Herod Agrippa, spanning the two ridges and creating a very approximate square. The best evidence that the present Old City represents fairly closely the extent of Aelia is the main elements in the street plan (fig. 44). There could not be a strictly symmetrical plan with the main north-south and east-west streets crossing in the centre, which was the standard form of Roman forts and the theoretical plan of towns, but with frequent divergences. At Jerusalem the obstacle to the plan was the great platform of the temple courtyard, which survived the destruction of the Temple itself. The main north-south axis can still be seen in the street plan running from the Damascus Gate, to intersect the main street from the west that entered the city by the present Jaffa Gate along the north wall of Herod's palace, of which the towers survived to be used as part of the defences of the headquarters of the Xth Legion, and partially survive today in the Citadel. This street is today David Street, running from the present Jaffa Gate to the principal entrance, the Bab el-Silsileh, of the Haram. The main street from the east was pushed north by the existence of the temple platform, and entered the city by the present St Stephen's Gate. Archaeological evidence supports the ascription of the street plan to the Hadrianic period at a number of points.

On the key point of the Damascus Gate, there was clearly a rebuilding of the partially destroyed or uncompleted Herod Agrippa Gate. Immediately over the original arch of the eastern pedestrian entrance is a stone with an inscription including the name Aelia Capitolina (see above, p. 243). As has been pointed out, the stone is not quite central over the keystone, but it may have been levered slightly out of position in the Crusader period. The courses above this stone belong mainly to a later rebuild, incorporating a number of re-used stones.

The main Hadrianic street from the north, therefore, entered the city at the same point as does the present street, but at a level

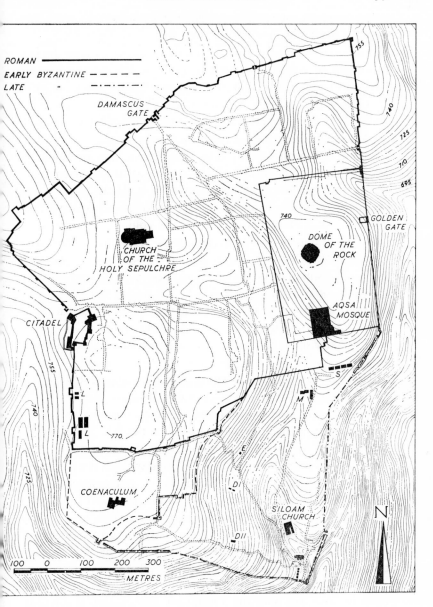

ROMAN
EARLY BYZANTINE
LATE

DAMASCUS GATE

CHURCH OF THE HOLY SEPULCHRE

CITADEL

COENACULUM

DOME OF THE ROCK

GOLDEN GATE

AQSA MOSQUE

SILOAM CHURCH

N

100 0 100 200 300
METRES

FIG 44   Plan of Jerusalem in the Roman and Byzantine periods

some 6 metres lower. The present main north-south road runs directly from this entrance, though there is a slight divergence immediately inside the gate. In the shops to the west of the line a number of columns of the colonnade which used to line the street in the typical lay-out of an Eastern Roman town confirms that this is the line of a Roman street. These columns provided shade for the pedestrian; Jerash provides an excellent illustration. At Madaba, to the south of Amman, the mosaic floor of a church of about the sixth century A.D. represents a map of Palestine. The plan of Jerusalem that it includes (Pl. 103) is fortunately well preserved, and shows this colonnaded street clearly. The present Arab name of the Damascus Gate, *Bab el-Amud* (Gate of the Column), is clearly derived from the column shown in the mosaic standing in a semicircular *piazza* inside the gate. It also shows another colonnaded street diverging to the south-east from the Damascus Gate, which is again a main thoroughfare today. It looks as though already by Byzantine times the direct continuation south of the main street to a south gate had been lost, if it ever existed, and also any direct continuation of the well-marked street from the east gate to meet the north-south street.

The main east gate was certainly St Stephen's Gate, to the north of the Haram. The main evidence of the Hadrianic date of the street from this gate is the considerable remains of a triumphal arch spanning it (Pl. 106), today known as the Ecce Homo Arch, for it adjoins the site of the Antonia; one theory has it that here Pilate judged Jesus (John 19:13). Adjoining the arch is a pavement of grooved stones which is shown today as the pavement or *lithostratos* of the Gospel story. Beneath the pavement is a double cistern with an elaborate vaulted roof. Père Benoit has recently shown[1] that the pavement and cistern roof must go together, and that the latter is much more likely to belong to the Roman than to the Herodian period, when he considers that there was an open pool here. He further gives grounds for believing that the pavement is associated with the Triumphal Arch, which is certainly

[1] op. cit., p. 223

Hadrianic. He believes that the pavement represents a small Forum, through which passed the street from the east gate. His arguments are persuasive, though the absolutely certain evidence is slight.

The main Forum probably lay in the area south of the Church of the Holy Sepulchre, where a further paved area overlying vaulted cisterns and traces of another arch have been found. The plan is, however, by no means clear. It was in this area that excavation has recovered the most impressive evidence of the large scale of the work involved in laying out Aelia Capitolina. The evidence from Site C has already been described (above, p. 228) in connection with the problem of the north wall at the time of the Gospels. The aim was clearly to level over the inequalities of the hilly site of Jerusalem to provide for the regular rectangular lay-out of Aelia. An enormous amount of earth was collected from two different sources, one a deposit of the seventh century B.C., the other of the first century A.D. There were hardly any stone or architectural fragments in the debris, so the deposits were not destruction levels, but more likely midden tips possibly outside the contemporary wall. The amount of material must have been really enormous. At Site C, the depth of the fill was 8·25 metres. To the north, Dr Ute Lux has recently been engaged in some remarkable excavations right beneath the Lutheran Church, at a distance of one hundred metres north from Site C. Her excavations there were on a similar scale to those at Site C, and the accomplishment of these beneath a standing building is why I call them remarkable. The results were identical with those of Site C, a tipped fill of material of the same dates, and eventually quarried rock, at the base. Presumably the whole area between the sites and beyond them, and of unknown extent east to west, was filled in and levelled over in this operation.

The methodical planning of Hadrian's architects is well illustrated by the drain found in Site C, running down to the west. When the required height was reached, filling was suspended, and the drain was built. Filling was then resumed, and in Pl. 96 one can see the change in the angle of tipping above the level

of the drain, which is to the left of Terry Ball, one of our surveyors, on the higher level. One can deduce that the drain was
part of a network, leading down to the main drain beneath the
main north-south street, which approximately follows the line
of the central valley. This main drain has been located in a number
of places, in addition to portions of the street-paving of the
period, and has in fact served as the main drain of Jerusalem down
to modern times.

The Damascus Gate gives a fixed point on the north wall of
Aelia, and excavations by R. W. Hamilton in 1937–38[1] further
east showed that the line of the Roman and present walls here
coincided. Since the east wall of the Haram and the evidence
of the Roman street plan running to St Stephen's Gate make the
line of the east wall certain, the boundaries of the north-east
sector of Aelia are clear. West of the Damascus Gate there is in
the present wall an irregular segment to a north-west angle
projecting a good deal to the west of the remainder of the west
wall. There is no dating evidence for any part of this wall.

The whole length of the west wall is in fact uncertain. The
towers of Herod's palace certainly continued in existence, and
the street plan indicated by David Street suggests that there was a
gate here, though it could have been further out. In Site L there
was no evidence at all for this period. The Byzantine wall beneath
the present one was built direct on the ruins of the Maccabean
wall. Doug Tushingham, who was in charge of this area, was
inclined to think that the terrace outside the present wall, above
the slope of the Hinnom, might suggest that the Roman wall
was further west. There is no evidence, for the wash-outs that
removed all evidence of the city of the first century A.D. were
later repeated (see below, p. 273).

It is certain that Aelia did not extend to the south of the present
south wall of the Old City. It is very likely that clearance to the
base of this wall would show that it was founded on Hadrian's
wall throughout. The only part of the wall that is exposed to a
low level is the stretch to the east of the Dung Gate, which after a

[1] QDAP X.

length of 212 metres, turns north and runs up to the Haram wall. It is certainly post-Herodian, for it is built against the Herodian temple platform. It would not be the work of Herod Agrippa, for his wall was far to the south. When Jerusalem began to grow in the Byzantine period (see below, p. 267), its walls also extended to the south, and in any case Byzantine buildings are everywhere characterized by mixed, re-used, masonry. The only place in the history of the city for this construction in enormous blocks, with excellent margins and bold irregular bosses, beautifully set (Pls. 89, 91), is in the Hadrianic building of Aelia. It has already been pointed out that in its return to the north it is built on the vertical edge of a quarry of Herodian date. It must therefore have had a predecessor on this line, which I have tentatively suggested (above, p. 114) may have had its origin in the Solomonic period.

The main evidence of the Hadrianic period is that of quarrying. In Site s, immediately outside the sector of the wall just described, second-century A.D. quarrying succeeded the Herodian, as the dumps of first-century debris made clear. In Site R, the story was the same. It seems in fact possible that Hadrian's architects in their search for stone completely stripped a part of the area south of their intended city. If one looks at the contours of the east side of the eastern ridge below Site s, one sees a noticeable bulge (Pl. 75), in which the looseness of the soil is emphasized by the erosion channels cutting down it. These channels are the happy hunting ground of scavengers for antiquities, especially coins. Many of the coins are of the period of the first Jewish Revolt (A.D. 66–70). It seems highly probable that Hadrian's architects 'bulldozed' the ruins of the first-century A.D. town destroyed in A.D. 70, and anything that lay beneath it, into the valley, to expose the rock for quarrying.

Quarrying also preceded the construction of a Byzantine building in the uppermost part of Site M; only as the rock started to slope steeply into the valley did earlier buildings survive. The most dramatic quarrying evidence is in the area excavated by Weill towards the southern end of the eastern ridge (see above, pp. 31–2). In our adjoining Area v, we were able to date this quarrying to the second century A.D.

Hadrian thus very literally abolished Jewish Jerusalem with his construction of Aelia Capitolina. Within his city he buried it to level up the site for his regular lay-out. Outside it he threw it away in order to use the very rock on which it was built for his own city.

★

CHAPTER FIFTEEN

Byzantine, Moslem, and Crusader Jerusalem

THE LENGTH of time covered by the title of this chapter is a confession that during it archaeology has only a small contribution to make to the history of the city. From the evidence of the written records, the political history is highly eventful, and I shall only deal with it in the broadest outlines.

For nearly two centuries after the foundation of Aelia Capitolina in A.D. 135, there is little to record from either historical sources or archaeological evidence. The archaeological evidence of structural developments would lie within the Old City, where the opportunities for investigation are scanty, and archaeology has contributed virtually nothing concerning this period. One might have expected the remains of buildings in Site C, but the earliest to survive above the Hadrianic fill were Byzantine. The wash-outs on Site L might have destroyed evidence, and in fact if there had been buildings of the second and third centuries A.D., they must have done so with great thoroughness. One is left with a surprising impression of a vacuum concerning what should have been an important and populous city.

One might in fact suspect that Aelia Capitolina merely ticked over. It was forbidden to the Jews, and perhaps had no particular attraction to others. The great revival came when Constantine the Great in A.D. 313 made Christianity the official religion of the Roman Empire, an empire whose capital he transferred to the ancient city of Byzantium, which he renamed Constantinopolis.

Jerusalem at one stroke became the religious centre of the civilized Western world.

The most immediate impact of this was the construction sponsored by Empress Helena, Constantine's mother, of a church covering the sacred spots of Calvary and the Holy Sepulchre. The evidence that the site of the church was outside the walls at the time of the Crucifixion has been given above (pp. 230–1). The evidence that from the foundation of Aelia Capitolina onwards the site was in the middle of the Roman city is discussed above (p. 261). There is in fact no conclusive evidence concerning the wall of the north-west sector of the city, but in our present state of knowledge one would expect that the present wall of the Old City in that area has a fairly close relation to the Hadrianic plan.

The probabilities therefore are that Helena accepted as the site of these two cardinal places in the Gospel story one that was completely within the walls of her time, therefore contravening the necessities that tombs and sites of executions should be outside the city walls. Unless there is a great error in these propositions (and, of course, here I am being very cautious), she chose an improbable site. All that one can say is that, this being so, she could well have been guided by tradition treasured by the small, often persecuted, but continuing Christian groups.

Evidence concerning the Church of the Holy Sepulchre almost comes into the story of Digging up Jerusalem. For a number of years now – I have not checked how long – but from early in the period of our 1961–67 excavations and still continuing, the religious communities jointly responsible for the church have been carrying out restoration work urgently needed. This restoration work demands a rigorous investigation of all substructures, and has resulted in the identification of the plan of the church of the Constantinian period, now almost completely overlaid by later structures, principally those of the Crusader period. I have been very much privileged to be shown over all the structural elements of the present and earlier churches by Père Couäsnon, the architect appointed by the Latin community.

On structural and archaeological evidence, the plan of the original Constantinian church can be firmly established. Père Couäsnon is about[1] to give the evidence that he has acquired for the Constantinian (and later) plans during the course of the reconstructive work.[2] The archaeological contribution concerning the church comes from the identification of the foundation trenches and the isolation of the pottery from them, which is, on my assessment, fourth century A.D.

Beyond this point, the first outburst in Jerusalem of the great period of Eastern Christianity, the evidence concerning the Church of the Holy Sepulchre does not help us. What is abundantly clear is that from the fourth to the sixth centuries A.D. there was a great expansion of Jerusalem to the south, ultimately reaching the limits of the city of Herod Agrippa, which in the first century A.D. encompassed the maximum previous area (see above, p. 241–7).

There is no doubt of occupation here (see below, pp. 270 ff.). Our knowledge about the extension of the defences to enclose this area comes from the Bliss and Dickie excavations of 1894–97. A great part of the wall that they traced south and then east from the south-west corner of the Old City was represented by a rock scarp only. It is reasonable to accept that the city wall stood on the top of the scarp, though the creation of the scarp may either have been with the object of increasing the height of the wall, or perhaps more likely that the area of subsequent quarrying was limited by the line of the city wall. In the portions of actual wall above the scarp discovered by Bliss and Dickie, the excavators identified two periods, very clearly stratigraphically separated. It is accepted (see above, pp. 202–3) that the earlier wall is Maccabean, with a tower in Herodian masonry (above, p. 235) added to it. The continuation in the time of Herod Agrippa is discussed above (p. 247).

I believe it is likely that in the later wall there were two periods, which are indicated on fig. 44. My suggestion is that the first

[1] September 1972.
[2] Given in the Schweich Lectures, 1972.

Byzantine expansion enclosed only the southern part of the western ridge, the area in which tradition places the Coenaculum and the House of Caiaphas. The basis for this suggestion is that in Bliss and Dickie's plan (fig. 6), some hundred metres to the south-east of the angle in the scarp that marks the beginning of the southern wall, there is a projecting tower. The masonry style[1] suggests that the tower could have been Maccabean. However, the continuation to the south-east was assessed by Bliss and Dickie as belonging to the later stage, certainly Byzantine.

We are left with a tower that on masonry evidence could be Maccabean, outside which the south-east surface rock has been intensively quarried.[2] This quarrying created a 'fosse' between the two sections of Bliss and Dickie's wall on a north-west–south-east alignment. This planning point is certainly of importance, for the line of scarp which the south-east wall of the tower follows can be traced in a curve to the north-east. If this curve is prolonged still further to the north-east,[3] a junction can be inferred with portions of what is certainly a town wall, of which the angular line is shown on the plan (fig. 44). This wall is late, for it was built on top of Roman and Byzantine buildings, and included in it were stones with characteristic Crusader dressing. It is therefore either late Crusader or Mamluk. Nevertheless, there is in the tower and 'fosse' evidence for the south-east angle of a wall enclosing the western hill, and its course must on topographical grounds have been approximately on this line. On historical grounds one can infer that this is to be dated to about A.D. 400, for at the time of the visit of the Bordeaux Pilgrim in A.D. 333 both the Coenaculum and the Pool of Siloam were outside the walls, and at the time of the visit of Eucherius towards A.D. 440, the Coenaculum was within the walls, but the pool was still outside them.[4]

---

[1] B. and D., Pl. 1.

[2] ibid., section B-H.

[3] The intervening area could not be excavated as it passed too close to the Coenaculum (B. and D., p. 74).

[4] This evidence is well summarized in B. and D., pp. 306 ff.

There is certainly a second stage to which belongs the length of wall continuing to the east of the Maccabean tower and 'fosse' in which the whole area of the Jerusalem of Herod Agrippa was brought once more within the walls. This was probably the work of the Empress Eudoxia, as it is explicitly stated by Antoninus Martyr that she enclosed the Pool of Siloam. It would seem that a gateway was created adjoining the angle of the suggested earlier wall, and beyond that was traced for a considerable distance a wall, mostly in a smooth-dressed masonry, that was in places built on top of the earlier wall. From the structures associated with it, this wall was certainly Byzantine. For instance, a paving stone in a street associated with a gate a little to the south-east of the 'fosse' has a Greek cross incised on its underside. An aqueduct that brought water into the city round the flank of the western ridge, which changes angle to enter the city at the line of the wall, was also Byzantine, since it skirts a tower-like building, roughly built with strong lime mortar and a filling that included Roman tiles.

The upper wall was not picked up east of the Jewish cemetery. At least parts of the gate at the extreme south-east angle, re-excavated by us, were certainly Byzantine. As can be seen in the photograph (Pl. 6), the butt end of the main wall line, on the left in the view, has clearly been rather roughly rebuilt. The masonry of the gate itself is smooth-dressed, and therefore probably Byzantine. The outer tower, only rather roughly attached to the rest of the structure, is certainly Byzantine, for it was built over a wall associated with a Roman bath-building to the south.

At this gateway, the wall turns north-east to cross the Tyropoeon Valley and join the eastern ridge. One can only estimate the date of this by the character of the masonry, well described by Bliss and Dickie. The length of wall between the angle and the great buttressed wall crossing the valley could well be later, since it seems[1] to include bossed stones of possibly Maccabean origin and some flat-dressed. The line of buttressed wall suggests that it

[1] B. and D., p. 98.

was in origin planned as a dam wall rather than part of the defences, for it does not run direct to the tip of the eastern ridge, but juts out down the slope. Bliss and Dickie's drawing[1] of the return of this wall to the eastern ridge suggests that it was Maccabean (see above, p. 246), but combined with it are patches of smooth-dressed masonry. It seems likely that the Byzantine city wall was carried across the valley on the earlier dam wall, which the Byzantine builders patched up; the strengthening by filling in between the buttresses may belong to the same period.

We thus have a wall certainly Byzantine running along the south side of the western ridge, and at the south-east angle a gate that was certainly Byzantine in use, if not in origin; Byzantine work can probably be identified as re-using the dam wall across the valley. The dam wall turns back to join the tip of the eastern ridge. From that point one must infer that the wall ran along the eastern crest of the eastern ridge on the line of the post-Exilic wall, though for some 425 metres nothing of the period has been found. The inference is justified both by the contours and by the fact that a length of 240 metres of Byzantine wall was traced by Warren running south from the south-east corner of the Haram (the so-called Ophel wall), where it is clearly built against the Herodian wall (Pl. 108). Bliss[2] remarks on the resemblance of Warren's Ophel wall to his later wall at the south of the western ridge, with rough rubble foundations and a superstructure of smooth-dressed masonry. In our trench in s II, only the foundations survived, undermined perilously by the trench by which Warren followed the line of the wall. In the photograph (Pl. 107), the centre of the wall is supported by an underpinning which we had hurriedly inserted. The Byzantine date of the foundations was certain.

Evidence of a fairly elaborate Byzantine lay-out on the western ridge was obtained by Bliss and Dickie. Running along the eastern flank of the western ridge was a paved street 18 feet wide, traced for a distance of 500 feet. Its Byzantine date was proved

[1] ibid., Pl. XIII.
[2] ibid., p. 128.

by the fact that it was built over mosaic pavements, but crossed by a tower of the Crusader wall enclosing the western ridge (see above, p. 268). A similar 18-feet-wide paved street, with an excellent underlying drain, has already been mentioned (above, p. 269) as passing through a gate in the south-west sector of the wall. It is possible that the other street turned west to join this one, and did not itself lead direct to a gate. The Byzantine date of the aqueduct running round the western ridge and within the heart of the city has already been mentioned.

Our own discoveries on the western ridge suggest a much less sophisticated lay-out. This is no doubt due to the fact that our excavations, Sites D I, D II, and E, were limited to the rather steep slopes of the ridge by the area of no man's land that included the summit of the ridge. In all the sites, caves formed part of the dwellings. They had originally been in use in the first century A.D. In the Byzantine period, in Site D II, at least, the original cave was transformed into a combination of troglodyte dwelling and free-standing house, with a reasonably well-built doorway in the wall enclosing the cave (Pl. 109). Adjoining the building was a paved street, running down the hill, with beneath it a well-built drain. It is very possible that the street cleared in the grounds of St Peter Gallicantu belongs to the same period. Thus, though the buildings on the steeper slopes of the western ridge may not have been very impressive in plan, the whole area may have been laid out with paved streets.

The remains we uncovered on the eastern ridge, on Sites S, R, and M, were much more impressive. They were all built on quarried rock, probably levelled over for the purpose, but scarps and the truncation of earlier features such as cisterns and baths, and the complete absence of any earlier occupation levels, are clear evidence of the preceding quarrying. On Site M, part of a spacious building with good plastered floors was uncovered, though the walls were destroyed to a low level (Pl. 110). The best-preserved area was Square S III to V, where there was a solidly built house with large rooms (Pl. 111). Much more impressive, however, are the houses being uncovered by Professor

Mazar farther up the slope, just south of the Haram. They stand in part up to the first storey, and show that in this area at least there was full urban development.

One very curious fact has, however, emerged from the excavation of our Sites s and r. Solid and pretentious buildings stood in areas surrounded by quarry dumps. The west wall of the building shown on Pl. 111 was cut down to a depth of 3 metres into the quarry and robbing debris to the west, which was then levelled over at 5 metres above the floor of the house. The evidence from Site R was even more remarkable. The earliest remains were cisterns probably belonging to the first-century A.D. town. Above them was a great mound of debris, in which the latest pottery is probably second century A.D. This dump of debris stood to *c*. 4·50 metres above rock. Into it was cut a substantial house which rested on the rock. Its walls were cut into the dump with a wide foundation trench, in which Byzantine sherds gave the date of the building. It is clear, however, that the rubbish in the dump was so unstable that slips from it tended to threaten the house, and to control them a rough revetment wall surrounding the house had to be introduced (Pl. 112). Piles of rubbish were therefore allowed to remain in areas of solid houses. This may sound improbable, but it is not all that unlike present-day Beirut, where beside each new skyscraper there is the debris of a collapsed earlier building or one that is in process of being pulled down.

This expansion of Jerusalem to the south was the result of the prosperity brought by the edict of Constantine that Christianity was to be the official religion of the Roman Empire. The greatest impetus to the expansion was probably the residence in Jerusalem of the Empress Eudoxia, wife of the Emperor Theodosius, who lived there in exile from A.D. 450 to 460. It has already been suggested that she was responsible for building the walls enclosing the whole southern and eastern circuit; in due course the archaeological evidence concerning this dating will be assessed, though unfortunately nearly all the uncovering of walls described above was in the days preceding stratigraphical excavation.

Naturally, in this expansion the building of churches played a great part. At the Pool of Siloam a church was discovered by Bliss and Dickie which can with considerable probability be ascribed to Eudoxia.[1] It was described in detail c. A.D. 560–70 by Antoninus Martyr. The church is not visible today, for it was excavated by a labyrinth of tunnels as described above (p. 28). In fact, when the villagers of Silwan heard that a church had been discovered, they hurriedly built a mosque on top, the minaret of which is visible in Pl. 67. The church was built over the northern side of the arcade that surrounded the Pool of Siloam. That this arcaded lay-out of the pool was earlier, is shown by the fact that the construction of the church involved alterations to the original flight of steps down to it. There is no other evidence of the date of the lay-out, but it may have been Roman, perhaps contemporary with the bath-house further south, mentioned above as being earlier than the Byzantine wall. The architecture of the church was rough, and it was floored with a simple mosaic in geometric pattern.

A fragment of a church not identifiable in any literary record was discovered in our excavations at Site L. The photograph (Pl. 113) shows how very much ruined it was. Only the foundations of the walls survived, and though they were very substantial, a great part even of the foundations had been carried away by the wash-out that accompanied successive destructions of the city wall to the west. The photograph shows part of the main east apse of the church, ending on each side in ragged destruction. Just enough fragments of walls survived to suggest that this apse was flanked by two smaller ones, and that the plan was basilical with a nave and side-aisles. One pleasing survival was a fragment of a charming mosaic (Pl. 114). A guilloche band divides a panel with fan-shaped ornaments, probably meant to be floral, from a very naturalistic panel in which a delightful rabbit sits and an unidentifiable quadruped stands beneath a tree. Below the guilloche is an inscription, incomplete and damaged, which can be read as associating the church with the noble Lady

[1] B. and D., pp. 191 ff.

Bassa. Bassa was a friend of the Empress Eudoxia's, and may have been responsible for inducing her to return from the heresy of Monophysitism to Orthodoxy. She built a chapel of St Menas, which is now part of the nearby Armenian Cathedral of St James, and a nunnery, to which this church could have been attached. It is sad that so little survives in this area of what must have been a very flourishing period in Jerusalem.

Indeed, these two churches are the only two of the Byzantine period revealed by excavation. This is a very small contribution to the vast number that certainly existed. Within the area enclosed by the Byzantine walls, the sites of thirty-five churches identifiable in pilgrims' records can be located,[1] and certainly there were many more originally.

In A.D. 638, the forces of Islam, though they needed another eight hundred years to overwhelm Eastern Christianity, captured Jerusalem. The city and the province of Palestine in general had been seriously weakened by the savage Persian attack in A.D. 614 and a short period of Persian control. The interlude of renewed Byzantine control was brief. In A.D. 638, Jerusalem fell finally to the Moslem Arab attack.

One of the most vivid pieces of evidence in the course of our excavations involved the only gold coin that we found. Gold is always in excavations a very great problem. Petrie's principle in making sure that all finds were handed in was to pay by results, and for gold he paid the weight of the gold. But of course these results, these finds, were divorced from their find spot when fished out of the finder's pocket at the end of the day. In my apprenticeship on the dig at Samaria between 1931 and 1935, I came very clearly to recognize a further danger of Petrie's *bakshish* system. I have a vivid recollection of my initiation into such matters at Samaria, when our most respectable basket-girl produced as a find claimed to be from an Israelite level a modern stamped tile from Marseilles. So at Jericho and Jerusalem we gave no *bakshish*. But one must recognize the particular temptation

[1] E. A. Moore, *The Ancient Churches of Old Jerusalem.*

of gold, so easily recognizable as valuable. So when the gold coin was produced, the astonished basket-boy was rewarded with £5. The coin is a beauty (Pl. 116). It is a gold *solidus* of Heraclius. On the reverse is a cross on a stepped plinth and CONOB shows that it was minted in Constantinople. On the obverse is Heraclius flanked by his sons Heraclius Constantinus, and Heraclonas. Heraclius is breathing defiance with every hair of his moustache, but to no avail. The date of the coin is A.D. 632, and Jerusalem fell to the Arabs in A.D. 638.

We have very few topographical details of the early Arab, Ommayad, Jerusalem. There can be little doubt that the city shrank in size, for there is no recognizable evidence of Ommayad occupation outside the present Old City, though the Christian pilgrims of the ninth century A.D. could still recognize the line of the wall built by Eudoxia. Jerusalem, however, retained its holy status, for in the Moslem record it was the place to which the Prophet Mohammed flew by night on his miraculous steed. The first conqueror, Omar, built a wooden-roofed mosque on the site, and in A.D. 691 the Caliph Abd-el-Malik completed the building of the Dome of the Rock, one of the most beautiful buildings in the world (Pl. 3), modelling it on the rotunda of the Church of the Holy Sepulchre.

Of the contemporary Jerusalem, we have little evidence. On our Site C, early Arab remains overlay the Byzantine levels, but they were of no great consequence. In the area west and south of the south-west corner of the Haram, however, it is claimed that the excavations at present in progress under the direction of Professor Mazar have revealed the plan of three imposing Ommayad buildings, one of which it is suggested was the palace of the Caliph el-Walid (A.D. 705–15), son of Abd-el-Malik.

I find myself in some difficulty about this. The excavation of this building was begun in 1961 by the Jordanian Department of Antiquities, because a wall incorporating immense re-used Herodian ashlars had been found beneath a school being built inside the Dung Gate. We were associated in these excavations as advisors. In 1962 we obtained permission from the Supreme Moslem Council to excavate in the area within the salient to the south from the Haram wall, which can be seen, for example, in fig. 36, and the work was continued in 1963. This area of our excavations was directed by Père Roland de Vaux, O.P., on behalf of the Ecole Biblique et Archéologique de Saint-Etienne, which in these seasons shared with the British School responsibility for the excavations. We had wished to continue in subsequent seasons, but unfortunately permission was refused.

The 1961 excavations show that the wall of enormous blocks found beneath the school had a return to the east running parallel to the Haram, forming the boundary of an area to the south some 4 metres lower. It was clear that this wall had two periods, as can be seen by a comparison between the photograph (Pl. 117) of the eastern of two soundings to the base of the wall and that of the western sounding (Pl. 118). In the eastern trench, the face of the wall is excellently built of smooth-dressed ashlar blocks. With it goes a colonnade, of which one monolithic column was still standing and others were found fallen. The association of the column with the wall is clear in Pl. 117, for it stands on a paving stone, part of a paving of which the bedding of the other slabs can be seen running up to the footing level of the wall. In the western sounding, the wall has been rebuilt with enormous re-used Herodian blocks. This rebuild can be seen in Pl. 119, cutting through the paved street that follows the face of the Haram, corresponding to the Herodian street many feet below. The wall in its final stage, therefore, belongs not to the street but to the level some 25 centimetres higher that can be clearly seen in Pl. 119.

In 1962 and 1963, Père de Vaux excavated a considerable area in the south-east sector of the salient. His conclusion was that he had located two Byzantine buildings, one running east-west, the other north-south, which he suggested were part of two hospices built by Justinian (emperor A.D. 527–65) for foreign pilgrims and for the indigent sick. This is the building that the present excavators identify as the eighth-century Ommayad palace.[1] I think that the explanation is the two periods of use for which evidence had already been found in 1961. Père de Vaux recognized that the building continued in use to a late date, for associated with a floor immediately above the earlier one[2] was a glass weight with the name of the Caliph al-Mustansir bi 'llah (A.D. 1035–94). He also recognized the traces of the robbing of the walls at various periods down to the fourteenth century A.D. It is doubtful whether any of this evidence was observed in the present excavations, for the clearance has been on much too rapid and large a scale for exact stratigraphy. We have, of course, only available preliminary reports of these excavations,[3] which, though they are full and detailed, cannot be expected to give more than an outline of the evidence. It seems, however, that the Ommayad dating is based on architectural fragments, wall-plaster, and pottery found in the destruction debris *above* the building. Finds above a building can never be conclusive as to its date unless care is taken to differentiate between destruction debris and occupation levels. When, as the 1961 evidence shows, a building has been rebuilt in parts to its foundations and the secondary floor-level is probably the same as the original one, such evidence has no bearing at all on the original date of the building.

I think likely that one should conclude that there was a large late Byzantine building complex here, possibly the hospice of the time of Justinian suggested by Père de Vaux, and that in the Ommayad period the area was taken over and the Byzantine walls re-used and in part rebuilt. One thing is clear: the street along the south wall of the Haram does not belong to the rebuilding, and therefore probably the other streets which divide the three buildings are also not contemporary; the failure of the

[1] The sad death of Père de Vaux in 1971 prevented him writing up his excavations, which he had promised to do in 1972. I have not yet had time to study his records, but I am naturally inclined to accept his conclusions.

[2] *RB* LXX, pp. 256–8.

[3] *Mazar,*

excavators to observe the foundation trench of the rebuild is disconcerting and must cause doubt about other conclusions. As, however, the excavators have not bothered to discuss or even mention our excavations in the area, one cannot judge of the grounds on which our evidence is dismissed.

It therefore seems that in the eighth century A.D. there was a grand reconstruction of this part of Jerusalem. Whether the whole area within the walls was rebuilt may be doubted, for in Site L there was no trace of Ommayad occupation at all, and the thirteenth- and fourteenth-century Mamluk buildings almost immediately overlay the remains of the Byzantine church. The Ommayads and the Abbasid dynasty which succeeded them were tolerant to the Christians – churches continued to exist and pilgrims continued to visit Jerusalem. This period of tolerance ended in A.D. 969 with the establishment of the rule of Egyptian Caliphs; and a century later the Seljuk Turks captured Jerusalem and completely disrupted the pilgrim routes. This was the immediate stimulus to the Crusades.

In 1099, the First Crusade captured Jerusalem, and the Latin Kingdom of Jerusalem lasted until 1187. For the Crusader period in the city the chief surviving remains are the churches. The Crusader rebuilding of the Church of the Holy Sepulchre is being unravelled and repaired in the present restoration, and its true character can now be appreciated. Inside St Stephen's Gate is the delightful church of St Anne, which could be an English village church of the Norman period. In the mid-nineteenth century it was offered to the Anglicans as a cathedral. It is difficult to understand why they were so idiotic as to turn the offer down. Fragments of other churches are incorporated in later buildings. The Dome of the Rock became the church of the Knights Templars, and it was on the model of this that the circular Temple Church in London was built.

It was by pure good fortune that Digging up Jerusalem has contributed anything to the Crusader period. On Boxing Day 1964 I received an urgent cable from Mrs Bennett, who was supervising excavations at the Damascus Gate on behalf of the

Jordanian Department of Antiquities. The complications of Bank Holiday and a week-end made visas and tickets difficult, but with some wangling I managed to fly to Jerusalem next day. The trip was well worth it, for in the area outside the present gate, between it and the western tower, remains had turned up that were certainly Christian and medieval. Fallen blocks had on them fragments of paintings, including heads with haloes (Pl. 120). Other fragments of paintings were still in position on the walls. The building as subsequently cleared was simple and the walls were crudely built, but it was certainly a chapel, with a lavabo in the wall just beside the emplacement of the altar.

The municipality of Jerusalem then took the remarkable decision to carry the road into the Damascus Gate on a bridge, in order to enable the whole area to be excavated. The present ugly concrete structure was intended to be temporary, but it looks as though it is going to be regrettably permanent. Once it was built, excavation, now under the direction of Dr Hennessy, was able to continue and the setting of the chapel was made clear. It was not, as we had first thought, extra-mural. In the Crusader period, the gate was set out to the north of the Roman gate. As the plan (fig. 40) shows, the entrance was dog-legged, the outer gate facing east, and beyond the inner gate the road then turned at right-angles to enter the city on the present line, dictated certainly by the street line of Aelia Capitolina. The chapel lay to the west of this road, from which it was approached, and was within the north wall of the period. It could have been the Church of St Abraham, known from Crusader records to lie just inside the gate. To the east another room was approached up a flight of steps opposite to those leading into the chapel (Pl. 121), the use of which is uncertain since the floor had collapsed into the underlying Ommayad cistern. The possibility that part of the Crusader south wall enclosed the southern part of the western ridge, on the line shown on fig. 44, has been mentioned above (p. 268).

Crusader Jerusalem was lost to the Christians when it was captured by Salah-ed-Din in 1187. For two brief periods, 1229–39 and 1243–44, it was recaptured by subsequent Crusades. From 1247 the Mamluks from Egypt asserted their power in the area against the kingdom of Damascus, and for three centuries Jerusalem was a Mamluk city.

Though Site L was disappointing for the earlier periods, it did provide us with an excellent area of Mamluk buildings (Pl. 122) of the fourteenth century. From this time on the city walls to the west must have remained intact, for the buildings suffered no erosion. They consisted of vaulted halls flanked by ranges of rooms. The lay-out is that of a *suq* or bazaar, and it may have been associated with the hostel of the people of Hebron, known from the records of the Armenian Patriarchate to have existed in this area.

As a whole, the Jerusalem of the period may have been rather dilapidated, for at the Damascus Gate (Pl. 121), entrance was apparently between stumps of the Crusader walls and over the rubble derived from them until the area was tidied up by Suleiman the Magnificent.

The Mamluk period comes to an end with the capture of Jerusalem by the Seljuk Turks in 1517. The city took its present form under the second ruler, Suleiman the Magnificent. Between 1538 and 1541 he rebuilt the complete circuit of the walls, and only minor repairs have altered its appearance today. From the time of Suleiman the Magnificent onwards it is no longer necessary to dig up Jerusalem to trace its history in its buildings, for so much of Suleiman's Jerusalem is still visible.

Index

Printed in Great Britain by The Garden City Press Limited, Letchworth, Hertfordshire SG6 1JS